Bloom's Modern Critical Interpretations

Tennessee Williams's
Cat on a Hot Tin Roof
New Edition

Edited and with an introduction by
Harold Bloom
Sterling Professor of the Humanities
Yale University

BLOOM'S
LITERARY CRITICISM
An imprint of Infobase Publishing

Bloom's Modern Critical Interpretations: Cat on a Hot Tin Roof—New Edition

Copyright © 2011 by Infobase Publishing
Introduction © 2011 by Harold Bloom

Bloom's Literary Criticism
An imprint of Infobase Publishing
132 West 31st Street
New York NY 10001

Library of Congress Cataloging-in-Publication Data
Tennessee Williams's Cat on a hot tin roof / edited and with an introduction by Harold Bloom. — New ed.
    p. cm. — (Bloom's modern critical interpretations)
  Includes bibliographical references and index.
  ISBN 978-1-60413-888-7 (hardcover)
  1. Williams, Tennessee, 1911–1983. Cat on a hot tin roof. I. Bloom, Harold II. Title: Cat on a hot tin roof.
  PS3545.I5365C3734 2010
  812'.54—dc22
                                            2010019264

Bloom's Literary Criticism books are available at special discounts when purchased in bulk quantities for businesses, associations, institutions, or sales promotions. Please call our Special Sales Department in New York at (212)967-8800 or (800)322-8755.

You can find Bloom's Literary Criticism on the World Wide Web at
http://www.chelseahouse.com

Contributing editor: Pamela Loos
Cover design by Takeshi Takahashi
Composition by IBT Global, Troy NY
Cover printed by IBT Global, Troy NY
Book printed and bound by IBT Global, Troy NY
Date printed: October 2010
Printed in the United States of America

10 9 8 7 6 5 4 3 2 1

This book is printed on acid-free paper.

All links and Web addresses were checked and verified to be correct at the time of publication. Because of the dynamic nature of the Web, some addresses and links may have changed since publication and may no longer be valid.

Contents

Editor's Note

My introduction meditates on the relative eminence of *Cat* among Williams's major plays.

M. Thomas Inge views the play as an agrarian tragedy that, in its film adaptation, became a comedy of salvation and regeneration. Gulshan Rai Kataria then turns his attention to Maggie, one of the embodiments of the Williams hetaira.

Robert J. Corber explores the cold war context of the play and the ways Williams's text is coded with sexual reference, after which Dean Shackelford suggests the play's rhetoric of oppression is linked to its portrayal of midcentury social convention and gay identity.

R. Barton Palmer notes the melodramatic distortions present in the original staging and subsequent film adaptation, while David A. Davis detects hints of King Lear in the formidable Big Daddy.

Jeffrey B. Loomis points to the presence of Pirandello in the work's various drafts, then Bruce McConachie returns to cold war influences in eliciting the play's embrace of the grotesque. William Mark Poteet concludes the volume by taking up, once again, the indeterminacy created by the play's varying versions, especially of the final act.

HAROLD BLOOM

Introduction

It is difficult to argue for the aesthetic achievement of Tennessee Williams's long, final phase as a dramatist. Rereading persuades me that his major plays remain *The Glass Menagerie; A Streetcar Named Desire; Suddenly, Last Summer;* and the somewhat undervalued *Summer and Smoke. Cat on a Hot Tin Roof* was a popular and critical success, onstage and as a film. I have just reread it in the definitive Library of America edition, which prints both versions of act 3, the original, which Williams greatly preferred, and the Broadway revision, made to accommodate the director, Elia Kazan. Here is the ambiguous original conclusion, followed by the revision:

Margaret: And so tonight we're going to make the lie true, and
when that's done, I'll bring the liquor back here and we'll
get drunk together, here, tonight, in this place that death
has come into . . .
—What do you say?
Brick: I don't say anything. I guess there's nothing to say.
Margaret: Oh, you weak people, you weak, beautiful people!—
who give up.—What you want is someone to—
(*She turns out the rose-silk lamp.*)
—take hold of you.—Gently, gently, with love! And—
(*The curtain begins to fall slowly.*)
I *do* love you, Brick, I *do!*
Brick: (*smiling with charming sadness*) Wouldn't if be funny if
that was true?

1

* * *

Margaret: And you lost your driver's license! I'd phone ahead and
              have you stopped on the highway before you got halfway
              to Ruby Lightfoot's gin mill. I told a lie to Big Daddy,
              but we can make that lie come true. And then I'll bring
              you liquor, and we'll get drunk together, here, tonight, in
              this place that death has come into! What do you say?
              What do you say, baby?
Brick: (*L to L side bed*)
              I admire you, Maggie.
              (*Brick sits on edge of bed. He looks up at the overhead light,
              then at Margaret. She reaches for the light, turns it out; then
              she kneels quickly beside Brick at foot of bed.*)
Margaret: Oh, you weak, beautiful people who give up with such
              grace. What you need is someone to take hold of you—
              gently, with love, and hand your life back to you, like
              something gold you let go of—and I can! I'm determined
              to do it—and nothing's more determined than a cat on a
              hot tin roof—is there? Is there, baby?
              (*She touches his cheek gently.*)

As Williams noted, his Maggie augments in charm between the two
versions; his Brick modulates subtly and is a touch more receptive to her.
Shakespeare demonstrates how difficult it is to resist vitality in a stage role,
by creating Sir John Falstaff with a vivacity and wit that carries all before him.
There is nothing Shakespearean about Williams: He sketches archetypes,
caricatures, grotesques and cannot represent inwardness. And yet, with all his
limitations, he writes well, unlike Eugene O'Neill, who is leaden, and Arthur
Miller, who is drab. Thornton Wilder, Edward Albee, and Tony Kushner also
have their eloquences, but Williams remains the most articulate and adequate
of American dramatists up to this moment.

Yet his inability to dramatize inwardness is a considerable limitation.
What is Brick's spiritual malady? His homoeroticism is palpably less a burden
than is his homophobia: He will not accept Big Daddy's earlier bisexual-
ity any more than he could yield to love for Skipper (or to Maggie). Brick's
narcissism is central to the play, but even more crucial would be his nihilism,
if only Williams could tell us something about it. As a Hamlet, Brick does
not work at all; he hasn't enough mind to express what most deeply torments
him, and I fear that Williams shares this lack. What deprives *Cat on a Hot
Tin Roof* of any authentic aesthetic eminence is its obscurantism, which may

be indeliberate, unlike Joseph Conrad's *Heart of Darkness*. It is as though both Williams and Brick were saying: "The horror! The horror!" without ever knowing what they were trying to talk about.

The ultimately benign and loving Big Daddy and the adoring Big Mama are *not* the cause of Brick's despair. Were it not for his nihilistic malaise, it seems likely that Brick eventually would turn into his dying father and would become pragmatically bisexual or pansexual. Brick's attachment to Maggie is ambivalent but so was his affection for Skipper. As a pure narcissist, Brick is autoerotic in the manner of Walt Whitman.

The play's epigraph, from Dylan Thomas's "Do Not Go Gentle into That Good Night," is a gesture of tribute to Big Daddy, who, with Maggie the Cat, saves the play. Brick, without them, would freeze the audience, particularly now, when homosexuality is no longer an issue for an audience not dominated by fundamentalists and assorted other mossbacks. Read side by side with the wistful *Summer and Smoke*, *Cat on a Hot Tin Roof* seems more a film script than an achieved drama.

M. THOMAS INGE

The South, Tragedy, and Comedy in Tennessee Williams's Cat on a Hot Tin Roof

Along with Eugene O'Neill, Arthur Miller, and Edward Albee, Tennessee Williams is considered one of America's major playwrights. While his reputation is national and international, he is also very clearly a Southern writer. Born in Columbus, Mississippi, into a family related to some prominent Tennesseans, as well as the Georgia poet Sidney Lanier and raised in St. Louis, Williams had a distinctly Southern home life. It was to this experience that he turned when he first began to write plays, and nearly all of his major dramas are set in the South and portray the problems of Southern families and individuals. Like his fellow Mississippian William Faulkner, Williams has raised these regional figures to a level of wider relevance by addressing tragic conflicts of universal significance and application. His Southerness is especially evident in such plays as *The Glass Menagerie* (1945), *A Streetcar Named Desire* (1947), *Summer and Smoke* (1947), *Suddenly Last Summer* (1956), *Sweet Bird of Youth* (1959), and, of course, *Cat on a Hot Tin Roof* (1955).

Whether in the stage or screen version, most critics have agreed that the appeal of *Cat on a Hot Tin Roof* resides in its powerful, dominating, realistic characters—Big Daddy, Maggie, and Brick. This is evident in Fidel Castro's preference for the play because he reportedly thought of himself as being a cat on a hot tin roof,[1] although the significance of his identification with

From *The United States South: Regionalism and Identity*, edited by Valeria Gennaro Lerda and Tjebbe Westendorp, pp. 157–65. Copyright © 1991 by Bulzoni Editore.

5

Maggie would be unusual material for political analysis. But another main reason for its success may be the work's recreation in modernized forms of old familiar Southern stereotypes.

Though time may pass and political climates may change, the larger American public loves its Southern stereotypes, perhaps because they enable it to make simplistic sense out of the complex incomprehensibility of the region. In his introductory comments to the published text of the play, Tennessee Williams clearly acknowledges his stance as a Southern writer dealing with Southern materials:

> I once saw a group of little girls on a Mississippi sidewalk, all dolled up in their mothers' and sisters' castoff finery, old raggedy ball gowns and plumed hats and high-heeled slippers, enacting a meeting of ladies in a parlor with a perfect mimicry of polite Southern gush and simper. But one child was not satisfied with the attention paid her enraptured performance by the others, they were too involved in their own performances to suit her, so she stretched out her skinny arms and threw back her skinny neck and shrieked to the deaf heavens and her equally oblivious playmates, "Look at me, look at me, look at me!"
>
> And then her mother's high-heeled slippers threw her off balance and she fell to the sidewalk in a great howling tangle of soiled white satin and torn pink net, and still nobody looked at her. I wonder if she is not, now, a Southern writer.[2]

If Williams is shouting "Look at me," he doesn't have to shout very loudly in this play. The setting is very Southern—a large plantation house in the Mississippi Delta—and the language approximates a Southern dialect, but the characters who arrest our attention have a familiarity about them which sustains our interest throughout the viewing experience. If Faulkner's *The Sound and the Fury* chronicles the fall of the aristocratic Compson family, in *Cat* we witness the deterioration of the Pollitts, Southern *nouveau riche* who have achieved position through wealth rather than good breeding.

Big Daddy is an epitome of Southern masculine virility and assertiveness. The son of a tramp who left his son nothing to remember him by but a smile (this we discover only in the film version), with the front door of life slammed in his face much as it was for Thomas Sutpen in Faulkner's *Absalom, Absalom!*, like Sutpen he wrests a fortune from the wilderness. Obtaining the plantation from the two homosexuals who had lived and died there, he reasserts the Agrarian dream and builds an empire, although as Maggie notes, "He hasn't turned gentleman farmer, he's still a Mississippi redneck...."[3]

Unless Brick, the true son of his father, can produce an heir, the entire dream threatens to sink back into the lush wilderness from which it came, or become in the hands of Gooper an efficient but sterile business operation.

Brick is the romantic and idealistic counterpart to Big Daddy's realistic aggressiveness. Having lived in the loving admiration of the public eye as an athlete and believed in a form of ideal friendship and love beyond the physical, his dreams are punctured when he discovers the lies which support illusion and his own sexual ambivalence. In his romanticism, he is akin to the effeminate Ashley Wilkes of Margaret Mitchell's *Gone with the Wind*, but in his penchant for self-destruction, he reminds us of Quentin Compson of *The Sound and the Fury*, whose chivalric illusions have been shattered by his perverse lust for his promiscuous sister. To the popular mind, Brick may serve as a symbol of the modern Southerner, emasculated and impotent because the sources of his vitality—physical force and blind belief in romantic notions—have been wiped out by the changing tides of history and circumstance.

Maggie, the most compelling character in the play, possesses the strong-willed tenacity which has characterized the Southern woman in the popular media. Like Scarlet O'Hara of *Gone with the Wind*, she is determined to survive and reassert the control of the land which Brick threatens to let slip through his ineffective fingers. She is associated with the goddess of the hunt (at Ole Miss she won the Diana Trophy in the intercollegiate archery contest), and has several of the characteristics of the pistol-wielding Drusilla Hawk who, in Faulkner's *The Unvanquished*, attempts to instruct young Bayard Sartoris in the traditional rigors and responsibilities of manhood through seduction (even though she is married to his father). Though in her own way as acquisitive and ruthless as Gooper and Mae Pollitt in her pursuit of survival, she emerges an admirably independent woman, and we can only respect her agility and cleverness as a cat who refuses to leap from the hot tin roof of domestic conflict.

It is possible to interpret the entire play as an Agrarian allegory of Southern history, a symbolic comment on the state of the modern South. In this allegory, Big Daddy would be seen as representative of the Old South, a would-be nation that has created itself out of the frontier wilderness by mastering the forest, felling the trees, and cultivating the land until it becomes a lush and profitable garden of Eden. The Pollitt plantation, we are told several times in the text, is "twenty-eight thousand acres of the richest land this side of the Valley Nile,"[4] something that could be said of the entire Southland. We are not told what crop has made the Pollitt family fortune, but cotton seems likely, and the presence of faithful black family servants seems to be a holdover from the days of slavery.

The attraction that the media hold for Brick, as football player and sports announcer, and the absorption of Gooper in the worlds of law and business, are symbolic of the lures of technology and industrialism for the generation building the postwar New South. The Civil War concluded the possibility of the South remaining largely an Agrarian society based on an agricultural economy. It was simply a matter of how fast or how fully the South would industrialize and adapt the scientifically developed ways of technology to a new life style. The intrusion of technology into the Agrarian way of life in the play is symbolized by what Williams describes in his notes for the stage designer as "a monumental monstrosity peculiar to our times, a *huge* console combination of radio-phonograph (Hi-Fi with three speakers) TV set *and* liquor cabinet, bearing and containing many glasses and bottles, all in one piece.... This piece of furniture (?!), this monument, is a very complete and compact little shrine to virtually all the comforts and illusions behind which we hide from such things as the characters in the play are faced with."[5] This console is anathema to Big Daddy, who curses and reviles it when it is turned on during the play.

Of the two sons who have been corrupted and lured away by the glitter and hedonism of the New South, the materialism represented by the console, Gooper is the most compromised, wedded as he is to the new world of business and a wife whose only concerns are how much money and land he will inherit after Big Daddy's death. Their children, little "no-neck monsters"[6] as they are called by Maggie, represent the hoards of acquisitive generations which will consume the South with their greedy appetites, the "consumers" in the new order of capitalism which will embrace the nation.

There is some hope for the rescue of the Pollitt Agrarian domain in Brick, who like the South after the Civil War is dispirited, caught in despair over the loss of a dream and an idea for which a war had been fought but finally lost. As did many Southerners after the war, Brick questions the basis for his actions, the worthiness of his dream, and the degree of his responsibility for the tragedy and death it brought. He is paralyzed by his inability to break free of the weight of his guilt over the death of his friend Skipper, something like the burden of guilt felt by some Southerners over having fought for the unjust cause of slavery.

What can save Brick from his spiritual despair and the Pollitt plantation from the new economic order offered by Gooper is, of course, Maggie, an embodiment of the Agrarian spirit, devoted to fertility and regeneration, willing to sacrifice herself to any extent to rescue Brick from his malaise. It is no accident that Williams associates Maggie with the aggressive spirit of femininity represented by Diana, goddess of the hunt. Will she be successful in her mission? We are not told but are left to speculate about the outcome, as we are about the South in general. Certainly the old Agrarian order is gone, but have the values of the old order survived in the new scheme of things? Or rather has greed and materialism won out over the spiritual benefits once associated with tilling the soil? Those questions are still being debated in the modern South.

While the symbolic overtones of these striking figures are conveyed in both the stage and film versions of *Cat*, Williams's final intentions are not solely to reexamine the psyche of the Southern mind but to create out of these familiar materials a tragedy in the modern mode. Like the classical tragic figure, Brick has achieved success in the world through pride (in the film he destroys a huge poster of himself playing football which he has kept in the basement), and his tragic flaw lies in his inability to accept responsibility for his own downfall. His close friend Skipper committed suicide not because of the ineffective attempt to make love to Maggie but because Brick had hung up on him when he called to confess his true love for Brick. The click he needs to hear in his head before liquor can bring him peace is a rehearsal of the sound of hanging up the receiver to deny the truth. The "mendacity" or deceitful lying that Brick scorns in the actions around him—Gooper and Mae's pretended devotion to Big Daddy, the pretense of filial respect for his father symbolized by the robe Maggie has purchased as a birthday present, and the lie told Big Daddy and Big Mama that he is suffering from a spastic colon rather than terminal cancer—his scorn is actually a form of self-hatred for his own rejection of the truth and inability to accept the love of another man.

Brick experiences his moment of recognition when he and his father exchange truths. Big Daddy asserts, "You have been passing the buck. This disgust with mendacity is disgust with yourself. You!—dug the grave of your friend and kicked him in it!—before you'd face truth with him!" In anger at the accuracy of the charge, Brick replies, "How about these birthday congratulations, these many, many happy returns of the day, when ev'rbody but you knows there won't be any!"[7] Yet a reconciliation was not intended in the original text of the play. When Elia Kazan insisted on a rewrite of the third act in the direction of allowing Brick some change or sign of regeneration, Williams wrote that "the moral paralysis of Brick was a root thing in his tragedy, and to show a dramatic progression would obscure the meaning of that tragedy in him and ... I don't believe that a conversation, however revelatory, ever effects so immediate a change in the heart or even conduct of a person in Brick's state of spiritual disrepair."[8] Except for the fact that we know Maggie will somehow see to his survival, Williams intended to leave Brick doomed to relive the terrible moment he shut out the voice of his best friend's plea for understanding and perhaps unable to regain his potency and selfhood.

Although in his adaptation of the play for his 1958 film Richard Brooks claimed absolute fidelity to the stage version, when Tennessee Williams saw it, he said it was "somehow, not quite what I meant to say."[9] Williams's quiet statement must go down as one of the great understatements in modern letters. Not quite what he meant to say, indeed. It is too little to say that Brooks turned the play inside out and converted what was a tragedy of existential despair into a comedy of salvation and regeneration. In fairness to Brooks, however, Williams had already taken steps in that direction in writing for Kazan a modified version of act three for the Broadway production, but Brooks took licenses which changed the entire form and structure of the drama.

Many of the superficial changes have merely to do with toning down the language and content for larger public consumption and opening up the play from the claustrophobic bedroom into other parts of the house for cinematic variety. Big Daddy's expletive "Crap!" is exchanged for the milder "Bull!" and the word "cancer" is carefully avoided in the film dialogue. What Maggie sees in Big Daddy as a "lech" for her becomes in the film merely "an eye for women," and her reference to the way he "drops his eyes to my boobs and licks his old chops"[10] disappears from the script. The religious satire is muted when the avaricious Reverend Tooker of the play, who is continually talking about building monuments for his church at the most inappropriate times, is changed in the film to a layman using the church affiliation for his own political motives.

Perhaps it was concern for public sensibility that led to one of the more radical changes which stripped the text of a part of its power. This was the deletion of all suggestions that the relationship between Brick and Skipper was a matter of latent homosexuality. In the film, Brick's basic heterosexuality is underlined, by the bathroom scene in which he lovingly caresses Maggie's slip still bearing the scent of her body. His reason for rejecting her becomes simply a matter of shock over her being unfaithful with his best friend, and his suppressed guilt a matter of refusing to hear out Skipper's confession and possibly prevent his suicide. Brick thus becomes the cuckolded and jealous husband (although Maggie insists that nothing more than a kiss passed between her and Skipper) and not the tragic victim of sexual uncertainty and metaphysical despair.

In Maggie's last-ditch effort to regain her husband and give Big Daddy the grandson he needs to feel sure his line will continue and his property expand, she unexpectedly announces she is pregnant. An even more radical change in the meaning of the text begins with Brick's response to this lie. With obvious admiration for her, Brick realizes that some lies can become truth by sheer grit and determination. "Truth is something desperate," he says, "an' she's got it." He has just ascended the basement stairs where he and Big Daddy have visited the underworld, and after exchanging platitudes about the importance of love, family, and life, had determined that Big Daddy has the guts to die if Brick has the nerve to live. The father says, "We can start by helping each other up these stairs." In continuing the symbolic rise, Brick supports Maggie in her lie and invites her to climb the next set of steps to the bedroom with him. Her little girl reply at this stage, as delivered by Elizabeth Taylor, a cowed "Yes, sir," is enough to irritate the mildest supporter of feminism, not to mention being uncharacteristic of the aggressive Maggie we have grown to admire. As if to underline the obvious by now, in the bedroom Brick throws his pillows on their bed. Maggie's locking away the liquor in the play is not necessary in the film as it moves to clear redemption through reproduction.

What this means is that Brooks has transformed Williams's study of sexual and moral despair into a celebration of reformation and salvation. Brooks has made a tragedy into a comedy, complete with ritual reunion and phallic demonstration. I would submit that a more radical transformation is not possible.

It may be argued that each work, the play and the film, has a separate integrity and unity. It is difficult, however, to agree with Maurice Yacowar, who concludes in *Tennessee Williams and Film* that the movie is "a creative, faithful performance of the text."[11] The film certainly has its own appeal— in the sultry performance of Elizabeth Taylor, the blue-eyed charm of Paul Newman as Brick, the dominating presence of Burl Ives in the best acting role of his career, and the sizzling sexual chemistry that occurs between them all (Big Daddy's lecherous looks are accepted by Maggie without shock or surprise). Jack Carson and Madeleine Sherwood create appropriate characters in Gooper and Mae which add a new dimension to the meaning of what Faulkner called Snopesism, or pure, unadulterated acquisitiveness. Nevertheless, it will be wise to view the film as a separate phenomenon from the play and to remember what we should know by now—that films based on works of literature insist on and must be allowed to follow their own aesthetic paths, which are not likely to cross except in incidental ways.

NOTES

1. Mike Steen, *A Look at Tennessee Williams* (New York: Hawthorne Books, 1969), 219.

2. Tennessee Williams, *Cat on a Hot Tin Roof* (New York: New American Library/Signet, 1955), vii–viii.

3. *Ibid.*, 41.

4. *Ibid.*, 65.

5. *Ibid.*, xiii–xiv.

6. *Ibid.*, 15.

7. *Ibid.*, 92.

8. *Ibid.*, 125.

9. Maurice Yacowar, *Tennessee Williams and Film* (New York: Frederick Ungar, 1977), 48.

10. Williams, 19.

11. Yacowar, 38.

Works Cited

Steen, Mike. 1969. *A Look at Tennessee Williams.* New York: Hawthorne Books.

Williams, Tennessee. 1955. *Cat on a Hot Tin Roof.* New York: New American Library/Signet.

Yacowar, Maurice. 1977. *Tennessee Williams and Film.* New York: Frederick Ungar.

GULSHAN RAI KATARIA

The Hetairas (Maggie, Myrtle, Blanche)

A brief reference was made to the hetaira earlier. It would be appropriate to know and understand here the hetaira's psychological characteristics both in her positive and negative manifestations. 'Hetaira' literally means 'courtesan' and by extension means a companion woman engaged in the service of love. Jung's collaborator Toni Wolff (and other Jungians too), considers her as a woman for whom love is an end for which she can subordinate all familial and social taboos and surmount all physical and material impediments.[1] Her relationship is with the man and really a decisive factor of her life. Lord Byron had none other than a hetaira woman in mind when he said, "Man's love is of man's life a thing apart / 'Tis woman's whole existence." A hetaira is permeated by the essence of love or probably breathes love itself.

She is the extreme opposite and furthest away from the maternal type. She is instinctively oriented towards the individual and relates with him for his own sake and not as a father of her children or for his social status. She gets her fulfillment in interpersonal relationship, by being companion to him on any plan—intellectual, spiritual or sexual—all three at once, but not necessarily all three. Such a woman is often seen in those marriages where procreation is assigned a secondary significance. Elsewhere, in extramarital relationships, she is the 'other' woman, constantly filling the gap which a maternally oriented wife leaves in a husband's psyche, giving him value in

From *The Faces of Eve: A Study of Tennessee Williams's Heroines*, pp. 67–96. Copyright © 1992 by Gulshan Rai Kataria.

13

himself over mere husband or father. Because a hetaira is concerned with the subjective individual aspect in man as well as in herself, she tends to address herself to the shadow side of the individual, to the same extent that a mother will tend to disregard it in favour of social persona. In other words, that part of the psychic life of her man which a mother woman suppresses, ignores or hides (such as his talent for poetry or his fondness for oriental philosophy or cricket, simply because it is not 'useful' for the family) is sedulously tendered by this woman. She cares for his needs, moods and ambitions, and loves him in spite of his weaknesses and failures.

Now a hetaira, like a mother can be of two types: in extreme positive cases she may be *femme inspiratrice*, guiding and motivating the man to higher goals. Ann B. Ulanov says in this context, "In its positive aspects, this type . . . *is* symbolized for Jungians in the images of the priestess dedicated to the service of love, the love deities, the hierodules, and the woman who inspires men to prodigious feats."[2] Such a woman understands her man: discusses, adds and abets his projects, whets and feeds his appetite, but never stands in the way of his advancement. It is one such woman who stands behind a successful man without taking credit for anything. Further, if/because such a woman operates from outside the marriage, she comes in direct confrontation with the family of the person, the law and society at large not to mention her need for financial independence. The hetaira role thus cannot be played by a weaker woman because of inherent difficulties. The woman remains constantly on the horns of dilemma: if she loves her man and seeks her own fulfillment in giving him fulfillment, she rankles like a wound in conventional societies. If, on the other hand, she accepts the latter's dictates she has to neglect her own genuine nature. It is here that a hetaira finds herself on shaky grounds and tries to change her status of mistress to that of a wife, mistakenly believing that marriage is inevitable for a lasting relationship. Jungians, however, believe that the moment she attempts to give herself a status she ceases to be a pure hetaira. Irene Claremont de Castillejo writes, "The hetaira woman who breaks other people's marriages in order to become the wife herself has not yet learned what belongs to her particular form of relationship."[3] In other words, she has to observe rules of her peculiar relationship and know that the man belongs to her only in a relationship which she has to respect more than her own needs for a legal status. She has to understand what does not belong to her relationship and has moreover "to know when a relationship has become fulfilled and complete."[4] Upon realizing the fulfillment this eros-motivated woman must leave without making demands. The onus on the hetaira is rather heavy.

An unadapted or negative hetaira can become a *femme fatale*. Because of the intimate knowledge of her man's unconscious—his needs, wishes and ambitions—she can lapse into the role of a seductress weaning him away from everything else. De Castillejo remarks, "if so she may lure him away from his real destiny or the practical necessities of outer life, in favour of some illusory anima ambition, and so ultimately ruin him."[5] She might try to keep him tied to her apron-strings, use all feminine wiles and guiles to emasculate his urge for achieving miraculous heights or at least his cherished goals. Her possessive love and inordinate solicitude might make him seek her image in other women and cripple him psychologically. Another characteristic of a negative hetaira woman is her lack of commitment to permanence in outer relationship. She might throw her hands up too soon and walk away to seek and give fulfillment to another man. Such a hetaira is the *puella aeterna*, the eternal daughter, seeking love wherever she can get it. Edward C. Whitmont comments, "Indeed, she may, like her male counterpart, *puer aeternus*, shy away from making any concrete commitment and forever lead a provisory life of emotional wandering."[6] Exhibitionism and egotism are other negative traits in such a woman: for a true hetaira mediates the personal unconscious of her man unobstrusively, quietly, without looking for credit or reward.

Lest the foregoing discussion should create an impression that a hetaira has to be a weak woman or a doormat, it may be repeated that that is not true. The woman has to be brave enough to face the world, work for her own financial independence, and simultaneously bring the best out of her man. She might use her maidenly softness now and alternate it with aggression and wilfulness then, all in the service of the relationship. Secondly, it is not necessary that a hetaira can only be the other woman and not one's wife. In fact, the converse is as true, though rare. Blessed is the man who has a wife with an overlay of hetaira personality in her. And lastly, the traits mentioned above are archetypal. Variations on the archetype are always possible depending upon the secondary personality which might be of the mother or medium.

Tennessee Williams created at least two pleasing and positive hetairas, viz., Maggie (in *Cat on a Hot Tin Roof*) and Myrtle (in *Kingdom of Earth*).

Maggie, the wife of Brick Pollitt, is companion to him at the sexual level. She is a beautiful, sleek, slender and a soft woman, immensely conscious and proud of her looks. Unlike the other heroines of Williams, who are, more often than not, past their prime, Maggie is youthful, lusty and vivacious. Williams describes her as a "pretty young woman"[7] with a voice that "has range and music," (p. 111) a "gay, charming smile," (p. 113) a woman who has "lovely bare arms" (p. 111), and "giggles with a hand fluttering at her throat and her breast and her long throat arched," (p. 114) and her speech is oddly funny, because her eyes "constantly twinkle and her voice shakes with laughter which is basically indulgent." (p. 113) She has a "bitchy" humour (p. 114), which Williams attributes to her estrangement with her husband for the nonce. In other words, she is a sensual, languorous and voluptuously appeasing hetaira woman, who has kept herself attractive for the conquest of her alienated husband. (p. 128) She is "Great: the greatest" (p. 172) in bed. She has an intense love for Brick, and she would not look at any other man: "I can't see a man but you! Even with my eyes closed, I just see you.... But don't continue my torture. I can't live on and on under these circumstances." (p. 123) Immediately after her marriage with Brick, she tries to obliterate her identity in his love and in his love for football. Brick recalls:

> She went on the road that with the Dixie stars. Oh she made a great show of being the world's best sport. She wore a—wore a—tall bearskin cap! A shako, they call it, a dyed moleskin coat, a moleskin coat dyed red!—Cut up crazy! Rented hotel ball rooms for victory celebrations, wouldn't cancel them when it—turned out—defeat.... (p. 172)

Maggie has been presented in the play as a hetaira woman for whom love of the man is supreme. She has sacrificed herself for him in the past and continues to do so when the play opens.

As a hetaira, Maggie is more into the power and allure of sex than into other components of the hetaira. She is aware of the spell she can cast upon men by her bewitching looks and figure. She has exploited them many a time to gain favour, love and attention. She is conscious of Big Daddy's eyes which seem to pry into her person. She flirts with him now and then knowing that the lascivious "Big Daddy harbours a little unconscious lech for me.... Way he always drops his eyes down my body when I'm talkin' to him, drops his eyes to my boobs an' licks his old chops! Ha ha!" (p. 113) This charming woman has exercised her powerful beauty in the past and forced Brick to marry her. (p. 172) She has deliberately exercised her charms on Big Daddy to circumvent the danger of being cut off from his inheritance in view of Brick's intemperance with alcohol. She relishes talking about the attentions she receives from men while walking on the roadside. She tells Brick about them:

> They still see me, Brick, and they like what they see. Un-huh. Some of them would give their—... Other men still want me.... Why, last week in Memphis everywhere that I went men's eyes burned holes in my clothes, at the country club and in the restaurants and department stores, there wasn't a man I met or walked by that didn't first eat me up with his eyes and turn around when I passed him and look back at me. Why, at Alice's party for her New York cousins, the best lookin' man in the crowd—followed me upstairs

and tried to force his way in the powder room with me, followed me to the door and tried to force his way in! (pp. 128–129)

She talks of this handsome man as a having a "lech" for her. By way of comment, one may add that her repeated babbling of others' "lech" for her comes from her idea that this way she can excite Brick's jealousy and also his desire for her. Brick who has not been sleeping with his wife ever since his friend Skipper died has made Maggie as nervous as a cat. She has begun to feel that Brick's deliberate casting her aside means her defeat and of her lack of charms, to provoke sexual desire in her man. She, therefore, talks of others' "lech" for her so as to arouse the sexual passion in him. She flaunts her powerful battery—her breasts and her hips—to Brick and says:

> You know, our sex life didn't just peter out in the usual way, it was cut off short, long before the natural time for it to, and it's going to revive again, just as sudden as that. I'm confident of it. That's what I'm keeping myself attractive for. For the time when you'll see me again like other men see me ... Look Brick! [*She stands before the long oval mirror, touches her breasts and then her hips with her two hands.*] How high my body stays on me! Nothing has fallen off me—not a fraction ... (pp. 128–129)

Her exhibitionistic use of her sexual lure also sets her up in the hetaira modality. But her exploitation of her sexual charms to gain her selfish ends makes her a powerful and dangerous hetaira.

To a perceptive reader, the animus of Maggie would clearly seem reflected in Big Daddy. Her lust for life, for love, for children, for money, for comfort and for talking, all would reveal her connection with the old man. Her aggressive, indefatigable spirit and strength are much like Big Daddy's who started from a scratch to become the biggest landlord of the Delta, just as Maggie has fought her way up to Brick. Her desperate but spirited attempts at the revival and restitution of her conjugal life are identical with Big Daddy's vigorous zest for life with which he seeks to defeat death. Her talk of others' "lech" for her can be equated with Big Daddy's bragging about his sexual potency, even on his deathbed, "I still have desire for women and this is my sixty-fifth birthday." (p. 155) When Maggie talks of sleeping with another man surreptitiously so that Brick could not cast her off for faithlessness and adultery, she echoes Big Daddy's desire which he vociferously announced to his derelict son Brick:

> All I ask of that woman [Big Mama] is that she leave me alone. But she can't admit to herself that she makes me sick. That comes of

having slept with her too many years. Should of quit much sooner but that old woman she never got enough of it—and I was good in bed . . . I never should of wasted so much of it on her. . . . They say you got just so many and each one is numbered. Well, I got a few left in me, a few, and I'm going to pick me a good one to spend 'em on! I'm going to pick me a choice one, I don't care how much she costs. I'll smother her in—minks! Ha ha! I'll strip her naked and smother her in minks and choke her with diamonds! (pp. 157–158)

Thus, Maggie combines in herself the sexuality and aggressiveness of Big Daddy. Moreover, she delights in Big Daddy's use of four-letter words, and laughs heartily at his jokes. She shares Big Daddy's love for Brick and hatred for Mae and Gooper, and their little children, whom she calls "no-neck monsters." (p. 109) She indulgently and delightfully reports Big Daddy's strong aversion of their children to Gooper. Maggie adds, "Well I swear, I simply could have di-ieed." (p. 110) The rapport between Maggie and Big Daddy is obvious from her remark:

Big Daddy dotes on you, honey; and he can't stand Brother Man and Brother Man's wife, that monster of fertility, Mae; she's downright odious to him. Know how I know? By little expressions that flicker over his face . . . (p. 112)

Moreover, Maggie's concern at Brick's alcoholism and avoiding sexual intercourse with her is echoed by Big Daddy. Only she and Big Daddy try to break into the wall of his composure to elicit the confession from him about his relations with Skipper. She succeeds only in part, but Big Daddy succeeds completely.

Being possessed by Big Daddy's animus, the animus of a sexually aggressive hero and not that of a wise old man, Maggie often acts in an aggressive and drastic manner. Her actions, when offended or irritated, are replete with willfulness and drive for power. Pointing out the negative facets of the hero animus, Ann Belford Ulanov says, "Negatively, the hero animus becomes unrelated aggression, ravaging her, severing ties both within herself and outside her in destructive ways."[8] This devastating aspect of her personality is seen in her destruction of the love affair between Skipper and Brick which threatened her conjugal harmony. She was aware of their attraction to each other at college. After their graduation Skipper and Brick decided to tie themselves together under the banner of one team so that their goings-on together would not be perceived. But with the help of her differentiated and perspicacious animus, Maggie focused on the problem and saw through the game that was designed to dupe the collective. She says:

> You married me early that summer we graduated out of Ole Miss, and we were happy. Weren't we, we were blissful. Yes, hit heaven together ev'ry time that we loved! But that fall you an' Skipper turned down wonderful offers of jobs in order to keep on bein' football heroes—pro-football heroes. You organized the Dixie Stars that fall, so you could keep on bein' team-mates forever! But somethin' was not right with it!—*Me included!*—between you. (p. 135)

Maggie, his anima since his college days, recalls that even in college they never dated exclusively. It was always double-dating with Skipper and his sweetheart. But Maggie reminisces that every date "was more like a date between you and Skipper. Gladys and I were just sort of tagging along as if it was necessary to chaperone you!—to make a good public impression—." (p. 134) With all these facts of the past in mind, Maggie set out to destroy the relationship which was so far disguised as an idyllic attraction. She stepped in with all her power and challenged their idyllic romance and their hanging on to the adolescent dreams of glory. She destroyed their idyllic Eden by telling Skipper about his homosexual feelings for Brick. Skipper then "made that pitiful, ineffectual little attempt to prove that what I had said wasn't true . . . ," (p. 135) by trying to sleep with her. When it did not work out he thought the charges were true. Skipper thereafter broke down and died. Maggie, the cat, thus achieved her goal and delivered her husband, Brick, from being seduced away. Indeed, Skipper paid heavily for his intrusion into the domain that belonged to the hetaira woman.

But Maggie also overreacted in exposing Skipper. She has not understood what belongs to her realm. As the carrier of Brick's anima, she should have been wary and careful. She lacks the scruples that a finely differentiated hetaira with a sense of psychology and ethics would have. Toni Wolff sounds a note of warning regarding the problematical ethical areas in the hetaira-power over the male. Ulanov explains her warning:

> The Hetaira's relation to the male stimulates and promotes his individual interests, his inclinations, and even his problems, thus effecting his shadow side and the subjective side of his anima. This can be dangerous if she has not learned what properly belongs to the relationship and what does not.[9]

By working on the destruction of her husband's homosexual friend, Maggie inadvertently slighted the shadow side of the former's personality. This was the side that Brick would have hidden from public view. She traces the reasons for his alcoholism, ennui and disgust with the world to a factor, which for reasons like exposure and scandal, Brick wants to conceal. Even Brick warns her off when she pricks him again and again by the mention of Skipper and their relationship. He says, "Look Maggie, what you're doing is a dangerous thing to do. You're—you're—you're fooling with something that nobody ought to fool with." (p. 133) Brick obviously means his shadow. As his anima, the contents of Brick's personal unconscious were available to her. She committed a mistake, therefore, by telling Brick about having tested and proved Skipper homosexual. She admits her mistake now:

> I've thought a whole lot about it and now I know when I made my mistake. Yes, I made my mistake, when I told you the truth about the thing with Skipper. Never should have confessed it, a fatal error, tellin' you that thing with Skipper. (p. 133)

Maggie is rightly penitent over having trifled with the shadow side of his personality, which as a mediatrix of his personal unconscious she should have avoided.

In fact, by having driven Skipper to death, by declaring and proving him homosexual, Maggie has put Brick also in a predicament where he has begun to feel afraid of being an unconscious homosexual himself. He has deteriorated so badly over the weeks after Skipper's death that he does not like sex being mentioned in his presence. Bernard F. Dukore has made interesting observations:

> To be sure, Brick is afraid that he is homosexual and this fear explains a great deal of the past and present action. He refuses to sleep with his wife. He is disgusted with even the mention of sex. "That kind of talk is disgusting," he says when Maggie describes Big Daddy admiring her body. When his father talks of having pleasure with women, "Brick's smile fades a little but lingers." He advises Maggie to take a lover. This would give him reasons for despising women, a justification for his homosexual fears. Since his close friend Skipper was homosexual, Brick doubts his own normalcy. Maggie realizes that Brick is not homosexual, but although he states that he is not, he inwardly fears that he is the one who is discussing his relationship with Skipper 'names it dirty' though he unjustly accuses Maggie of doing so.[10]

To avoid the risk of being tested sexually like Skipper, Brick begins to soak himself in alcohol. He uses drink to, what is called in Gestalt psychology, "desensitize" himself. His dissociation from the quotidian reality is thus designed to insulate himself against being hurt. His withdrawal, his nonchalance about Big Daddy's huge property, cash or his pathological problems can be construed as his desperate attempts to check his neurosis from turning into psychosis. In other words, by swamping his brain with liquor, he is using a kind of defence mechanism to alleviate his ego-injury, his neurotic anxiety.

When Maggie set out to explore and explode the relationship between Brick and Skipper, she was not conscious of the repercussions. Now faced with them, with Brick hitting the bottle, drifting away and lapsing into a state of dissociation, Maggie becomes cautious and nervous. It seems that Brick's state of anxiety has infected her mind and body. In other words, she becomes the 'cat on a hot tin roof' of the title. She admits that she has "gone through this *hideous!—transformation* become—*hard*! *Frantic*!. . . . cruel!" She adds, "I'm not-thin-skinned any more, can't afford t'be thin-skinned any more." (p. 116) Her use of the word 'afford' probably signifies that now she is aware of the troubles ahead if Brick continues with his intemperate behaviour, which has compelled her—the Cat—to fight a defensive battle. Cat is the symbol of the sensual hetaira, as also of the mystery, jealousy, savagery, vindictiveness and guilefulness associated with the Feminine. The "hot tin roof" of the title not only signifies that a highly sensual woman, believing intensely in man–woman relationship, has been suddenly denied the pleasure of the senses; the denial intensifies her sexuality till it burns in an infrared manner. She really becomes a cat sizzling on a hot tin roof. It also alludes to the troubles under the tin roof on which she stands. There is Big Daddy dying of cancer, there are claimants to his inheritance already in the house clamouring hard to cut Brick and Maggie off from the legacy, simply because Maggie is childless and Brick an alcoholic. On top of it, there is her husband, Brick, indifferent to the tough times ahead, if Mae and Gooper succeed in their designs. Consequently, Maggie is obliged to fight for her husband, and by implication, for herself too. She cannot afford any complacency because the war is on. Nancy M. Tischler defines Maggie beautifully: "She is a scrappy little fighter, spitting at the enemy, purring for the master, clawing for survival."[11] In taking up the defence for her crippled husband, Maggie becomes the amazonian hetaira. On the other hand, she reminds one of the mother-cat carrying her kitten lovingly by the neck, coaxing him back to life, attempting to reconstitute and revive his interest in reality.

But her repeated attempts, her overtures, her entreaties meet with the unruffled 'cool' of the man. Her attempts recoil on herself and the cat on a hot tin roof becomes even more nervous. She notices his detachment which throws her off her balance. She becomes even more catty and tries all the feminine wiles and guiles on him. She envies his coolness and says, "But one thing I don't have is the charm of the defeated, my hat is in the ring and I am determined to win!" She asks, "What is the victory of a cat on a hot tin roof? I wish I knew ... Just staying on it, I guess, as long as she can. . . ." (p. 118) Her vigorous spirit coupled with her unflinching determination makes her a real fighter. She proceeds in a cool and calculating manner to break into his composure and elicit the information regarding his neurosis which manifests itself in his dissociation from reality. She tells him about the conspiracy afoot to send him away to Rainbow Hill, where "dope fiends" are lodged. (p. 112) Then she tells him about being repeatedly taunted for childlessness. She reports, "It goes on all the time, along with constant little remarks and innuendoes about the fact that you and I have not produced any children, are totally childless and therefore totally useless." (p. 110) Then she talks of others' "lech" for her and includes Big Daddy and Sonny Boy Maxwell who have eyed her with lascivious desire. But she finds that the mention of these three details fail to move, disturb or pierce the impervious wall of his composure. Then she talks of Skipper and succeeds. Brick suddenly loses his enviable cool and shouts at her. Maggie's delight at finding out the root cause of his troubles is obvious in these lines:

> We mustn't scream at each other, the walls in this house have ears ... but that's the first time I've heard you raise your voice in a long time, Brick. A crack in the wall?—Of composure?—I think that's a good sign ... A sign of nerves in a player on the defensive! (p. 119)

She tells him to cathart, so that the burden is lifted and shared. She wants to extricate him from the whirlpool of detachment and withdrawal. She wants him not to give in to defeat and passivity. Rather, she wants him to fight his way out of the labyrinth of despair and noninvolvement. She enthuses and provokes him to grapple with life. Like a true *femme inspiratrice* she says:

> Laws of silence don't work. . . . When something is festering in your memory or your imagination, laws of silence don't work, it's just like shutting a door and locking it on a house on fire in hope of forgetting that the house is burning. But not facing a fire doesn't put it out. Silence about a thing just magnifies it. It grows and festers in silence, becomes malignant ... (p. 119)

Like a true hetaira, the carrier of his anima, she wants to share his problems. She smashes his composure and enters into the fortress and advises him, "My only point, the only point that I'm making, is life has got to be allowed to continue even after the *dream* of life is-all-over . . ." (p. 134) She tells him that the only way to protect the inheritance and their interests is by exploiting the love that Big Daddy has for both of them. But Big Daddy would make reservations in his legacy unless they beget a child. For the sake of inheritance, for the sake of future life and comfort they have to make love and have a child. She says, " . . . there is no reason why we can't have a child whenever we want one. And this is my time by the calendar to conceive." (p. 137) She forewarns him of the dangers of his intemperance in drinking—it can cut them out of the legacy which would mean growing old without money. She says:

> You can be young without money but you can't be old without it.
> You've got to be old *with* money because to be old without it is just
> too awful, you've got to be one or the other, either young or *with*
> money, you can't be old and *without* it. (p. 132)

Another danger that she foresees is that Gooper is going to be given the purse and the power of attorney to "dole out remittances" to them, which would mean complete dependence because then he would be able to "cut off our credit wherever, whenever he wanted". (p. 112) She wants him to wake up to the emergency of the situation by reconnecting him to the reality principle. With these facts in mind, it is difficult to agree with Jeanne M. McGlinn who thinks of her as a selfish, self-centered, manipulative and destructive woman who acts out of the motivation to benefit herself.[12] Maggie, though not entirely altruistic, yet acts out of a profound love and concern for her husband. She wants a child not only to protect the inheritance, but also because it would mean making Brick a responsible man once again. Moreover, the begetting of a child would stem the tide of the taunting attacks and also fulfil her—"'cause I'm consumed with envy an' eaten up with longing?" (p. 122) She has not given up hope of emerging victorious. Defeat is not for her. She would rather die or kill herself before facing defeat. She says:

> You know, if I thought you would never, never, never make love to
> me again—I would go downstairs to the kitchen and pick out the
> sharpest knife I could find and stick it straight into my heart, I
> swear that I would! (p. 118)

To seduce Brick back into life, she alternatively entreats, mocks, curses, warns, goads, harangues and even threatens suicide. Like a zealous mother, she tries to plan and provide for his future, like a lawyer she fights for him and like a priestess of love, a hierodule, she invites "the godlike being" (p. 133) to consummate with her, beget a child and save himself.

In order to get perhaps at the deepest layer of meaning in the Maggie–Brick relationship, one has to take recourse to the Sphinx myth. Sphinx the Egyptian deity adopted by the Greeks had a cat's body with face and breasts of a woman. She was the archetype of the all-enveloping and all-deluding mysteries associated with the Feminine. She is the deepest level of the Archetypal Feminine. She, it is said in the myth, would pose riddles and put to death those who failed and rewarded those who succeeded in meeting the challenge posed by her. The riddles of the Sphinx could not be answered by those who denied life. For answering her riddles one was supposed to know life experientially. She was the hetaira of Matriarchy who would question a man's shadow and kill his anima in case he failed. In her all authority of life was vested. Moreover, a Sphinx was housed on an elevated platform from where she shot questions at victims. Maggie is also a "cat"—a Sphinx—on a "hot" tin roof. Both the symbols ("Cat" and "hot") signify lust and sex. The question of the Sphinx in this play, therefore, is whether Brick can answer Maggie's lust in order to save himself. Skipper could not answer her riddle and perished. Brick, too, cannot individuate unless he answers her sexuality. Towards the end of the play when Maggie tells a lie about having conceived, he seems to answer one of her riddles by "keeping still", (p. 195) to save her face, and implicitly affirming her lie. His surrender to Maggie at the end of the play is surrender to the Feminine, which means dropping the ego in order to reconnect with the springs of life. He drops his ego and walks into her arms which hold him "gently, gently with love", (p. 197) in order to rejuvenate and reconstitute him.

Like Maggie, Myrtle Ravenstock (née Kane) in *Kingdom of Earth* is not only central to the play but also a positive hetaira woman. At the beginning of the play, however, she appears maternal—but that is merely a persona to hide her real nature. Her maternal role first.

Myrtle, one discovers, meets her one-lunged husband, Lot Ravenstock, on a television programme, quickly accepts his proposal for marriage in her attempt to bunk from "show business."[13] She wishes to put an end to the life of emotional wandering and the life of a prostitute she has led, to give herself "a quiet and happy married life", (p. 189) to fulfill her dream of "settl'n down somewhere sometime". (p. 209) Her keenness to settle down with a man-with-property in order to have social security, stability and 'decency' blinds her to the future on the conjugal front. She does not pause to reflect on the prospects that her marriage with a sickly man (who unknown to herself is a transvestite and also tuberculoid) would offer her. For both Lot and Myrtle marriage is the most expedient measure: while Myrtle gets the coveted status of a wife, Lot hopes to retrieve his property from his half-brother Chicken. The latter, a mulatto, hated by Lot's mother as a 'nigra' had made Lot sign a document bequeathing all property to himself. Unable to win over Chicken in a straight fight, Lot has now married so that the property passes on to her, a white woman, after his death giving the souls of the mother and son (Lot) eternal peace.

Finding her husband in a desperate situation, Myrtle quickly steps into the maternal role of a nurse. She coddles him with "Lot Baby" and "Sugar", puts his head in her lap, strokes his forehead affectionately and sings him a lullaby:

"Cuddle up a little closer, baby mine.
Cuddle up and say you'll be my clinging vine!"
Mmmm, Sugar! Last night you touched the deepest chord in my nature, which is the maternal chord in me. Do you know, do you realize what a beautiful thing you are? (p. 135)

She assuages his regret over his failure in bed on their first night by cooing words of endearment, "Baby, last night don't count. You was too nervous. I'll tell you something that might surprise you. A man is twice as nervous as a woman, and you are twice as nervous as a man". (p. 135) His insistent references to his mother, Miss Lottie, make her jealous and she tells Lot that she would have none of it. "Now, baby, this mother-complex, I'm gonna get that out of you, Lot, 'cause I'm not just your wife, I'm also your mother and I'm not daid, I'm livin'." (p. 130)

Her new found role of a wife, mother and nurse has also made her decency-conscious, so to speak. An "elegant" blonde man for a husband, "a little dream of a parlor" (p. 137), and so much of property have made her rise to the occasion and behave with "self respeck an' decency as a woman!" (p. 178) Her loud protests against indecency stem from her compensatory need to drown her promiscuous past in over-genteel mannerisms and affectations. For instance, she chastises Chicken for carving an indecent picture on the kitchen table, "An' you ought to know it's insulting to a clean-livin' woman who is not interested or attracted to indecent things in life." (p. 164) She complains to Lot against him and his vulgarity, "Decent people have got to be protected, flood or no flood, yes, come hell or high water. I'm going down there and try to phone the police." (p. 167) What one needs to see through is her attempt to disguise her real sensual nature under compulsion from the

newly acquired role of a housewife. Jerrold A. Phillips also notes that she tries
to "repress her own elemental nature—her sexuality—as she tries to reform
her promiscuity to wifely virtue and motherly kindness."[14] It is only when she
meets Chicken that she realises that her husband is an impotent child, her
house no home, her marriage no security. It is then that she decides to give up
all pretence and returns to her own essential nature, which is that of a woman
who enjoys giving love and receiving attention from men.

Myrtle is a voluptuous young woman, one who would arouse "curious
attention". Williams, her creator, conceived Myrtle as "a rather fleshy young
woman, amiably loud-voiced. . . . wearing a pink turtle neck sweater and tight
checkered slacks. Her blonde-dyed hair is set up in a wet silk-scarf, magenta
colored. Her appearance suggests an imitation of a Hollywood glamor girl
which doesn't succeed as a good imitation." (p. 127) Later when she goes
downstairs on instructions from Lot to trounce Chicken and get the papers
from his pocket, she changes into a rather flamboyant costume "a sheer blouse
sprinkled with tiny brilliants and a velveteen skirt." (p. 156) She says she
never wears slacks after dark, which tells about her past life in show-business
where she was billed as a 'Petite Personality Kid'. Her confident boast, "I've
yet to meet the man that I couldn't handle" (p. 137), and "I'm not scared of
that man [Chicken], or any man livin'! No, Sir!" (p. 141) obviously stem from
her promiscuous experience with men. Chicken minces no words when he
tells her for what he takes her, "You kick with the right leg, you kick with the
left leg, and between your legs you make your living?" (p. 147) Even Lot calls
her a "whore" (p. 195), when he finds her mesmerised by Chicken and return-
ing to him on one pretext or another. From her assumed mother role she once
again returns to her vital self. Jerrold A. Phillips' remarks corroborate these
observations, "Myrtle's seven descents also reveal a changing definition of
love that occurs during the course of the play. She moves from her sacrificial
motherliness to a resumption of her real self."[15]

Being thus in the hetaira modality, Myrtle makes no mistake in recog-
nising Chicken as a powerful masculine figure who will finally bring her
emotional stability and deep instinctual fulfillment. In this context it would
not be beside the point to recapitulate Myrtle's confession at the first sight of
Chicken in the story entitled "Kingdom of Earth" published in *The Knightly
Quest and Other Stories* (1966): "The minute I laid eyes on you, the first glance
I took at that big powerful body, I said to myself, Oh, oh, your goose is cooked,
Myrtle! . . . Well, I said, when somebody's goose is cooked the best way to
have it is cooked with plenty of gravy."[16] To Chicken, who needs affirmation
and love of a woman, she gives the best compliments in the play. She says,
" . . . and another thing, I pride myself on is noticin' an' appreciating a man's
appearance. Physical. I notice such things about him as a strong figure, in fine

proportion. Mouth? Full. Teeth? White. Glist'nin', why, you look like a man that could hold back the flood of a river." (p. 208)

Chicken, a deprived young man, begotten out of wedlock on a coloured woman, has been despised by the neighbourhood and rebuffed even by the white trash (the prostitutes) to stay in his place. "That's how it is with me an' wimmen around here. Talk, suspicion, insult." (p. 206) He is naturally suspicious of Myrtle's gooey words and remains stiff and unresponsive even when passion tears him within. He responds to her only when she volunteers to abdicate the 'kingdom of earth' he is after, and which he fears she will grab from himself. Only after she writes "All's Chicken's when Lot dies", (p. 200) that he makes love to her on the kitchen table. He is thrilled at having been powerfully desired by a woman. His passionate love-making leaves Myrtle in a daze: "she looks as if she had undergone an experience of exceptional nature and magnitude." (p. 203) He gradually opens up and confesses that he is a mulatto, that he has got a raw deal out of life, and that he holds a woman's love as the highest and the most enviable gift a man could ever have. Nothing could compare with "what's able to happen between a man and a woman, just that thing, nothing more, is perfect." (p. 211) The woman he desperately needed, one who would look up to him for love, protection and satisfaction, he finds in Myrtle. The latter gives him value in himself by praising his physical attributes and declaring him her "saviour". (p. 183) With her head leaning on his shoulder, she says the very words he always yearned to hear:

> I pray for your protection, and right now I feel like that prayer is going to be answered. Go on talking in that deep voice of yours. I don't just hear it. It, it—it gives me a sensation in my ears and goes all through my body—it vibrates in me. I don't even hear the river. (p. 211)

The uncouth youth, Chicken, who acquired the name when he bit off the heads of chickens to quench his thirst with their blood as he perched atop the roof of their house one time when the Mississippi flooded the entire area, finds a woman who pays tribute to his boorish virility. The Mississippi is flooding once again and Chicken with his Herculean prowess seems to her the only one who would save her from this catastrophe. A gratified Chicken promises to save her and requests, "Produce me a son. Produce a child for me, could you? Always wanted a child from an all-white woman." (p. 214) A child from Myrtle will symbolise emergence from a life of deprivation to a life of wholeness, helping him overcome the sense of injury from the society at large. The Kingdom of Earth would then prosper to fruition with both Chicken and Myrtle happy in their garden of love.

The symbols in *Kingdom of Earth* though complicated yet bring us to the core of the play's meaning. The flood recalls the deluge of the Old Testament that washed away Sodom and Gomorrah: only Lot was saved along with his two daughters while his wife turned into a pillar of salt. In a grotesque inversion of these stories, Lot the transvestite here is the weak and corrupt who tries to cheat Chicken through getting married and one who is likely to be washed away by the surging waters leaving the Kingdom of Earth clean. The flood at the same time also symbolises the human passions. Myrtle tells that she is a passionate woman who has been taking pills from a Memphis doctor to restrain her natural inclination to give herself in service of all comers. Her sensual nature is also hinted at in the diagnosis of her asthma which said that she "was living with a cat and had an allergy to it." (p. 171) Cat, as mentioned in the analysis of Maggie, represents the feminine principle—mysterious, playful, jealous and loving. She is probably allergic to cats because she has not entered into a comprehensive relationship with the attributes that cat signifies and has only lived her animal nature. On arrival in Lot's house she tries to repress the latter as well in favour of wifely virtue only to find the inexorable flood of passions rising and asking for someone who would have the strength to tame it. Chicken the "bull of a man," (p. 168) and "a suitable antagonist to a flooding river", (p. 125) rechannelises her sexuality and reconnects her with her essential nature.

The play is suggestively subtitled "Seven Descents of Myrtle". A perceptive reader would understand that each descent takes her closer to Chicken. Her first descent is to the Mississippi delta house, to the Kingdom of Earth, from Memphis. Her second descent is coming downstairs with Lot to the kitchen for coffee: here she tells Chicken all about her past life, giving Chicken a playful little slap on the shoulder, (p. 102) which surprises the latter. She comes down alone during her third descent smelling hot French fries and expresses the wish to be "better acquainted" with each other. (p. 163) Her fourth is on Lot's persuasion to make Chicken drunk and steal away the legal papers about the property from his wallet. This time she sings some old favourite numbers with him and plays on the "mansize instrument", the guitar, which he gives her. She runs away screaming this time when Chicken throws the cat in the water. Her fifth descent to fill the 'hot water bottle' for warming Lot messes up her life. She has difficulty with heating the water which suggests her attempt to repress her own elemental nature. Chicken furnishes her with fresh rain water from the barrel outside which probably is suggestive of the invigorating freshness she may have from him outside her marital life. Chicken coolly talks of the flood, of Lot's imminent death and her own death by water unless he saves her. Even as she implores him to rescue her, he does not promise safety unless she brings to him their marriage licence. The tables are thus turned on herself: she came downstairs a while earlier to steal away the legal papers but goes upstairs now to bring her marriage certificate, with which she returns in her sixth descent. Her seventh is her surrender to Chicken: she writes as dictated by him. Chicken now consummates with her for he does not fear her as a rival but accepts her as a partner in his kingdom of earth. Number seven, symbolic of perfection, signifies the union of the high with the low, the 'decent' with the boorish, the white with the 'nigra' and archetypally speaking of fire with water. Through each descent the hetaira modality is progressively constellated till through surrender comes wholeness.

II

In the second part of this chapter a negative hetaira woman, Blanche DuBois, shall be analysed. 'Negative' here is neither any attempt to denigrate her status as an excellent artistic creation of Williams nor is it used in any moral sense. 'Negative' is merely restricted to the archetypal manifestation of the hetaira where one lacking in emotional centring attracts the label. While Blanche too is engaged in the service of eros, enjoys giving and taking of love, hers is not necessarily with someone to whom she is emotionally drawn. A drift characterises the numinous core of her personality. And that is not all for categorising her as negative: several other reasons shall be mentioned as exploration and analysis unfolds her inherent personality.

Blanche DuBois, by far the greatest creation of Tennessee Williams, is the heroine of *A Streetcar Named Desire*. Born into an old agrarian Southern family of French extraction, she was raised at Belle Reve (meaning "Beautiful Dream") the ancestral mansion outside Laurel, Mississippi. She and younger sister Stella (and possibly a third, Margaret, who died) had the best of a pampered and comfortable childhood what with all the affluence, black slaves and courteous attention from gentlemen. Their adolescence, however, saw the rich plantation going to seed as a price for the "epic fornications"[17] that the men of the family indulged in, leaving only the house and some twenty acres of land.

Blanche's downhill journey also seems to begin around this time. She fell in love with an extremely good-looking young poet Allan Grey and eloped with him. She "adored him and thought him almost too fine to be human", (p. 140) until one day she discovered his homosexuality. Sexually innocent then, she could not understand that the boy needed her help through his half-spoken pleas to be saved from his perversion. Shocked and repelled, Blanche accused him publicly precipitating his suicide a few minutes later by the shore of the lake. The grievous loss and how it came about left a deep trauma in her psychic life. In close succession to her husband's death came the deaths of her father, mother, sister Margaret and an old cousin Jesse, each contributing to her loneliness and fear of death and disease. Stella by then had left and settled with a Polish master-sergeant Stanley Kowalski, visiting only briefly for funerals. Blanche who had to pawn the estate to meet the medical and funeral expenses soon found it slipping from her fingers and had no means to retrieve it.

It was around this time that her loneliness began to overwhelm her leading to the beginning of her search for distraction in eros, the opposite of thanatos. Fleeting intimacies with younger companions seemed to take the sting out of her loneliness, at least momentarily, and seemed to neutralise the feeling of guilt over having caused young Allan's death. Young trainee soldiers, young schoolboys and other young (*Evening Star* collector is one such) boys began to fill her life. Her grief drove her to drink, hysteria and nymphomania. All this was supposed to be anodyne to assuage the pain and grief of her miserable life. Her physical relationship with one of her students, her one-night stands with strangers, made her a town character, leading to her dismissal from school and eviction from the hotel and town both.

Blanche having lost her all—husband, family, financial security from inheritance, her job, her youth as also her fair reputation reaches New Orleans to look up her sister Stella. Her "delicate beauty ... that suggests a moth" (p. 117), her fragile nerves and her uncertain manner, show her as a sensitive woman in a brutal world, in desperate need of refuge. She finds one such person in those shabby surroundings too—the mother coddled Mitch—but throws away her chance of finding stability mainly because she cannot any-more commit herself to a man. She thinks the best way to get a man is by using the trappings of her ante-bellum charm. She sees in Mitch an oppor-tunity to prove her allure and score an easy sexual conquest. She fools the gullible Mitch by feeding him on magical details about herself. To arouse his desires, she passes for a coy virginal old-fashioned Southern belle and does not allow him any other liberties than a kiss. She dupes him regarding her age and declares herself younger to Stella, tries to fool him regarding her drinking habits, avoids going out with him until after dark and manages to avoid being seen in direct bulb-light. She buys a paper lantern to avoid detection of her true age. All these deceptions she considers necessary for fanning the flames of love in Mitch: she adopts a cool dignified posture calculated at achieving the desired results. "I want his respect: And men don't want anything they get too easy. But on the other hand men lose interest quickly. Especially when the girl is over thirty." (p. 171) She believes reality kills the romantic spirit, while illusion is necessary to keep the flame kindled. "Yes, yes, magic! I try to give that to people. I misrepresent things to them. I don't tell the truth. I tell what ought to be truth." (p. 204)

Blanche's sexuality cannot function as an expression of psychic relatedness. She remains caught up in the persona reality of her jazzed up and fantasized Belle Reve past. While a true hetaira would meet her lover, naked, denuded of pretensions, Blanche never tires of game-playing. She continues to delude and misrepresent things, hiding facts about herself. She cannot open herself to the relationship as a process, as an exploration, as a continuing communion. She relishes the projections and desires of men to get affirmation of her own existence. Every relationship for her is an adventure, a fresh occasion to have her sexual superiority and charms confirmed. She exploits her manners and genteel past as art to gain easy conquests on men.

Her lurid past uncovered by Stanley, coupled with the explanations offered by Blanche herself, points towards the past of a whore, at best "a sentimental prostitute" as Signi Falk calls her.[18] The trauma of young Allan's death, followed by those of several others, compelled her to glut herself sexually as she says, in order to forget the hovering spectre of the tragedy. This indiscriminate indulgence has helped her escape from loneliness as also alleviated her sense of worthlessness. But it has made her neglect the much needed centring of her emotions through commitment to one person. The biological energies thus gratified have left no scope for emotional maturity. Jeanne M. McGlinn's observation corroborates this point of view. McGlinn regards Blanche sexually immature and inadequate "because of which she avoids adult sexual relationships but actively seeks affairs with adolescents."[19] Blanche becomes, to adapt a phrase from D.H. Lawrence's *The Plumed Serpent*, the "Aphrodite of frictional ecstasy", revelling in the fulfillment of temporary unions. Williams very aptly selected the epigraph for the drama from Hart Crane's "The Broken Tower":

And so it was I entered the broken world,
To trace the visionary company of love, its voice
An instant in the wind (I know not whither hurled)
But not for long to hold each desperate choice.

Early in the play Stella describes Blanche as "flighty" (p. 189), probably alluding to her incapacity to experience love as a relationship. The epigraph does not refer to the "theme of the soul's quest for ideal love in the most unlikely of places—the broken world of actuality," as Leonard Quirino interprets it.[20] The epigraph, on the other hand, clearly points out the gratification that Blanche seeks in the arms of "each desperate choice" to refurnish the broken quality of her life, looking for closeness, perhaps kindness in that physical contact. "I've run for protection, Stella, from under one leaky roof to another leaky roof—because it was storm—all storm, and I was—caught in the centre." (p. 164) It is also for this reason that she does not see herself as a mere prostitute. Her moral vision blurred by her desperate need to be with someone, with ancestors for models who indulged in "epic fornications" with impunity, she moves through the world filling the void in her life with lust. "Yes, I had many intimacies with strangers. After the death of Allan—intimacies with strangers was all I seemed to be able to fill my empty heart with . . . I think it was panic, just panic, that drove me from one to another, hunting for some protection. . . ." (p. 205) It is this need that blinds her to her moral reality. Normand Berlin aptly says, "She cannot see herself a whore because sexual activity was for her a temporary means for needed affection, the only refuge for her lonely soul."[21]

Erich Fromm in his famous book *The Art of Loving* divides human love in five categories: brotherly, motherly, erotic, self and Love of God. Among these erotic love is "the craving for complete fusion, for union with one another person." This union is the "souls' union" if the craving matures into caring, mutual respect, tenderness or flowers into understanding the psychic needs or what Lawrence calls the 'otherness' of the partner. The true union comes if the partners relate with each other's intrinsic nature. Such a relationship becomes an exploration into the infiniteness of finite love. In mystical writing such love partakes of the divine. Only the pure hetairas are capable of such love. However, in the absence of these values, the union is merely physical and the happiness shortlived. Sexual contact in such cases does not touch, much less involve the soul. The contact thus is no better than the mating of animals. In the light of this latter observation, if one looks at the sexual conquests of people like Blanche one is struck by Fromm's telling observation, "Since they experience the separateness of the other person primarily as physical separateness, physical union means overcoming separateness."[22] Each new affair brings freshness, intensity and exhilaration along with an illusion that the new love will be different from the earlier one. Blanche has been chasing this mirage in ever new affairs, even in the brief one-night-stands because only physical contact seemed to her the antidote to her pathetic existence. For her the conquests have to go on, so that she goes on living without getting time to reflect on her life. The mere thought of being alone with herself frightens her, because it would mean confrontation with her own sordid reality. Sex in the name of anxiety of aloneness, gratification of vanity, expiation of guilt, or seeking refuge (or "protection" as she calls it) are prompted by a desire to seek in the world of romance that which is hopelessly bleak all around herself. She flirts with Stanley, Mitch and the *Evening Star* collector boy almost simultaneously. Among them she pursues Stanley for the gratification of her vanity because he poses a challenge she has not had before. The "gaudy seed bearer", (p. 128) she has for a brother-in-law, feels insulted by her pose of superiority and decides to put her in her place by making "her recognise that she is the same as he, a sexual animal."[23] So her customary hope of seeing him wilt before her flamboyant manners, apparel and charm bounces back leaving her badly shaken. He piece by piece unravels her past and confronts her with the reality she sought to deny in herself. She had always been on the brink of lunacy but finds herself even closer to it. The second hope was in Mitch. She hoped that overwhelmed by her charms he would rebel against the stories of Stanley and would not desert her. Her hopes of protection, because it is all that she seeks in him, a house, "a cleft in the rock of the world that I could hide in!" (p. 205), bounce when despite her hopes and probably fervent prayers he does not come on her birthday party. He was the man who had "stopped that polka tune that I had caught in my head", (p. 201) the tune which played when Allan committed suicide, the tune that always haunted her, that tune now comes back. She finally realizes to her dismay that she has lost her reputation, a place to go to, and what is worse, her charms. This realisation, painful as it is, coupled with the rape, sends her reeling into a world of shadows, from which she was never really far away.

Elsewhere in this chapter it was pointed out that the dominant archetype of the hetaira is The Great Father to whom the former relates as a *puella aeterna* (or eternal daughter). True to the archetype, Blanche seeks mainly one thing from her lovers—"protection". She sees them as refuge, even though "leaky", (p. 164) from the "panic", (p. 205) "the storm", (p. 164) all around. She sees Mitch as a sanctuary where she can take rest. "I want to rest! I want to breathe quietly again! Yes—I want Mitch . . . very badly! Just think! If it happens! I can leave here and not be any one's problem. . . ." (p. 171) She no longer wants journeys because "travelling wears me out." In other words, journeys on the streetcars named desire, the abnormal sexual activation since adolescence, have cloyed her now. She needs a cosy nook to squirm herself into because more than physical aggrandisement she requires the protection and security of a home. Mitch fits into her requirement like one made to order: he has a big heavy frame which promises to protect her and he is tender and mother-complexed which assures her compassion. Leonard Berkman's words aptly sum up her need, "It is specifically the intermingling of sex with compassion that Blanche longs for; sex without compassion that she cannot accept."[24] She genuinely thanks God for Mitch who seems to her as "the poor man's paradise" where she can have her "peace" (p. 205) from the cruel world.

Blanche's ambivalent attraction towards Stanley and her attempts to fight it down also require discussion. In the very first scene together, Blanche regards Stanley's half-naked torso with awe as he changes his T-shirt in front of her. Roger Boxill comments, "It is because she is torn between attraction and repulsion, that she thinks she is going to be sick. The 'Varsouviana', echoing the guilt she bears for the suicide of her young husband filters through the dialogue."[25] She flirts with him, sprays him with her atomizer, asks her to button up her blouse prompting Stanley's blunt remark, "If I didn't know that you was my wife's sister I'd get ideas about you!" (p. 138) Some hours later, however, she violently criticises him as 'primitive', 'sub-human', 'apelike', 'madman', 'brute' (Scene IV). What, however, betrays her reaction formation (a Freudian term which means you criticise something bitterly in others that you yourself desperately want) are two speeches in this very scene. The first reads, " . . . I saw him at his best! what such a man has to offer is animal force and he gave a wonderful exhibition of that! But the only way to live with such a man is to go—go to bed with him! And that's your job—not mine!" (p. 161) The speech barely conceals an intense wish. The next speech repeats the motif in the previous one a trifle more vehemently, "I am not being or feeling at all superior, Stella. Believe me I'm not . . . A man like that is someone to go out with—once-twice-three times, when the devil is in you. But live with! Have a child by?" (p. 162) Both speeches showing Blanche's strong hatred of Stanley's animalism are indeed only in the nature of subterfuge to disguise her own immense need of raw passion and sexuality. It is borne out by the fact that she too would like to settle down with a "wolf" (p. 146) from the pack of Stanley. The latter, however, is not the kind to understand the psychological reason for Blanche's virulent attack against himself. He can only understand that the latter is trying to ruin his marriage by prompting Stella to get away and that he must pay back, eye for an eye, by destroying the chances of her marriage with Mitch. In any case, her attempt to break Stella's marriage because she cannot get Stanley would be considered, according to Jungian psychology, an obvious deflection in her hetaira personality. A woman who breaks or attempts to break others' marriage has not understood the limits within which a hetaira is to operate: breaking homes is a negative trait. Roger Boxill, however, has a different opinion as to why Stanley destroys Blanche's marriage with Mitch. Adducing evidence from the early drafts of the play he writes, "In retrospect neither his uxoriousness nor his protestation of friendship for Mitch rings true. Stanley's underlying motive for warding off Blanche's only suitor, we are bound to conclude, has been to remove the obstacle in the way of keeping his 'date' that he has had with her from the beginning."[26] Boxill's opinion finds support in how Stanley is portrayed in the Stage Directions. "Since earliest manhood, the centre of his life has been pleasure with women . . ." (p. 128), which implies that he is not a faithful husband and that he is a liar too. He denies rape which is "a greater lie than any Blanche ever told."[27]

At another level the encounter between Stanley and Blanche can be seen as a clash between two contrary ontologies. Mythically, Stanley is Pan, the Greek god of all enveloping cosmic energy manifested in human' terms through sexuality and libido. In several mythologems, based on stories and depth experience of the psyche, Pan is deemed to have a duplex nature—he is the god of erotic ecstasy, libidinal virility, art, creativity and transformation on the one hand, and on the other, of violence, rape, nightmare, alienation and madness. Stanley in *Streetcar* represents the chthonic principle and is characterised by fire. In comparison Blanche is in the modality of nymph who archetypally embodies grace, delicacy and elegance and is characterised by water. Their ambivalent attraction leading to abrasive encounter is thus always on the cards. A fuller discussion would clarify these points.

Stanley Kowalski is the primal blacksmith of the flaming "red hot" (p. 141) milieu, The Elysian Fields ("Stanley" or "Stone-lea" suggests the Stone Age man and Kowalski is Polish for "smith").[28] He is the rough hewn lord of his house, immensely proud and possessive of his things: his liquor, his bathroom, his game, his team, his wife, his child, "everything . . . that bears his emblem." (p. 128) He quotes from Huey Long's 'Every Man is a king', and believes rather intensely in it. He believes it is his right to flaunt his brutal life force through all kinds of barbarism including smashing things, bellowing at people, hitting his wife and insulting others. Williams describes him and his friends as "men at the peak of their physical manhood, as coarse and direct and powerful as the primary colours." (p. 143) He gives Stanley Capricorn as his birth sign and gives him animal habits. Boxill's recapitulations of Marlon Brando as Stanley show that brutish force and fire as also sexual attractiveness was combined by him in his lively portrayal of the character. "The first Stanley had the face of a poet, the body of a gladiator and the vocal placement of a whining adolescent. Brando's performance was a mosaic of sexual insolence, sullen moodiness, puckish good humour and terrifying rage. His slurred delivery and loutish stances added to the grammar of acting."[29] Audiences still remember the tiger-like suddenness with which Brando, in the birthday party scene smashes plates, stalks out onto the porch, shouts while continuing to pick his teeth and lick his fingers.[30]

Blanche, however, is not the youthful but an aging nymph ("A gargoyle" as Henry Popkin, "a witch" as Nancy M. Tischler call her). Her name means "white woods", like an "orchard in spring" which is ironic because she knows she has lost her youthful vitality and looks. Like her ironic name she has an ironic birth sign, Virgo or the virgin, with the background of a whore. She is fond of water which refreshes her, makes her a "brand new human being." She frolics for long hours in the bathroom, soaking her frayed nerves in hot water. Her "hydrotherapy" is necessary for her probably to wash away the feeling of guilt as also the stains of her promiscuous life. While locomotive journeys wear her out she views the prospect of voyage on the Caribbean with Shep Huntleigh with pleasure, "I can smell the sea air. The rest of my time

I'm going to spend on the sea. And when I die, I'm going to die on the sea."
(p. 220) Before her last journey from the Elysian Fields, she questions Stella
from the bathroom, "Is the coast clear?" As Eunice and Stella assist her to
dress, Blanche treats them like handmaidens in the service of a water nymph.
The climax of her fantasies is also connected with the sea. She hopes, "And I'll
be buried at sea sewn up in a clean white sack and dropped overboard into an
ocean as blue as . . . my first lover's eyes!" (p. 220) Water which dominates her
lively fantasies has always dominated her life. Water principle which manifests itself through drift, dependence and buoyancy, has kept her on the move,
to one lover from another, to one leaky roof from another, without allowing
her to experience the much needed cathexis to her emotions, to find time to
introvert and see her psychic life as it really is.

No discussion of *A Streetcar* can be complete without a sideways glance
at the character of Stella, who in Jungian terms is a typical mother woman
wallowing in the bliss of animalistic life, much as Serafina before Rosario's
death. Stella, unlike Blanche, lives in the present and does not raise her eye-
brows over the quality of her sordid existence. What matters more to her is
the security and sense of fulfillment in the love of Stanley. Emerging from the
cocoon of plantation life, Stella adopted her husband's way of life with equanimity. Blanche is intrigued by her stolid indifference over life with Stanley, "Is this a Chinese philosophy you've cultivated?" (p. 158) Like a tolerant
mother woman she casually observes that Stanley is the smashing type, that
a house in which men are drinking violent things do happen, that men and
women have to get used to each other's ways of life. She gets up with a smile
to fix the things in the house, stow away the beer bottles, and clear the mess
the poker players made and be ready for him when Stanley returns home.
She forgives Stanley for hitting her because "he was as good as a lamb when
I came back", (p. 157) and because he promised never to play poker again in
the house. Her absolute acceptance of Stanley on his word is seen when she
wakes up next morning: "Her face is serene. . . . Her eyes and lips have that
almost narcotized tranquillity that is in the faces of Eastern idols." (p. 156)
That Williams wanted Stella to be passive, physically and imaginatively static,
is understood from a note he wrote to Elia Kazan, the first director of the
New York Production, "I think her natural passivity is one of the things that
make her acceptance of Stanley acceptable. She naturally 'gives in', lets things
slide, she does not make much effort."[31] For Stella, passive by conditioning in
a house in which the elder Blanche dominated, taking things as they came has
been a way of life. It is for this reason, she is cool and peaceful and sits with
her "little hands folded like a cherub in choir!" (p. 123) unruffled by things
that could have shaken anyone else. Her contentment with her lot stems from
profound satisfaction at the sexual level, "But there are things that happen

between a man and a woman in the dark—that sort of make everything else seem—unimportant." (p. 162) Like Serafina, she too is proud of the potency of her husband and believes that "Stanley is the only one of his crowd that's likely to get anywhere," (p. 146) because he has the "drive" (p. 147) in him. She is proud of his physical attributes, his captaincy of the bowling team and his status at the plant. She tells Blanche of course, that Stanley comes from "a different species" (p. 124) than they have known.

Stella has, if one considers her affluent plantation background and compares her with Blanche who cannot get away from her view of herself, made a radical compromise with life. She does not complain against the ram-shackle two-room apartment or meagre income of Stanley. It is she, rather than Blanche who claims, "I'm very adaptable—to circumstances", (p. 150) who has adjusted with the sweeping winds of change and thus found contentment. The climax of her rejection of the past and acceptance of the new comes when she has to choose between Stanley the rapist and Blanche who needs love and attention. She chooses Stanley and lets Blanche slip away into insanity. In this process she, as Bigsby says, "opts for the future over the past, for potency over sterility. And if that also means accepting a world bereft of protective myth and cultural adornments this is a compromise which she has the strength to make. Blanche cannot and is broken."[32] Stella, thus, in spite of her seeming indolence and passivity, must be seen as a more practical and sane woman. Her categorical rejection of Blanche derives from her the need to "go on living with Stanley", (p. 217) because nothing to her is greater than marital bliss.

And finally it would be wrong to consider her, like Elia Kazan did, as "Stanley's slave."[33] She may not have succeeded in monopolising her husband's love, but has certainly been able to extract his dependence on herself. He loves and needs her which is seen in his hollering as he finds her gone with Blanche to a neighbour's to spend the night after the fracas of the poker night. He kneels to her and carries the sobbing Stella inside the bedroom. Some time later when he finds her upset over Blanche he reassures her, "Stell, it's gonna be all right after she goes and after you've had the baby." (pp. 195–196) He cares for her, in spite of his arrogance and loud mouth.

In every conceivable way Stella offers a contrast with the character of Blanche and helps as a foil in bringing it out. In another essay C.W.E. Bigsby pays a profound tribute to Stella when he says, "The real hero of the play, therefore, is Stella, for she alone is prepared to offer the necessary comfort and understanding. Like Connie Chatterley she discovers a genuine fulfillment based on sexuality but, more significantly, she thereby stumbles on the urgent need for that tenderness and compassion which, to both Williams and Lawrence, is the key to the human predicament."[34] In the world of *A Streetcar*, in other words, she is the only sign of humanity because both Stanley (too bestial) and Blanche (too delicate) with their mutual sparring row and vehement antagonism present a bleak vision of life. And Williams wanted people to believe that love is the only answer in this world bristling with anger and discontent. He believed that "the only satisfactory thing we are left with in this life is the relations—if they're sincere—between people, love being "the closest we've come to such a satisfying relationship."[35] Stella is a woman committed to dependence on her man in family relationship: to her everything else is secondary.

Maggie, Myrtle and Blanche have been grouped under the hetaira category in view of eros as the driving force of their life. Their fulfillment lies in the giving and receiving of love. While the positive ones, Maggie and Myrtle, are fortunate to find men they could love, whose psyches they could mediate, whose shadows they could penetrate into without resistance: they have in the process stabilised, their emotions have found apt cathexes and their lives acquired a meaning. Made in the hetaira modality Blanche has been unfortunate in losing her blue-eyed, adorable, lover-husband simply because she did not understand him and his needs. She has been trying to give meaning to her life by indulging with younger boys or softer men in the vain hope of finding another Allan she could adore, and thus have a fulfilled existence. That path, however, has led to moral degradation, at least in the eyes of society at large. Inability to find one more Allan despite desperate search, makes her depend on "the kindness of strangers," and finally even in the public asylum.

Notes

1. Toni Wolff, "Structural Forms of the Feminine Psyche", trans. Paul Watzlawik (Zurich: Students Association, C.G. Jung Institute, 1956), p. 6.

2. Ann B. Ulanov, "Descriptions of the Feminine", *The Feminine in Jungian Psychology and in Christian Theology* (1971; Evanston: North Western Univ. Press, 1978), p. 203.

3. Irene Claremont de Castillejo, *Knowing Woman: A Feminine Psychology* (1973; New York: Harper and Colophon, 1974), p. 66.

4. Wolff, p. 7.

5. De Castillejo, p. 65.

6. Edward C. Whitmont, *The Symbolic Quest: Basic Concepts of Analytical Psychology* (1969; New York: Harper and Colophon, 1973), p. 179.

7. Tennessee Williams, *Cat on a Hot Tin Roof* in *Cat on a Hot Tin Roof* and *The Milk Train Doesn't Stop Here Anymore* (1955; Harmondsworth: Penguin, 1969), p. 109. All subsequent refs. to the text are from this edn.

8. Ulanov, "Descriptions . . . ," p. 205.

9. ibid., p. 204.

10. Bernard F. Dukore, "The Cat Has Nine Lives", *Tulane Drama Review*, 8 (Fall 1963), p. 97.

11. Nancy M. Tischler, "A Gallery of Witches", *Tennessee Williams: A Tribute*, ed. Jac Tharpe (Jackson: Univ. Press of Mississippi, 1977), p. 501.

12. Jeanne M. McGlinn, "Tennessee Williams's Women: Illusion and Reality, Sexuality and Love", ibid., pp. 517–518.

13. Tennessee Williams, *Kingdom of Earth: Seven Descents of Myrtle*, Vol. V, *The Theatre of Tennessee Williams* (1967; New York: New Directions, 1975), p. 143. All subsequent refs. to the text are from this edn.

14. Jerrold A. Phillips, "Kingdom of Earth: Some Approaches", *Tennessee Williams: A Tribute*, p. 352.

15. Phillips, p. 353.

16. Tennessee Williams, "Kingdom of Earth", *The Knightly Quest and other Stories* (New York: New Directions, 1966), p. 161.

17. Tennessee Williams, *A Streetcar Named Desire in Sweet Bird of Youth, A Streetcar and Menagerie*, ed. E. Martin Browne (1947; rptd. Harmondsworth: Penguin, 1976), p. 140. All subsequent references to the text are from this edn.

18. Signi Falk, "The Profitable World of Tennessee Williams", *Modern Drama*, 1 (December 1958), p. 158.

19. Jeanne M. McGlinn, p. 513.

20. Leonard Quirino, "The Cards Indicate a Voyage on *A Streetcar Named Desire*", *Tennessee Williams: A Tribute*, p. 80.

21. Normand Berlin, "Complementarity in *A Streetcar Named Desire*", *Tennessee Williams: A Tribute*, p. 98.

22. Erich Fromm, *Art of Loving* (1957; rptd. London: Unwin Paperbacks, 1978), pp. 48–49.

23. McGlinn, p. 514.

24. Leonard Berkman, "The Tragic Downfall of Blanche DuBois", *Modern Drama*, 10 (Dec. 1967), p. 254.

25. Roger Boxill, *Tennessee Williams* (New York: St. Martin's Press, 1987), p. 82.

26. Boxill bases his argument on Vivienne Dickson, "*A Streetcar Named Desire*: Its Development Through the Manuscripts", *Tennessee Williams: A Tribute*, pp. 154–71.

27. Bert Cardullo, "Drama of Intimacy and Tragedy of Incomprehension: *A Streetcar Named Desire* Reconsidered", *Tennessee Williams: A Tribute*, p. 150.

28. Leonard Quirino, p. 79.

29. Boxill, p. 88.

30. ibid.

31. Tennessee Williams to Elia Kazan in Toby Cole ed., *Directing the Play* (Indianapolis, 1953), p. 306, rptd. in C.W.E. Bigsby, *A Critical Introduction to the Twentieth Century American Drama*, Vol. II (London: Cambridge, 1984), p. 65.

32. Bigsby, p. 66.

33. Elia Kazan, quoted in Bigsby, p. 65.

34. C.W.E. Bigsby, "Tennessee Williams: Streetcar to Glory", in Harold Bloom, ed. Tennessee Williams's *A Streetcar Named Desire* (New York: Chelsea, 1988), p. 47.

35. Bigsby, "Streetcar to Glory", p. 47.

ROBERT J. CORBER

Tennessee Williams and the Politics of the Closet

You still want to know why I don't write a gay play? I don't find it necessary. I could express what I wanted to express through other means. I would be narrowing my audience a great deal. I wish to have a broad audience because the major thrust of my work is not sexual orientation, it's social. I'm not about to limit myself to writing about gay people.

—Tennessee Williams

Critics often cite Tennessee Williams's short story "Hard Candy" (1954) as typical of the evasive and indirect way in which he treated gay male experience in his work.[1] In "Hard Candy," Williams is careful not only to avoid explicitly stating that the elderly protagonist, Mr. Krupper, is homosexual but also to shroud in mystery his visits to the Joy Rio, a "third-rate cinema" situated near the waterfront where he engages in anonymous sexual encounters with young boys in exchange for a few quarters and a bag of hard candy.[2] Before disclosing what Mr. Krupper does in the upper galleries of the once elegant theater, Williams interrupts the story to prepare the reader for the shock of what he is about to reveal: "In the course of this story, and very soon now, it will be necessary to make some disclosures about Mr. Krupper of a nature too coarse to be dealt with very directly in a work of such brevity" (355). Although he realizes that his circumspection may confuse the reader,

From *Homosexuality in Cold War America: Resistance and the Crisis of Masculinity*, pp. 107–34, 221–25. Copyright © 1997 by Duke University Press.

41

he refuses to deal more explicitly with the ailing Mr. Krupper's visits to the Joy Rio. If he were to approach Mr. Krupper's clandestine sexual activities more directly, he might shock the reader, and he is determined to avoid "a head-on violence that would disgust and destroy and which would actually falsify the story" (355) by misrepresenting the mysterious Mr. Krupper. Williams does not want the reader to come to the reductive conclusion that Mr. Krupper is a dirty old man who preys on innocent young boys, even though there is ample reason for the reader to do so.

Williams's desire to avoid shocking the reader by dealing openly with Mr. Krupper's anonymous sexual encounters has led a number of critics to treat "Hard Candy" as a product of his internalized homophobia.[3] According to these critics, Williams's equivocations about Mr. Krupper's surreptitious visits to the Joy Rio can be attributed to his inability to come to terms with his own sexual promiscuity, which he did not openly acknowledge until the publication of his *Memoirs* in 1975.[4] They are particularly troubled by Williams's unflattering descriptions of Mr. Krupper, which threaten to reduce homosexuality to a form of bodily corruption. Williams tells us that Mr. Krupper is "a man of gross and unattractive appearance" (353) and that he is "shameful and despicable even to those who tolerate his caresses, perhaps even more so to them than to the others who only see him" (363). But this reading ignores the way in which Williams's evasions seem designed to implicate the reader in Mr. Krupper's "mysterious" activities. The indirection and obscurity of Williams's language encourage a pornographic interest in Mr. Krupper. Despite the fact that Mr. Krupper is a dirty old man whose sexual activities are potentially exploitative, the reader eagerly devours the story. Indeed, the more evasive Williams's language becomes, the more eager the reader is to finish the story so that s/he can learn the "truth" about Mr. Krupper's pilgrimages to the Joy Rio. That Williams's evasions are intended to implicate the reader in Mr. Krupper's "mystery" becomes clear at the end of the story, when he abruptly breaks off the narrative just before Mr. Krupper is about to give a blow job to the beautiful and odoriferous "dark youth" (362) he encounters in the upper galleries on his final visit to the theater. In marking with a blank space the place in the text where the description of the blow job should occur, Williams intensifies the reader's pornographic interest in Mr. Krupper. Williams refuses to satisfy the reader's desire to experience gay male sex vicariously, thereby leaving her/him feeling cheated.

But Williams's mockery of the reader is not limited to encouraging a pornographic interest in Mr. Krupper's sexual activities, despite his gross and unattractive appearance. The obscurity of Williams's language reduces the reader to engaging in the sort of reading practices that negotiating the gay male subculture often necessitated in the Cold War era. In an influential essay on the semiotics of homosexuality, Harold Beaver has argued that gay men's marginal position in relation to the dominant culture forces them to become "prodigious consumer[s] of signs."[5] We can use Beaver's argument about gay men's privileged relation to the commodity form to speculate about the emergence in the fifties of a distinct gay male reading formation in relation to the closet. According to Beaver, gay men are constantly besieged by signs, making them particularly skillful readers. The structures of secrecy and disclosure that organize gay male experience lead them to scrutinize constantly the behavior of other men for signs of homosexuality. For them, the slightly effeminate gesture or intonation of voice becomes fraught with meaning. Moreover, practices such as cruising require them to interpret signs on multiple levels. A meaningful look, a brush of the leg, a touch of the hand—all can be interpreted as signs of sexual solicitation. Thus for gay men there is no escaping "the urge to interpret whatever transpires, or fails to transpire, between [themselves] and every chance acquaintance."[6] But gay men do not just consume signs, they also produce them. To mark their identities, they appropriate a variety of signifiers from the dominant culture (leather jackets, blue jeans, flannel shirts, key rings), which they invest with new meanings by redeploying them in a homosexual context.[7] These signifiers comprise a complex system of signs the meaning of which only those initiated into the gay male subculture are wholly capable of decoding. To negotiate the subculture, gay men must learn how to interpret signs provisionally and on multiple levels.

Beaver's analysis essentializes gay male identity by grounding it ontologically. He does not adequately consider the changes that have occurred in urban gay communities since the Stonewall rebellion in 1969, which led to the emergence of the gay liberation movement, and thus he removes gay men from the historical process.[8] Not only is contemporary gay male experience less governed by the structures of secrecy and disclosure that defined the closet in the fifties, but the AIDS crisis has radically altered gay male practices such as cruising. Still, Beaver's argument provides a fairly accurate description of the semiotics of postwar urban gay communities. In "Hard Candy," Williams foregrounds Mr. Krupper's role as both a consumer and a producer of signs. After thirty years of attending afternoon matinees at the Joy Rio, Mr. Krupper has become a particularly skillful reader of signs. Although his experiences in the upper galleries of the movie theater have taught him to exercise caution, he has also learned that "there are certain pursuits in which even the most cautious man must depart from absolute caution if he intends at all to enjoy them" (361). Thus when he discovers that the place where he usually sits has been taken by an unusually attractive boy who emits a "warm animal fragrance" (362), he carefully maps out a course of action. He initiates contact with the boy by offering him a piece of candy. Shortly before the lights come up, he jingles the quarters he has brought with him "ever so lightly in his fist so that they tinkle a bit" (363), thereby indicating to the boy that he is pre-pared to pay him for his sexual favors. In case he has misinterpreted the boy's presence in the upper galleries of the movie theater, he then leans toward the railing so that the boy will think that he is interested in what is happen-ing below. When the boy remains seated after the lights go down again, Mr. Krupper interprets it as a sign that he is willing to submit to his caresses in exchange for the quarters. He then offers the quarters to the boy who, in tak-ing them, signals that "the contract is sealed between them" (364).

Given the obscurity of Williams's language, the only way in which the reader can make sense of the story is by mastering the sort of reading practices in which Mr. Krupper has learned to engage. Williams's refusal to shock the reader by divulging the "secret" of Mr. Krupper's visits to the Joy Rio requires her/him to occupy a gay male subject-position. To understand the meaning of the story, the reader must demonstrate a mastery of gay male reading prac-tices; that is, s/he must fill in the blanks—quite literally, as we will see shortly. Williams does not fully test the reader's ability to read as a gay man until the end of the story, where he does not explicitly state how Mr. Krupper died but refers to it indirectly, thus shrouding it in mystery. The reader knows only that Mr. Krupper died in "an attitude of prayer" (364) and with discarded candy wrappers stuck to his clothes. Williams stresses the different ways in which Mr. Krupper's death can be interpreted. Unaware of the sort of activities the patrons of the Joy Rio engage in, the "spinsterly reporter" (364) who writes Mr. Krupper's obituary gives it unusual prominence. She is impressed by "the sentimental values of a seventy-year-old retired merchant dying of thrombosis at a cowboy thriller with a split bag of hard candies in his pocket and the floor about him littered with sticky wrappers, some of which even adhered to the shoulders and sleeves of his jacket" (364). Mr. Krupper's cousins similarly mis-interpret his death. For them, it is poetic justice. Mr. Krupper has constantly pilfered their stock of hard candy. When the daughter reads his obituary in the local newspaper, she exclaims gleefully: "*Just think, Papa, the old man choked to death on our hard candy!*" (365).[9] Here it becomes apparent that deciphering Williams's veiled references to the way in which Mr. Krupper dies requires reading as a gay man. Neither the spinsterly reporter nor Mr. Krupper's cous-ins have mastered the codes of the gay male subculture, and so they do not know that they must read between the lines in order to interpret correctly the meaning of his death. It does not occur to them that Mr. Krupper died in a state of bliss, transfigured by his encounter with the unusually attractive boy.

Although given the position of his body there can be little doubt about the circumstances under which Mr. Krupper dies, Williams continues to shroud his homosexuality in mystery. I have already noted that he does not describe the blow job that makes possible Mr. Krupper's transfiguration but marks the place in the text where it occurs with a blank space, thus requiring the reader literally to fill in the blanks. In this respect, critics seem justified in claiming that Williams's evasions reproduce the epistemology of the closet.[10] Despite the fact that Williams encourages us to read "Hard Candy" as a narrative of disclosure, he never fully divulges the "secret" of Mr. Krupper's pilgrimages. Mr. Krupper's homosexuality remains an open secret, known only to the reader who is capable of reading between the lines. Although I agree with critics who read Williams's circumspection as an indication that he was heavily invested in maintaining the closet, I am not persuaded by the argument that his refusal to shock the reader by fully disclosing Mr. Krupper's "secret" was a product of internalized homophobia. To propose an alternative reading of Williams's relation to the closet, I want to examine more closely the structures of secrecy and disclosure embedded in his representation of gay male experience in "Hard Candy."

Until Williams interrupts the narrative to warn us that he will soon have to disclose something about Mr. Krupper that is "too coarse to be dealt with very directly," there is nothing in the text that would lead us to suspect that Mr. Krupper regularly engages in anonymous sex at the Joy Rio. Williams describes Mr. Krupper as a seventy-year-old retired businessman who is "almost like any other old man" (356) in that he spends the mornings in the park reading the newspaper. Only readers initiated into the gay male subculture would on the basis of their knowledge of Mr. Krupper's visits to the theater suspect that he is not like other old men but is a "bird of a different feather" (357). Williams remarks that even the most penetrating observer would have difficulty discovering "what it was that gave Mr. Krupper the certain air he had of being engaged in something far more momentous than the ordinary meanderings of an old man" (356). Thus even Mr. Krupper's cousins do not suspect that he leads a double life. Although their dislike of him might lead one to conclude that they had "penetrated to the very core of those mysteries" (356) that Williams insists on approaching only indirectly, they are not even curious about his activities. Indeed, they do not even speculate about what he does with the candy that he pilfers from their store. "The comments and the stares and the faughs of disgust betrayed no real interest or curiosity or speculation about him, only the fiercely senseless attention given to something acknowledged to have no mysteries whatsoever" (356). Their utter lack of curiosity about Mr. Krupper is more disturbing than their dislike of him because it reduces him to an "insensibly malign object" (356). In refusing to speculate about Mr. Krupper's activities or to show the slightest interest in them, they deny his humanity.

This may explain why in "Hard Candy" Williams did not hesitate to reproduce the epistemological structures of the closet. Although his refusal to deal more openly with Mr. Krupper's homosexuality reduces it to an open secret, the evasiveness of his language enables him to establish Mr. Krupper's subjecthood. Williams's equivocations about Mr. Krupper's homosexuality have the paradoxical effect of rendering it visible. Insofar as they transform Mr. Krupper's sexuality into an impenetrable mystery, they reverse the effects of his cousins' indifference. This is not to deny that one of the dangers of Williams's refusal to treat Mr. Krupper's visits to the Joy Rio more openly is that our interest in them will remain at the level of the pornographic. But Williams averts this possibility by breaking off the narrative at the point at which Mr. Krupper is about to give a blow job to the boy, thus arousing but not satisfying the reader's curiosity about gay male sex. Williams's hesitation to approach Mr. Krupper's homosexuality more directly guarantees that, unlike his cousins, we do not assume that we know "practically everything of any significance about him" (355). Because he refuses to describe Mr. Krupper's encounter with the anonymous youth, the "mystery" of Mr. Krupper's identity continues to elude us, forcing us to acknowledge that we can never fully know him. In reproducing the structures of the closet, in other words, Williams prevents our curiosity about Mr. Krupper from reducing him to an "insensibly malign object." Mr. Krupper's homosexuality becomes a sign not of his corruption but of his subjecthood, thereby discouraging us from positioning him as sexually other.

Many readers will no doubt object that Williams's strategies for establishing Mr. Krupper's subjecthood are as politically retrograde as his investment in the structures of secrecy and disclosure that organized gay male experience in the Cold War era.[11] In treating Mr. Krupper's homosexuality as a mystery that can never be wholly solved, Williams attributes to him a form of selfhood that in the wake of the poststructuralist critique of the subject we have learned to dismiss as an Enlightenment fiction designed to guarantee white male heterosexual privilege. Although we eventually learn Mr. Krupper's "secret," our knowledge does not provide us with the key to his subjectivity, which remains inaccessible to us. As we saw above, even after Williams makes his disclosures about Mr. Krupper's visits to the Joy Rio, he continues to equivocate about his homosexuality, merely describing the position in which his body was found, and thus he prevents us from thinking that Mr. Krupper's identity can be reduced to his homosexuality. To be sure, Williams's attempt to establish Mr. Krupper's subjecthood by shrouding his homosexuality in mystery is highly problematic from a political point of view: It reveals a liberal humanistic belief in the uniqueness and autonomy of the individual. To avert the possibility that the reader's interest in the story will remain pornographic, Williams is forced to relegate Mr. Krupper's homosexuality to the private realm where it can remain a secret. Although Mr. Krupper's encounter with the youth occurs in the public space of a movie theater, it is a private act, which, as I have already noted, not even the reader is allowed to witness.[12] Moreover, it is committed furtively and in the dark, thereby enabling Mr. Krupper and his partner to maintain their anonymity.

Despite its political limitations, however, Williams's strategy of attributing to Mr. Krupper a form of selfhood that in capitalist social formations is usually reserved for white, middle-class, heterosexual men seriously challenged the dominant understanding of gay male identity in the fifties. Williams's focus on a character whose sexual practices even many critics writing from an otherwise antihomophobic perspective see as morally reprehensible bespeaks his unwillingness to compromise his project by making his representation of gay male experience more palatable for straight middle-class readers. To clarify the politics of Williams's treatment of Mr. Krupper, it is necessary to compare his strategies in "Hard Candy" for contesting the hegemonic construction of gay male identity with those adopted by the Mattachine Society, the first gay rights organization founded in the postwar period.[13] Although, according to its charter, the Mattachine Society was established to lobby for the repeal of sodomy laws and to make "common cause with other minorities in contributing to the reform of judicial, police and penal practices," for the most part it limited its activities to the gay male equivalent of racial uplift. It wanted to see gay men assimilated into mainstream American society, and so it sought to dispel "the fears and antagonisms of the [larger] community" by establishing that gay men did not differ significantly from straight men.[14] It discouraged gay men from engaging in camp and other controversial practices that reinforced negative stereotypes and threatened to undermine the homophile movement.[15] It also insisted that only the "fringe" of the gay male community engaged in anonymous sexual encounters and that the majority of gay men were capable of sustaining long-term, monogamous relationships. By contrast, Williams was unwilling to disavow the practices and forms of identity that gay men had created in response to their oppression. Mr. Krupper is the Mattachine Society's worst nightmare, a promiscuous gay man who engages in anonymous sex in public places. Rather than repudiating his sexual practices or showing that they were not typical of the gay male community, Williams attributed to Mr. Krupper a complexity that made it difficult for the reader to see him as a stereotype.

Williams's strategies also differed from those adopted by Vidal and Baldwin, the other gay male writers we will be examining in this part of *Homosexuality in Cold War America*. As we will see in subsequent chapters, Vidal and Baldwin contested the dominant construction of homosexuality by foregrounding the construction of gay male subjectivity across variable axes of difference. They sought to define a mode of resistance that exploited gay men's fractured relation to identity. For them, the multiplicity of gay male identity did not entail a loss of agency but enabled a mobility in solidarity. The fragmentation and dispersal of their subjectivity meant that gay men could engage in opposition from multiple locations.[16] By contrast, Williams sought to reverse gay men's fractured relation to identity. On the one hand, his representation of gay male experience seemed to deny that gay male subjectivity is necessarily decentered. Because gay men must survive in the interstices of the dominant culture, they do not enjoy the luxury of having unified and coherent selves but must construct their identities from an atomized historical experience. On the other hand, Williams's treatment of Mr. Krupper as a mysterious figure whose inner world remains inaccessible to us indicates his recognition that achieving subjecthood can be a key moment in the radicalization process.[17] He understood that mobilizing gay men in opposition to postwar structure of oppression required a strategic stabilization of their identities, a stabilization that would enable them to see themselves as members of a collectivity. At the same time, however, he did not treat the achievement of a coherent self as an adequate substitute for liberation, and his investment in Enlightenment conceptions of identity should be understood as purely strategic.

I have dwelt at such length on "Hard Candy" because in this chapter I want to compare its treatment of gay male experience with that of *Cat on a Hot Tin Roof* (1954). A number of critics have recently argued that what they perceive as Williams's inability to come to terms with his homosexuality resulted in a split in his work between public and private forms of literary discourse.[18] According to them, whereas Williams did not hesitate to deal openly with gay male experience in his short stories and poetry, he refused to do so in his plays because they reached a broader audience and might expose his homosexuality to public scrutiny. The only way in which Williams was supposedly willing to express his gay identity in his plays was by refracting it.[19] We glimpse it in his treatment of sexual encounters that transgress racial, ethnic, and class boundaries; in his creation of strong female characters; and in his emphasis on the erotic in general. This argument positions Williams as a casualty of the closeted gay male subculture of the fifties and reproduces a view of his work that first gained currency in the early years of gay liberation Following the emergence of the gay liberation movement, which led to the removal of many of the obstacles on Broadway to the production of plays that dealt openly with homosexuality, gay male critics began to attack Williams for not being more "out" in his work. In their view, Williams had not yet written a "gay" play, by which they meant a play that focused exclusively on gay male characters.[20] They saw Broadway as Williams's closet, the site where he could simultaneously reveal and conceal his gay identity, thus insuring that it remained an open secret.

What is particularly disturbing about this view is that it does not adequately consider the place of the closet in postwar gay male experience and
thus seriously misrepresents Williams's hesitation to acknowledge his homosexuality publicly. Many critics are especially troubled by Williams's refusal
to come out publicly until 1970, when he admitted somewhat coyly on the
David Frost Show that he had "covered the waterfront."[21] They assume that
closeted gay men are necessarily maladjusted or suffer from internalized
homophobia.[22] The argument that Williams was unable to accept his homosexuality foregrounds the limitations of gay male criticism written from a
narrow feminist perspective. John M. Clum, for example, argues that Williams's representation of gay male experience in "Hard Candy" is politically
problematic because Mr. Krupper's anonymous sexual encounters are always
with "poor, beautiful (of course) young men," as though gay male sex that
cut across generational and class lines were inherently exploitative.[23] More
troubling, however, from an antihomophobic perspective, is the way in which
the criticism reproduces the very categories deployed by the national-security
apparatus in the 1950s to position gay men as security risks. In constructing
Williams as the stereotypical closeted gay man who was consumed by self-
hatred, such arguments underestimate the degree to which the emergence of
the national-security state made remaining in the closet a necessity for the
vast majority of gay men in the postwar period. In light of the Cold War construction of homosexuality as a threat to national security, we need to avoid
concluding that gay men who, like Williams, were unwilling to come out of
the closet publicly suffered from internalized homophobia.

To locate Williams's work more firmly in its Cold War context, I want
to compare his treatment of gay male experience in "Hard Candy" and *Cat
on a Hot Tin Roof*. Many critics regard Williams's examination of the closet
in *Cat on a Hot Tin Roof* as an example of the way in which his fear of public
exposure led to a split in his work. Clum, for example, argues that of all of
Williams's plays, *Cat on a Hot Tin Roof* provides "the most vivid dramatic
embodiment of [his] mixed signals regarding homosexuality and his obsession with public exposure."[24] Clum also sees a parallel between Williams and
Brick, the former athlete and heir apparent in the play who is tortured by
the possibility that his relationship with his college roommate, Skipper, was
homosexual. Clum reads Brick's determination to remain in the closet as an
indication that "homosexuality . . . is terrifying for him because it is inevitably public."[25] Although it is true that none of Williams's plays from the fifties concerns unequivocally gay male characters, I want to show that there is
more continuity in his work than critics have acknowledged. Written around
the same time as "Hard Candy," *Cat on a Hot Tin Roof* manifests a similar
investment in the structures of secrecy and disclosure that organized postwar

gay male experience. What distinguishes *Cat on a Hot Tin Roof* from "Hard Candy" is that its examination of the closet is part of a larger critique of post-war structures of oppression. Williams seems to have understood that one of the ways in which the discourses of national security contained opposition to the Cold War consensus was by homosexualizing it. In *Cat on a Hot Tin Roof*, the closet emerges as a space in which not only gay men but also Communists and other groups targeted by the national-security apparatus can find political refuge while continuing to engage in their subversive activities.

Williams and the Political Economy of Anal Eroticism

Many critics interpret Big Daddy's confrontation with Brick in act 2 of *Cat on a Hot Tin Roof* as a deliberate reversal of the audience's expectations which is meant to highlight Brick's inability to accept his homosexuality.[26] Whereas Brick vehemently denies that "there was something not exactly right" about his relationship with Skipper, Big Daddy tries to convince him that he has no reason to feel ashamed of being homosexual.[27] Big Daddy reacts angrily when Brick derisively calls gay men "queers," "sissies," and "dirty old men" and urges him not to condemn those who are different from him. When Brick claims to be shocked by the ease with which Big Daddy discusses sodomy and the other "dirty things" (87) gay men do together, Big Daddy lectures him on the importance of tolerance: "Always . . . lived with too much space around me to be infected by ideas of other people. One thing you can grow on a big place more important than cotton!—is *tolerance!*—I grown it" (89). But perhaps the most surprising reversal occurs when Big Daddy acknowledges his own homosexual past. According to the stage directions, Big Daddy leaves "a lot unspoken" (86) when he reminisces about his youth, thereby authorizing us to fill in the blanks.[28] Big Daddy tells Brick that he was hired by Jack Straw and Peter Ochello, the gay male lovers from whom he inherited the plantation, after they found him asleep "in a wagon of cotton outside the gin" (86). In conjunction with his revelation that he "knocked around in [his] time" (85), the gaps in Big Daddy's reconstruction of his past seem intended to convey to Brick that his relationship with Straw and Ochello was sexual as well as professional. Big Daddy implies that Straw and Ochello hired him purely on the basis of his good looks and athletic build.

Despite the way in which this scene deliberately reverses the audience's expectations, however, Williams seems to have been primarily interested in establishing Brick's desire to inherit the estate on his own terms. This is not to deny that Brick's ranting about gay men is unspeakably homophobic, nor that he seems genuinely tortured by his memories of his relationship with Skipper. Rather, my point is that his refusal to acknowledge his homosexuality should be seen as all indication that he is determined to redefine the terms of his unstated contract with Big Daddy concerning the estate. Big Daddy wants to learn the "truth" about Brick's relationship with Skipper because he is afraid that Brick's homosexuality will disrupt the system of property relations he embodies. In many respects, Brick's claims to the estate are more tenuous than those of his brother, Gooper. After all, Gooper is Big Daddy's first-born son and has produced a male heir, thereby insuring that the estate will remain in the family; he has even managed the estate during Big Daddy's illness. Despite the strength of Gooper's claims, however, Big Daddy does not want to leave the estate to him and his wife, Mae, "since I hate [them] an' know they hate me" (81). Big Daddy clearly thinks that Brick is more his son than Gooper is. According to the stage directions, Brick has inherited his "virile beauty" (103) from Big Daddy and thus bears the marks of his lineage more than Gooper does. But Brick's drinking has led Big Daddy to reconsider leaving the estate to him. He asks Brick why he should "subsidize a goddam fool on the bottle" (82).

But the chief obstacle to Brick's inheriting the estate is his failure to produce an heir. Big Daddy tells Brick pointedly: "Gooper's wife's a good breeder, you got to admit she's fertile" (60). On the one hand, Big Daddy is willing to acknowledge that Maggie's exchange-value is superior to Mae's. Despite his disappointment in Maggie's failure to provide Brick with an heir, he admits: "That woman of yours has a better shape on her than Gooper's" (59). On the other hand, he compares her use-value unfavorably to Mae's. He assumes that Brick and Maggie have not yet produced an heir because Maggie is not a "good breeder," and so he urges Brick: "If you don't like Maggie, get rid of Maggie" (63). That Brick's homosexuality represents a violation of his "contract" with Big Daddy becomes clear when Big Mama pleads with him to have a son before Big Daddy dies: "Oh, Brick, son of Big Daddy! Big Daddy does so love you! Y'know what would be his fondest dream come true? If before he passed on, you gave him a child of yours, a grandson as much like his son as his son is like Big Daddy!" (117). Brick's claim to the estate, in other words, is contingent on his willingness to reproduce the patriarchal order Big Daddy represents.

Brick's desire to remain in the closet indicates that he is unwilling to repress his homosexuality in exchange for securing his claims to the estate. Despite Big Daddy's willingness to acknowledge that he too "knocked" around in his youth, we should be careful not to confuse his homosexuality with Brick's. Big Daddy entered into a homosexual relationship with Straw and Ochello on condition that he would eventually inherit the plantation, and thus his homosexuality does not pose a threat to the patriarchal order but expresses the laws by which it operates. Although in his relationship with Straw and Ochello Big Daddy functions as an object of desire, he does not forfeit his claims to masculinity because he repairs their breach of patriarchal law. Straw and Ochello's ownership of the plantation threatens the transmission of patriarchal law, because, as gay male lovers, they cannot produce an heir. They further violate patriarchal law by failing fully to exploit the plantation's resources. They do not try to improve the plantation's productivity by accumulating more property but allow much of it to lie fallow. When Big Daddy becomes overseer, however, he reclaims the plantation for the patriarchal order. He not only provides Straw and Ochello with an heir, but he significantly increases the plantation's productivity, eventually becoming the delta's richest cotton planter. As he proudly reminds Big Mama in act 2, under his management and with "no goddam help" (58) from her, the plantation got "bigger and bigger and bigger and bigger and bigger!" (58), demonstrating that he is its rightful owner. Thus Big Daddy's homosexuality does not prevent him from fulfilling the patriarchal injunction to reproduce, an injunction that is at once biological and economic.[29]

To further clarify the differences between Big Daddy's and Brick's homosexuality. I want to examine briefly Luce Irigaray's analysis of the patriarchal economy of exchange, in which women function as commodities. According to Irigaray, in patriarchal societies the very foundation of the social and economic order depends on the exchange of women among men. Although men engage in the commerce of women, they do not enter into exchanges with them. Male heterosexual privilege is defined by an ability to engage in transactions with other men, and thus to retain their access to patriarchal power, men must renounce the desire to circulate as commodities. In this system of exchange, men's relations with women are governed by a homosexual economy of desire. Women have value only insofar as they "serve the possibility of, and potential benefit in, relations among men."[30] Thus heterosexuality merely provides "an alibi for the smooth workings of man's relations with himself, of relations among men."[31] To mark both the differences and the similarities between this system of exchange and homosexuality, Irigaray invents the neologism *hom(m)o-sexuality*. According to her, homosexuality differs from *hom(m)o-sexuality* in that it "openly interprets the law according to which society operates."[32] Moreover, in homosexual relations, the penis no longer functions symbolically but is merely a means to pleasure. For Irigaray, this is why homosexuality is so threatening to the patriarchal order and must be suppressed. Once the penis becomes a means to pleasure, "*the phallus loses its power.*"[33]

Although, as a number of critics have pointed out, Irigaray does not adequately distinguish between homosexuality and hom(m)o-sexuality, her analysis provides a useful theoretical framework for understanding the differences between Brick's and Big Daddy's sexual identities.[34] Big Daddy's homosexuality is clearly grounded in a hom(m)o-sexual economy of desire. Although he enters into a relationship in which he circulates as a commodity, he retains access to patriarchal power by repositioning himself as the subject of a transaction. His willingness to function as an object of desire in exchange for inheriting the plantation transforms a homosexual relationship in which the penis does not function as a sign of patriarchal power into a hom(m)o-sexual one that is based on an exchange. Thus in Big Daddy's relationship with Straw and Ochello the penis is not a means to pleasure but provides Big Daddy with an instrument for obtaining control of the plantation. This analysis of Big Daddy's hom(m)o-sexuality casts his desire to learn the "truth" about Brick's relationship with Skipper in a wholly new light. Although Big Daddy *seems* to be more tolerant of homosexuality, he is willing to accept homosexual relations only insofar as they do not impede the reproduction of the hom(m)o-sexual system of exchange on which patriarchal property relations are based. He readily admits that he too "knocked" around in his youth because he used his homosexuality to contain the threat Straw and Ochello's relationship posed to the smooth workings of the patriarchal order.

Williams expresses the differences between Brick's and Big Daddy's homosexuality symbolically by making Big Daddy die from bowel cancer. In Williams's work, bowel cancer is a recurrent trope for gay male promiscuity. For example, in "The Mysteries of the Joy Rio," which was written in 1941 but not published until 1954, Pablo Gonzales, the gay male protagonist, visits the upper galleries of the Joy Rio theater several times a week in order to engage in anonymous sex with young boys. Like Big Daddy, he is dying from bowel cancer, a disease his late benefactor, Emiel Kroger, also died from and that he seems to have bequeathed to Gonzales along with his watch repair shop. Moreover, in "Hard Candy," a story that closely resembles "The Mysteries of the Joy Rio," we are told that Mr. Krupper suffers from "unhealthy intestines" (362), a condition that links him to Gonzales and Kroger. The recurrence of this trope has led critics to see Big Daddy's cancer as a sign of the homosexual excess of his youth. But I think it is better understood as an indication of his desire to repress his homosexuality. Big Daddy's transactions with Straw and Ochello transform the anus into a reproductive organ, thereby containing its potential to disrupt the hom(m)o-sexual system of exchange. In his relationship with Straw and Ochello, the anus functions as a means not to pleasure but to capital accumulation. We know from Freud that the genital organization of sexuality requires the repression of anal eroticism.[35] We also know from Freud that the repression of anal eroticism makes possible the accumulation of capital.[36] Freud's analysis enables us to construe Big Daddy's cancer as retribution for his betrayal of his homosexuality. Big Daddy is willing to disavow anal pleasure in exchange for the accumulation of property. Thus it seems fitting that he should be dying from a disease that Gooper describes as a "poisoning of the whole system due to the failure of the body to eliminate its poisons" (113). Big Daddy's desire to repress his homosexuality has transformed it into a "poison" that corrodes his body from within.

Big Daddy's willingness to disavow anal pleasure is key to understanding the differences between him and the other gay male characters in the play. Straw and Ochello, for example, refuse to instrumentalize the anus. Their homosexuality is not embedded in the exploitative structures of patriarchal capitalism; nor can it be reduced to the phallic binarisms that regulate the production of sexual difference. As we saw above, until Big Daddy intervenes in their relationship, they do not participate in the hom(m)o-sexual system of exchange. In their relationship, the penis does not function symbolically but is akin to the Lacanian Real. As a means to pleasure, it resists symbolization and thus threatens to disrupt the symbolic order. We know from the stage directions that their relationship "must have involved a tenderness which was uncommon" (xiii). This would seem to suggest that their desire for each other cannot be plotted along an active/passive axis in which anal penetration produces a relation of inequality. Straw and Ochello do not occupy gendered positions in relation to desire but have a relationship that is based on a reciprocity of desire and a mutual access to pleasure.

Insofar as it involves an "uncommon tenderness" that is not grounded in a phallic economy of desire, Straw and Ochello's relationship differs significantly from the other relationships in the play. Unlike those relationships, it does not provide an alibi for the smooth workings of the hom(m)o-sexual economy but represents an alternative ungoverned by the terms of the phallus. This is made clear by Williams's description of the bed-sitting-room in which the play takes place as a space that is "gently and poetically haunted [by the] pair of old bachelors who shared [it] all their lives" (xiii). The play's setting, in other words, serves as a constant reminder that the characters have betrayed Straw and Ochello's legacy, a legacy that includes an alternative mode of structuring relationships. In providing such an alternative, Straw and Ochello's relationship exposes the way in which patriarchal capitalism instrumentalizes the male body. Whereas from a hom(m)o-sexual point of view their failure fully to exploit the plantation's resources is a sign of their arrested sexual development, from a homosexual one it is a sign of their unwillingness to disavow anal pleasure.

Having clarified the differences between homosexual and hom(m)o-sexual economies of desire and their relation to patriarchal capitalism, I want to return to the point I made at the beginning of this discussion, namely, that Brick's refusal to acknowledge his homosexuality indicates his determination to redefine the terms of his "contract" with Big Daddy. Unlike Big Daddy, Brick is unwilling to repress his homosexuality in exchange for the accumulation of property. He occupies an ambiguous subject-position, one that is neither homosexual nor hom(m)o-sexual. Whereas Big Daddy bases his relationship with Straw and Ochello on a transaction, thereby insuring that it does not deprive him of access to patriarchal power, Brick refuses to hom(m)o-sexualize his relationship with Skipper. Although Maggie is willing to function as an object of exchange between him and Skipper so that their relationship will remain "one of those beautiful, ideal things they tell about in the Greek legends" (43), Brick rejects her attempt to provide a conduit for his desire. Maggie explains to Brick that she and Skipper made love not because they were attracted to each other but because "it made both of us feel a little bit closer to you" (43). Unlike Big Daddy, however, Brick has no interest in participating in the hom(m)o-sexual system of property relations, and so he refuses to triangulate his relationship with Skipper through Maggie. He resents Maggie's attempt to mediate his relationship with Skipper and blames her for Skipper's suicide. He tells Big Daddy that Maggie was jealous of Skipper and sought to destroy him: "Y'know, I think that Maggie had always felt sort of left out because she and me never got any closer together than two people just get in bed, which is not much closer than two cats on a—fence humping" (91).

At the same time, however, he also refuses to remove himself wholly from the hom(m)o-sexual economy. Because he is unwilling to relinquish access to patriarchal power, he resists entering into an unequivocally homosexual relationship with Skipper. When Skipper calls him long-distance and makes a drunken confession, Brick hangs up on him, precipitating his suicide. Moreover, Brick refuses to believe that Skipper was attracted to him and blames Maggie for making Skipper doubt his sexuality. According to Brick, Skipper did not really believe he was gay but Maggie "poured in his mind the dirty, false idea that what we were, him and me, was a frustrated case of that ole pair of sisters that lived in this room, Jack Straw and Peter Ochello!—He, poor Skipper, went to bed with Maggie to prove it wasn't true, and when it didn't work out, he thought it *was* true!" (91). Brick's determination to retain access to patriarchal power prevents him and Skipper from experiencing the uncommon tenderness that marked Straw and Ochello's relationship. On the one hand, Brick wants to avoid forfeiting his claims to masculinity by entering into a relationship in which the penis is merely a means to pleasure and does not function as a sign of male heterosexual privilege. On the other hand, he does not want to destroy the "good clean thing" (89) between him and Skipper by structuring their relationship hierarchically. Brick has no desire to enter into a homosexual relationship in which access to pleasure is not mutual. He would prefer to have a relationship with Skipper in which the phallus does not operate than one in which the anus functions purely as use-value. Thus he refuses to structure his relationship with Skipper in a way that would allow him to recuperate his masculinity.

Brick's refusal to participate in the hom(m)o-sexual economy surfaces most fully in his refusal to engage in a transaction with Big Daddy. As we saw above, Big Daddy confronts Brick about his relationship with Skipper to determine whether he is willing to hom(m)o-sexualize his desire. Unless Brick overcomes his reluctance to disavow anal pleasure, Big Daddy does not want to leave the estate to him. Brick's claim to the estate, in other words, is contingent on his willingness to instrumentalize the anus by relegating it to the status of use-value. Engaging in a transaction with Big Daddy would complete the hom(m)o-sexual system of exchange Big Daddy instituted when he inherited the plantation from Straw and Ochello. Brick's determination to remain in the closet, however, enables him to inherit the estate without fulfilling the terms of his "contract" with Big Daddy. He neither confesses his desire for Skipper nor produces a male heir in exchange for inheriting the estate. If at the end of the play he finally agrees to make love with Maggie, he does so not to show Big Daddy that he is willing to hom(m)o-sexualize his desire but rather because he is determined to remain in the closet. In the final scene, when Gooper and Mae refuse to believe that Maggie is pregnant because they "hear the nightly pleadin' and the nightly refusal" (155), Brick asks them: "How d'y'know that we're not silent lovers? Even if y'got a peep-hole drilled in the wall, how can y'tell if sometime when Gooper's got business in Memphis an' you're playin' scrabble at the country club with other ex-queens of cotton, Maggie and I don't come to some temporary agreement? How do you know that—?" (156). In producing an heir, Brick hopes to leave unresolved the question of his sexual identity. Once he has become a father, Gooper and Mae will be unable to determine whether he is homosexual or hom(m)o-sexual.

Brick's refusal to engage in a transaction with Big Daddy marks the emergence of a new social and economic order in which neither the penis nor the anus functions as use-value. By inheriting the estate without fulfilling his agreement with Big Daddy, Brick disrupts the smooth workings of the patriarchal order. His unwillingness to reduce the anus to its use-value restores the plantation to its original condition and thus makes restitution for Big Daddy's betrayal of his homosexuality, a betrayal that violates Straw and Ochello's legacy. As I have already noted, insofar as Straw and Ochello's relationship deinstrumentalizes the male body, it threatens to disrupt the hom(m)o-sexual system of exchange. As gay male subjects, Straw and Ochello do not occupy fixed positions in relation to desire but are simultaneously active and passive, desired and desiring. Thus their relationship cannot be reduced to the binary structure of heterosexual relations, as they were normativized in the Cold War era. The positions they occupy in relation to desire cannot be understood in terms of the binary opposition male/female. Nor does their desire correspond to the heterosexual mapping of the body into differentiated erotic zones coded as male or female.[37] As gay male subjects, their bodies contain multiple possibilities for achieving pleasure. In their relationship, pleasure does not remain localized at specific sites but is dispersed across the body. It is simultaneously genital, oral, and anal, and thus it cannot be understood in terms of the heterosexual economy of desire.

Although Brick and Maggie's relationship is not based on a mutual access to pleasure, it resembles Straw and Ochello's in that it undermines the binary logic of sexual difference. Like Straw and Ochello, Brick and Maggie do not occupy gendered positions in relation to desire. Unlike Big Daddy, Brick refuses to judge Maggie according to her exchange-value or her use-value. Moreover, by the end of the play he no longer tries to thwart her will but allows her to assert control over their relationship. According to the stage directions, in the final scene he watches her "with growing admiration" (157) as she throws away his liquor bottles and places his pillow on the bed next to hers, indicating her determination to make love with him. Insofar as it reverses the hierarchical structure of heterosexual relations, Brick and Maggie's relationship has the potential to impede the transmission of patriarchal law. Like Straw and Ochello's relationship, theirs cannot be understood in terms of the binary opposition male/female. Brick and Maggie's relation to desire is not fixed but constantly shifting. Brick's lack of interest in Maggie forces her to position herself as a desiring subject. Indeed, Brick seems to encourage Maggie to treat him as an object of desire. Maggie tells him that she has no interest in taking a lover because she "can't see a man but you! Even with my eyes closed, I just see you! Why don't you get ugly, Brick, why don't you please get fat or ugly or something so I could stand it?" (31). Brick's indifference seems calculated to increase Maggie's determination to have him. She tells him repeatedly that "one thing I don't have is the charm of the defeated, my hat is still in the ring, and I am determined to win!" (25), and thus he knows that she is unlikely to concede defeat.

Deinstrumentalizing the Female Body

To show more fully how Brick and Maggie's relationship disrupts the hom(m)o-sexual economy, I want to examine in some detail the construction of Maggie's subjectivity. Many critics treat Maggie as the archetypal phallic woman, claiming that she functions as a sign of both desire and castration.[38] To be sure, the stage directions consistently describe Maggie in masculine terms. They state, for example, that when Maggie's voice drops low, we "have a sudden image of her playing boys' games as a child" (18). This does not mean, however, that her subjectivity is grounded in a phallic economy of desire. As a married woman who has a better shape on her than Mae does, Maggie occupies an ambiguous position in the hom(m)o-sexual economy: she cannot be easily reduced to her exchange-value or to her use-value. Though married, she does not wholly remove herself from circulation as a commodity. As we saw above, she encourages Brick and Skipper to treat her as an object of exchange so that their relationship can remain like one of those "beautiful, ideal things" in Greek mythology. At the same time, however, she does not allow herself to be relegated to the status of exchange-value. She is well aware of her desirability as a commodity and even brags about it. She tells Brick that when she was in Memphis shopping for Big Daddy's birthday present, "there wasn't a man I met or walked by that didn't just eat me up with his eyes and turn around when I passed him and look back at me" (38). She is also proud of the fact that Big Daddy has a "lech" (19) for her, bragging that when he talks to her, he "drops his eyes to my boobs an' licks his old chops!" (19). Despite her pride in her ability to arouse male desire, however, she is determined to remove herself from the hom(m)o-sexual economy. She refuses to take a lover, even though Brick encourages her to do so.

She similarly does not allow herself to be reduced to her use-value. She resents the pressure placed on her to provide Brick with an heir and refuses to take the blame for their childlessness. She rejects the position assigned to her in the hom(m)o-sexual economy as a "breeder" whose primary function is to insure the reproduction of patriarchal property relations. She complains bitterly that the family treats her and Brick as though they were "totally use-less" (16) simply because they have not yet had a child. Nor does she respect Mae, who allows the family to see her wholly in terms of her use-value. Maggie describes Mae as a "monster of fertility" (19) and makes fun of her claim that "motherhood's an experience that a woman ought to experience fully" (19), repeating it with mock solemnity. Nor does Maggie try to conceal her dislike of Mae's children, describing them as "no-neck monsters" (15) who do not know how to behave properly. As I noted above, she is even proud that she continues to have exchange-value, despite her status as a married woman. Maggie also violates patriarchal law by refusing to cede control of her body to Brick. She does not allow the hom(m)o-sexual economy to instrumental-ize her body by exploiting its reproductive capacity. She insists that she has as much right to experience sexual pleasure as Brick does. When Big Mama asks her if she makes Brick happy in bed, implying that she is to blame for their childlessness, Maggie retorts: "Why don't you ask if he makes *me* happy in bed?. . . . *It works both ways!*" (37). According to Maggie, husbands and wives should have equal access to pleasure.

Maggie's ambiguous position in the hom(m)o-sexual economy can be attributed to her desire to function simultaneously as a subject and an object of desire. Insofar as Brick's sexual indifference enables her to position herself as a desiring subject, it reinforces her attraction to him. Maggie has no reason to fear that Brick will reduce her to an object of desire and thus return her to the hom(m)o-sexual system of exchange. She does not resent his indifference, because it enables her to occupy an active position in relation to desire that does not phallicize her. Maggie tells Brick that his lovemaking is "more like opening a door for a lady or seating her at a table than giving expression to any longing for her" (25) and thus does not place her in a subordinate position in relation to him. That Maggie's masculine position in relation to Brick does *not* phallicize her becomes clear at the end of the play. In the final scene, when Brick expresses admiration for her refusal to concede defeat, thus indicating his willingness to submit to her, she exclaims: "Oh, you weak, beautiful people who give up with such grace. What you need is someone to take hold of you— gently, with love, and hand your life back to you, like something gold you let go of" (158). Maggie's language here recalls Williams's descriptions of Straw and Ochello's uncommonly tender relationship. Although she asserts her will over Brick, she does so "gently" and "with love," suggesting that the position she occupies in their relationship is simultaneously masculine *and* feminine, active *and* passive. According to the terms of the play, such a position is gay.

Maggie's insistence on occupying a position in relation to desire that is simultaneously active and passive helps to explain why her attempt to function as an object of exchange between Brick and Skipper ultimately fails. Maggie's willingness to allow Brick to triangulate his desire for Skipper through her bespeaks her determination to dismantle the binary opposition male/female. In trying to provide a conduit for Brick's desire, she redefines her place in the hom(m)o-sexual economy. As an object of exchange, she occupies both an active and a passive position in relation to desire. Because she is the one who initiates the transaction, she does not function purely as a conduit for Brick's desire but participates in the exchange as one of the contracting parties. She readily admits that she made love with Skipper so that she could feel closer to Brick. When she recalls why she and Skipper made love, she does not exclude herself from the transaction, but stresses that she participated in it fully: "And so we made love to each other to dream it was you, *both of us*" (43; emphasis added). Thus it is hardly surprising that Skipper is unable to perform sexually when he and Maggie make love. Participating in the transaction requires him to forfeit his access to patriarchal power. In making love to Skipper, Maggie treats him as a conduit for *her* desire.[39]

In light of Maggie's desire to occupy a subject-position that is simultaneously masculine and feminine, her determination at the end of the play to provide Brick with a male heir is problematic and requires explanation. If Maggie is eager to redefine her place in the hom(m)o-sexual economy, why does she want to establish her use-value? Despite her resentment of the way in which the system of property relations relegates women to the status of use-value, why is she willing to provide Brick with a male heir in exchange for solidifying his claims to the estate? Does she want to perpetuate the system of exchange Big Daddy instituted when he inherited the plantation from Straw and Ochello or dismantle it? I think Maggie's eagerness to fulfill Big Daddy's "fondest dream" is best understood as indicating her determination to consolidate her position as a desiring subject. Her claim at the end of the play that she is pregnant shows her determination to participate in the hom(m)o-sexual economy *on her own terms.* This does not mean, however, that like Gooper and Mae, she tries to deceive Big Daddy so that he will leave the estate to Brick. She resents the way in which Gooper and Mae try to manipulate Big Daddy with their "monstrous" fertility and complains that they behave like "a couple of cardsharps fleecing a sucker" (20). Moreover, despite the fact that he embodies patriarchal law, Maggie feels an affinity for Big Daddy. Big Daddy is not ashamed of his working-class background, and she genuinely admires him because he "*is* what he *is*, and makes no bones about it. He hasn't turned gentleman farmer, he's still a Mississippi red neck, as much of a red neck as he must have been when he was just overseer here on the old Jack Straw and Peter Ochello place" (41).

That Maggie should feel an affinity for Big Daddy is hardly surprising, given the similarities between them. Like Big Daddy, Maggie comes from an impoverished background, which she is determined to overcome through the accumulation of property. She resents the way in which as a young girl she "always had to suck up to people I couldn't stand because they had money and I was poor as Job's turkey" (41). She recalls bitterly how her father's drinking forced her mother to "maintain some semblance of social position, to keep appearances up, on an income of one hundred and fifty dollars a month on those old government bonds!" (41). And she is still bitter that when she was a debutante, she had only two evening dresses, "one Mother made from a pattern in *Vogue,* the other a hand-me-down from a snotty rich cousin I hated!" (41). Thus she does not hesitate to hom(m)o-sexualize her relationship with Big Daddy. Despite her resentment of the position the hom(m)o-sexual economy assigns to women, she willingly renounces her body as a means to pleasure and exploits its reproductive capacities in order to fulfill the conditions of Brick's "contract" with Big Daddy. She does not try to conceal her determination to do so but openly declares it to Brick: "Born poor, raised poor, expect to die poor unless I manage to get us something out of what Big Daddy leaves when he dies of cancer!" (45). Here Maggie's resemblance to Big Daddy surfaces fully. Although her desire has the potential to disrupt the smooth workings of the patriarchal order, she is willing, like Big Daddy, to repress it in exchange for inheriting the estate.

But it is also here that the similarities between her and Big Daddy end. For despite her willingness to participate in the hom(m)o-sexual economy, she does not allow herself to become its instrument. She does not share Big Daddy's desire to secure the transmission of patriarchal law but enters into the system of exchange in order to subvert it from within. Her determination to establish her use-value enables her to remove herself from circulation as a commodity. To be sure, she is eager to show Big Daddy that she is as good a "breeder" as Mae is so that he will acknowledge Brick as his rightful heir. But in acting as a kind of proxy for Brick, she positions herself as the subject of a transaction. Moreover, as we saw above, Big Daddy enters into the hom(m)o-sexual system of exchange in order to contain the threat the anus poses to the reproduction of the patriarchal order. His willingness to repress his homosexuality in exchange for inheriting the plantation reduces the anus to its use-value and thus restores it to its status as a reproductive organ that guarantees the transmission of patriarchal law. Maggie, on the other hand, renounces her body as a means to pleasure *only temporarily*. Participating in the hom(m)o-sexual system of exchange enables her to occupy a masculine position in relation to desire that does not phallicize her because it is both active *and* passive. Her access to pleasure becomes contingent on her willingness to function, albeit temporarily, as pure use-value.

Elia Kazan, the Closet, and the Politics of Naming Names

Having shown that Brick and Maggie's participation in the hom(m)o-sexual economy is deceptive, I want to conclude this chapter by examining the differences between the original and the Broadway versions of the play. Clarifying the differences between the two versions will help us to locate Williams's treatment of the closet more firmly in its Cold War context. In the "Note of Explanation" Williams included in the published version of the play, he recalled that he rewrote act 3 after the director, Elia Kazan, criticized the way in which the play ended. According to Williams, Kazan objected in particular to Williams's treatment of Brick, who Kazan thought should experience "some apparent mutation as a result of the virtual vivisection that he undergoes in his interview with his father in Act Two" (124). Although Williams was eager to have Kazan direct the play and respected his opinion sufficiently to "re-examine the script from his point of view" (125), he was reluctant to have Brick experience a transformation, as he did

not "believe that a conversation, however revelatory, ever effects so immediate a change in the heart or even conduct of a person in Brick's state of
spiritual disrepair" (125).

Kazan's criticisms of Williams's treatment of Brick do not seem to have
been motivated purely by artistic considerations. Kazan had become a controversial figure both on Broadway and in Hollywood because he had repu-
diated his left-wing past and named names when he appeared before the
House Un-American Activities Committee in 1952.[40] He later claimed that
he had cooperated with the committee in order to protect his career and avoid
the blacklist.[41] Although his willingness to inform on former friends and
colleagues who had been members of the Communist party in the thirties
made him the target of left-wing attacks, he adamantly refused to apolo-
gize for his testimony and went to great lengths publicly to justify it. His
film *On the Waterfront* (1954), for example, which won numerous Academy
Awards including Best Picture and Best Director, examined union corruption
and waterfront racketeering in a thinly veiled attempt to justify informing
on the former Communists and fellow travelers who had been targeted by
HUAC.[42] Although the film did not draw an explicit analogy between the
corrupt union officials and the Communist party hierarchy, the union-busting
hero, a Catholic priest played by Karl Malden, persuades one of the dockers,
Terry Malloy (Marlon Brando), to testify before the crime commission about
the union's corrupt activities. Malloy's willingness to confess to his criminal
past and to inform on his former buddies leads to his moral regeneration,
and the film ends happily with him marrying Edie Doyle (Eva Marie Saint),
the film's courageous and principled heroine who encourages him to follow
Father Barry's advice and inform on the union.

I have briefly summarized the plot of *On the Waterfront* in order to suggest that Kazan's criticisms of the original version of *Cat on a Hot Tin Roof*
were motivated by a desire to have the play provide further justification for
those who, like him, had named names before HUAC. Kazan's criticisms of
the original ending indicate that he wanted Brick to experience the sort of
moral regeneration Malloy experiences in *On the Waterfront* as a result of his
testimony before the crime commission. Such a regeneration would justify
Big Daddy's attempt to "straighten" Brick out by forcing him to acknowledge the "truth" about his relationship with Skipper and by extension exoner-
ate former fellow travelers such as Kazan who had confessed their political
"crimes." But this is clearly not what happens in the Broadway version of the
play. Although Williams insisted that he took "no attitude about [Kazan's
testimony], one way or another" and partially rewrote the play in response to
Kazan's criticisms, he was unwilling to endorse informing on former friends
and colleagues, even in the name of national security.[43] As we saw above, he

stated quite clearly that he did not think it was possible for a conversation, however "revelatory," to bring about the sort of transformation that Kazan wanted Brick to undergo. Despite Williams's desire to have Kazan direct the play, Brick remains closeted in the Broadway version. As we saw above, Brick makes love with Maggie at the end of the play not because he has undergone a moral transformation and is no longer homosexual but because he refuses to relinquish the protection afforded by the closet. Big Daddy makes clear that for Brick to inherit the estate he must hom(m)o-sexualize his desire, which he has no intention of doing.

A number of critics have noted the resemblance between the bed-sitting-room in which the play takes place and the homosexual closet.[44] Like the closet, the bed-sitting-room is a permeable space whose borders are not clearly defined but constantly shifting. According to the stage directions, it is barely distinguishable from the upstairs gallery. It includes "two pairs of very wide doors" that open onto the gallery and that provide a glimpse of "a fair summer evening that fades into dusk and night during the course of the play" (xiii). Williams also thought that the walls below the ceiling "should dissolve mysteriously into air" and that the set "should be roofed by the sky" (xiv). Moreover, the bed-sitting-room fails to protect its occupants from the intrusive gaze of others. In the scene in which he confronts Brick, Big Daddy complains that "the walls have ears in this place" (63). Although it is unusually hot, he closes the doors because "I hate eavesdroppers, I don't like any kind of sneakin' an' spyin'" (62), and he knows that Gooper and Mae are trying to overhear what he and Brick are talking about. Like the closet, in other words, the bed-sitting-room constantly exposes its occupants to public scrutiny. Family members enter it without knocking, complain bitterly when Brick and Maggie lock the doors, and listen through the walls to their personal conversations.

But in light of the wave of anti-Communist hysteria unleashed by the McCarthy hearings, the bed-sitting-room's permeability, its lack of fixed boundaries, has another possible meaning. Gooper and Mae's methods for exposing Brick as a homosexual who has broken his "contract" with Big Daddy are reminiscent of the surveillance practices of the national-security apparatus. Williams renders the similarities explicit when in act 2 he has Maggie exclaim, "Sister Woman! Your talents are wasted as a housewife and mother, you really ought to be with the FBI" (54). These references to the emergence of the national-security state make possible another reading of the play, one that links it to other plays written at about the same time, such as Arthur Miller's *The Crucible* (1953), which were more explicit in their criticisms of Kazan and the other so-called friendly witnesses who testified before HUAC.[45] Williams's representation of the bed-sitting-room as a space in which Brick and Maggie are constantly threatened with exposure suggests that he too wanted to critique the emergence of the national-security state. This may explain more fully why Kazan objected to the original ending of the play. Gooper and Mae's attempts to expose Brick could be read as an indirect reference to Kazan's controversial testimony. In the play, the closet emerges as a space in which Communists, gays, and other groups targeted by the national-security apparatus can escape detection. In confronting Brick with the "truth" about his homosexuality, a truth Brick denies not because he is ashamed of it but because he does not want to forfeit his claims to the estate, Big Daddy only reinforces his determination to remain in the closet.

Williams, then, did not allow his desire to have Kazan direct the play deter him from criticizing those who had cooperated with HUAC. Despite Kazan's criticisms, Williams did not delete his allusions to McCarthyism. The few changes he did make in response to Kazan's criticisms, such as having Brick express admiration for Maggie in the final scene, did not prevent Gooper and Mae's constant spying on Brick and Maggie from recalling the McCarthy witch hunts. Williams's strategies were not unlike those Maggie and Brick adopted to subvert the hom(m)o-sexual economy from within. His "Note of Explanation" and the few minor changes he made to act 3 functioned as a kind of screen that enabled him to protest the government's violation of basic civil liberties (the right to free speech and freedom of association) without alienating Kazan. His criticisms of Kazan are sufficiently veiled that they can easily go undetected. Brick's homosexuality is not the only open secret in the play. Williams's oblique references to the national-security state simultaneously reveal and conceal his criticisms of those who, like Kazan, had betrayed former friends and colleagues in order to protect their careers.[46]

Given his exploration in *Cat on a Hot Tin Roof* of the open secret that governed gay male experience in the Cold War era, it is hardly surprising that when in the early years of gay liberation Williams was criticized for not having written a "gay" play, he responded angrily, claiming that he had not found it necessary to write one because "I could express what I wanted to express through other means."[47] Many critics have seen Williams's desire to avoid limiting his audience by focusing exclusively on gay male characters as an indication that he conceived of homosexuality as a private or civil rights issue that did not have important political and social repercussions.[48] Yet in light of his treatment of gay male experience in *Cat on a Hot Tin Roof*, this understanding of his plays seems unwarranted and ignores their thematic continuity with his more sexually explicit short stories. In *Cat on a Hot Tin Roof*, Williams explored, albeit indirectly, the linkage between homosexuality and Communism in the Cold War political imaginary. If he refused to limit his audience, that is because he understood that in the Cold War era not only gay men but also "promiscuous" women, Communists, and other groups who rejected the postwar American dream of owning a home in the suburbs were forced to inhabit the closet.

NOTES

1. See in particular Edward A. Sklepowich, "In Pursuit of the Lyric Quarry: The Image of the Homosexual in Tennessee Williams's Prose Fiction," in *Tennessee Williams: A Tribute*, ed. Jac Tharpe (Jackson: Univ. Press of Mississippi, 1977), 525–44, and John M. Clum, "'Something Cloudy, Something Clear': Homophobic Discourse in Tennessee Williams," in *Displacing Homophobia: Gay Male Perspectives in Literature and Culture*, ed. Ronald R. Butters, John M. Clum, and Michael Moon (Durham, N.C.: Duke Univ. Press, 1989), 149–67. See also David Savran, *Communists, Cowboys, and Queers: The Politics of Masculinity in the Work of Arthur Miller and Tennessee Williams* (Minneapolis: Univ. of Minnesota Press, 1992), 111–14.

2. Tennessee Williams, "Hard Candy," in *Collected Stories* (New York: Ballantine, 1986), 359. Hereafter all references are to this edition and are cited by page number.

3. See Sklepowich, "In Pursuit of the Lyric Quarry", and Clum, "'Something Cloudy, Something Clear.'"

4. This is not to suggest that gay male critics were happy about Williams's revelations in his *Memoirs*. Whereas earlier Williams had concealed too much, now he concealed too little. He discussed his experiences of cruising for sex after the death of lover, Frank Merlo, *too* openly and in *too* much detail. On the reception of Williams's *Memoirs*, see Savran, *Communists, Cowboys, and Queers*, 131 and *passim*.

5. Harold Beaver, "Homosexual Signs," *Critical Inquiry* 8 (August 1981): 99–119.

6. Ibid., 105.

7. Beaver limits his discussion of gay male semiosis to camp. On the gay macho style as another important form of gay male semiosis, see Richard Dyer, "Getting Over the Rainbow: Identity and Pleasure in Gay Cultural Politics," in *Silver Linings: Some Strategies for the Eighties*, ed. George Bridges and Rosalind Brunt (London: Lawrence & Wishart, 1981). See also chapter 5 below.

8. In emphasizing the changes that have occurred in urban gay communities since Stonewall, I do not mean to legitimize the received narrative of postwar gay male politics. Although contemporary urban gay communities are less closeted and more politicized than earlier ones, I hope to show that in the fifties gay male resistance was not limited to camp, which is to say that there were gay men who were political before Stonewall.

9. This sentence, which is emphasized in the original and concludes the story, is clearly meant to function as a kind of punch line. Only the reader who is willing to read as a gay man will fully appreciate its humor, with its pun on choking and hard candy.

10. For a discussion of the epistemological structures of the closet and the way in which they continue to govern gay male experience, see Eve Kosofsky Sedgwick, *Epistemology of the Closet* (Berkeley and Los Angeles: Univ. of California Press, 1990), esp. 67–90.

11. D. A. Miller has written compellingly about the double bind Enlightenment constructions of the subject place gay men in when extended to them. See D. A. Miller, "Secret Subjects, Open Secrets," in *The Novel and the Police* (Berkeley and Los Angeles: Univ. of California Press, 1988), 192–220.

12. At the same time, however, it is also important to stress that precisely because they occur in a public place, Mr. Krupper's sexual activities transgress the privatization of sexuality, its confinement to the bedroom, and help to colonize public space for gay men.

13. On the history of the Mattachine Society, see John D'Emilio, *Sexual Politics, Sexual Communities: The Making of a Homosexual Minority in the United States, 1940–1970* (Chicago: Univ. of Chicago Press, 1983), and Toby Marotta, *The Politics of Homosexuality: How Lesbians and Gay Men Have Made Themselves a Political and Social Force in Modern America* (Boston: Houghton Mifflin, 1981).

14. Quoted in Jonathan Katz, *Gay American History: Lesbians and Gay Men in the U.S.A.* (New York: Harper & Row, 1976), 410.

15. On the way in which the Mattachine Society compromised its own founding principles by attempting to propitiate a hostile suburban mainstream, see Savran, *Communists, Cowboys, and Queers*, 84–88.

16. For a fuller discussion of the way in which the subaltern's fragmented relation to identity can be enabling rather than disabling from a political perspective, see Chela Sandoval, "U.S. Third World Feminism: The Theory and Method of Oppositional Consciousness in the Postmodern World," *Genders* 10 (spring 1991): 1–24.

17. Recent critiques of essentialism have tended to minimize the role the stabilization of minority identities has played in the consolidation of political collectivities. For an important defense of the strategic use of essentialism in contemporary theory and politics, see Diana Fuss, *Essentially Speaking: Feminism, Nature, and Difference* (New York: Routledge, 1989). See also Katie King, "Local and Global: AIDS Activism and Feminist Theory," *Camera Obscura* 28 (January 1992): 80–98.

18. See Sklepowich, "In Pursuit of the Lyric Quarry," Clum, "'Something Cloudy, Something Clear,'" and Savran, *Communists, Cowboys, and Queers*, 81–84.

19. What is disturbing about this argument is that it does not differ significantly from the virulently homophobic critique of Williams's plays that first emerged in the late fifties when it became widely rumored that Williams was gay. According to this critique, Williams did not express his homosexuality in his plays directly but indirectly. It surfaced most fully in his creation of strong female characters who were really gay men in drag. Critics dubbed Williams's strategies of indirection the "Albertine strategy," after Albertine, the sexually ambiguous lover of the narrator in Marcel Proust's *A la recherche du temps perdu*. For an example of this critique, see Stanley Edgar Hyman, "Some Trends in the Novel," *College English* (October 1958): 1–3. Hyman's criticism of Williams recalls the Cold War construction of "the homosexual" in that it positions Williams as the enemy within who must be exposed because he is secretly undermining the nation's morality.

20. See, for example, Lee Barton, "Why Do Playwrights Hide Their Homosexuality?" *New York Times*, 23 January 1972, 27.

21. Quoted in Savran, *Communists, Cowboys, and Queers*, 81–82.

22. For a more detailed discussion of the problems with this understanding of the closet, see Sedgwick, *Epistemology of the Closet*, 67–90. As Sedgwick notes, although coming out of the closet can be a powerful and disruptive act, its effectiveness as a political strategy is limited. To begin with, the closet is a structure that

is imposed on gay people, not one they have created to protect themselves from an intrusive public gaze. Even the most openly gay people find reasons for reentering the closet when they apply for a job or a bank loan, petition the courts for visiting or custody rights, or encounter a homophobic authority figure who is in a position to determine a job promotion or a salary raise. Moreover, individual acts of disclosure necessarily have a limited effect on structures that are institutionally embodied and collectively enforced.

23. Clum, "'Something Cloudy, Something Clear,'" 154. It is not at all clear to me in what way Mr. Krupper's sexual activities might be considered exploitative. After all, the six quarters he gives to the young men he encounters at the Joy Rio are hardly a large sum (even by postwar standards). The purpose of the quarters seems to be to provide an alibi that allows the young men to engage in a forbidden activity they find pleasurable without feeling guilty.

24. Ibid., 158.

25. Ibid., 159.

26. See Clum, "'Something Cloudy, Something Clear,'" 159, and Savran, *Communists, Cowboys, and Queers*, 100–101.

27. Tennessee Williams, *Cat on a Hot Tin Roof* (New York: Signet, 1985), 84. Hereafter all references are to this edition and are cited by page number.

28. Williams's emphasis on the "unspoken" here and elsewhere in *Cat on a Hot Tin Roof* provides another important link between it and "Hard Candy." As in "Hard Candy," Williams evasions seem meant to position the spectator as a gay man. To understand fully the play's meaning, the spectator must master gay male reading practices, that is, fill in the blanks and read between the lines.

29. In stressing that the patriarchal injunction to multiply is economic as well as biological, I mean to foreground the way in which patriarchal capitalism instrumentalizes the male body, in particular the penis and the anus, which it relegates to the status of use-value. For a discussion of the way in which homosexuality violates the *biological* injunction to multiply under patriarchal capitalism, see Beaver, "Homosexual Signs."

30. Luce Irigaray, "Women on the Market," in *This Sex Which Is Not One*, trans. Catherine Porter (Ithaca: Cornell Univ. Press, 1985), 172.

31. Ibid.

32. Luce Irigaray, "Commodities among Themselves," in *This Sex Which Is Not One*, 193.

33. Ibid.; emphasis in the original.

34. See Eve Kosofsky Sedgwick, *Between Men: English Literature and Male Homosocial Desire* (New York: Columbia Univ. Press, 1985), 21–27, and Diana Fuss, *Essentially Speaking*, 48–49. Many critics writing from an antihomophobic or gay affirmative perspective have identified Irigaray's work as the *locus classicus* of a recent strand of feminist theory that conceives of authoritarian regimes as even more homosexual than gay male culture. See, for example, Eve Kosofsky Sedgwick, *Epistemology of the Closet*, 154, and Lee Edelman, *Homographesis: Essays in Gay Literary and Cultural Theory* (New York: Routledge, 1993), 130–31. This rejection of Irigaray's work strikes me as a particularly costly theoretical move because her understanding of homosexuality as a form of male bonding in which the penis does not operate symbolically can be used to distinguish between patriarchal and nonpatriarchal forms of homosexuality, as I am doing here in my discussion of the differences between Brick and Big Daddy.

35. Sigmund Freud, "Three Essays on the Theory of Sexuality," in *The Standard Edition of the Complete Psychological Works of Sigmund Freud*, ed. James Strachey et al., 24 vols. (London: Hogarth Press and the Institute of Psychoanalysis, 1953–74), vol. 7.

36. Sigmund Freud, "On Transformations of Instinct as Exemplified in Anal Eroticism," in *The Standard Edition of the Complete Psychological Works*, 17:127–33.

37. For a fuller discussion of the way in which gay male desire exceeds the heterosexual mapping of the body and thus has the potential to disrupt patriarchal capitalism, see Guy Hocquenghem, *Homosexual Desire*, trans. Daniella Dangoor (Durham, N.C.: Duke Univ. Press, 1993), esp. 93–112. See also Gilles Deleuze and Felix Guattari, *Anti-Oedipus: Capitalism and Schizophrenia*, trans. Robert Hurley, Mark Seem, and Helen R. Lane (Minneapolis: Univ. of Minnesota Press, 1983).

38. See in particular Savran, *Communists, Cowboys, and Queers*, 106–10.

39. In this respect, Maggie's attempt to intervene in Brick and Skipper's relationship represents an interesting variation on the triangulation of male desire Sedgwick maps in *Between Men*.

40. For a discussion of the impact of Kazan's testimony on his reputation both on Broadway and in Hollywood, see Peter Biskind, *Seeing Is Believing: How Hollywood Taught Us to Stop Worrying and Love the Fifties* (New York: Pantheon, 1983), 169–82. See also Brian Neve, *Film and Politics in America: A Social Tradition* (London and New York: Routledge, 1992), 188–98.

41. See Michel Ciment, *Kazan on Kazan* (New York: Viking, 1974).

42. For a fuller discussion of *On the Waterfront* as a kind of apologia for Kazan's controversial testimony, see Biskind, *Seeing Is Believing*, 169–82.

43. St. Maria Just, *Five O'Clock Angel: Letters of Tennessee Williams to Maria St. Just, 1948–1982* (New York: Knopf, 1990), 56.

44. See in particular Savran, *Communists, Cowboys, and Queers*, 102–10.

45. Although Miller's opposition to McCarthyism was courageous—unlike Kazan, he refused to name names when he appeared before HUAC in 1956—he does not seem to have understood or been troubled by the way in which the discourses of national security contained resistance to the Cold War consensus by linking questions of gender and sexual identity directly to issues of national security. Nor did he express opposition to the Cold War construction of "the homosexual" and "the lesbian" as security risks.

46. In the present context, it seems particularly telling that Kazan refused to acknowledge the political content of Williams's plays. In the early seventies, he told an interviewer who asked him to compare Williams to Arthur Miller: "Williams, by the way, is political in the sense that he supports any cause that is truly liberal, in every way he can. But it's always pure, it's always immediate, it's not calculated. And it's always personal." Michel Ciment, *Kazan on Kazan*, 79. In other words, Williams's political commitments were stereotypically feminine. They were intuitive rather than intellectual and thus remained at the level of the "personal." Unlike the macho Miller, he was supposedly incapable of engaging in a systematic analysis of Cold War America. Thus his treatment of the closet in *Cat on a Hot Tin Roof* could not possibly have a political resonance that extended beyond the merely personal.

47. Quoted in Donald Spoto, *The Kindness of Strangers: The Life of Tennessee Williams* (New York: Viking, 1986), 319.

48. See in particular Clum, "'Something Cloudy, Something Clear,'" 151–52.

DEAN SHACKELFORD

The Truth That Must Be Told: Gay Subjectivity, Homophobia, and Social History in Cat on a Hot Tin Roof

Because important gay writers like Tennessee Williams were courageous during past homophobic times, a positive gay identity has evolved. Although it could be said that novelists of the first half of this century took more liberty in writing about homosexuality than dramatists, no American writer who wished to establish a reputation with a widespread audience could "come out" in public without facing censure or even rejection as an artist, a fact which gay critics John Clum and Nicholas de Jongh seem to ignore when considering the element of the closet in Williams's plays. Recognizing the complex ways in which gender and sexuality play a role in Williams, David Savran is the most understanding of these gay-oriented critics.

To comprehend fully Tennessee Williams's courageous "outing" of the subject of homosexuality, the critic should interpret gay subjectivity contextually within the period when Williams wrote and originally saw his plays produced. As Neil Miller notes in *Out of the Past*, a study of modern gay and lesbian history, homosexuals in the 1950s faced the growing influence of Senator McCarthy and his "witch" hunts. Gay men and lesbians were considered security risks; in fact, it was believed that homosexual spies could easily betray the U.S. government—as the name of the McCarthy-inspired House Committee on Un-American Activities, reveals. Being homosexual was associated with subversive, un-American behavior, as it had been during World War II.

From *The Tennessee Williams Annual Review* 1 (1998): 103–18. Copyright © 1998 by *The Tennessee Williams Annual Review*.

When Roy Cohn, a closeted homosexual himself, assisted Senator McCarthy in prosecuting and persecuting men and women of questionable repute according to the smug, middle-class America of the 1950s, the stage was set for a homosexual witch-hunt. Soon, the entire nation became involved in government-inspired persecution of those not only who were perceived to be communists but also homosexuals, who in the minds of many, were communists any way. As a result, many gays and lesbians in the federal government lost their jobs. Also inspired by McCarthyism, a legislative committee sought to rid Florida of any perceived homosexual, for being gay was not only perversion of the highest magnitude but, more importantly, also tantamount to being a traitor (Miller 271–272). For most of Tennessee Williams's life, the popular opinion was that homosexuals were capable of the worst crimes against their own country and God.

In addition, for much of this century, gay men and lesbians were considered mentally ill. Before 1971, when the APA officially removed homosexuality from its list of mental disturbances, being gay or lesbian also branded one as "abnormal" and "maladjusted." In the first *Diagnostic and Statistical Manual, Mental Disorders* (*DSM I*), homosexuality was considered a serious personality disorder despite the position of the father of psychiatry, Sigmund Freud, that homosexuality was neither an asset nor a liability. Few psychologists or psychiatrists openly questioned the official position of *DSM I* before the work of pioneer Evelyn Hooker in the 1950s.

Williams's *Cat on a Hot in Roof*, the focus of this discussion, was written and first produced during a time of reactionary politics. Because of the social, governmental, and institutional taboos against homosexuality, being an "out" gay writer was problematic during this time. As a result, when Clum and others attack Williams for internalized self-hatred and ambivalence toward homosexuality, they offer an anachronistic, post-Stonewall reading of his canon. Even more so, they seemingly overlook the playwright's courageous efforts to bring the subject "out of the closet" in a repressive era of American history.

As Michel Foucault has argued in *The History of Sexuality*, the lack of discussion of sexuality in a repressed society has typically indicated that "perverse" sexual permutations are rampant and that the more society renders taboo the unspeakable, the more such diversity is inscribed and reinforced. Considering the role of the unspoken as important as the uttered, gay (and other) critics should recognize that Williams's works have much more positive things to say about homosexuality and the gay subject than some contemporary gay critics give him credit for. This observation especially applies to *Cat on a Hot Tin Roof*, one of Williams's greatest works—the first major American play to confront the taboo subject of homosexuality directly and without apology. Winner of the 1955 Pulitzer Prize for Drama, *Cat on a Hot Tin Roof* is Williams's most gay play before *Small Craft Warnings* (1972).[1] Not only is *Cat on a Hot Tin Roof* a plea for tolerance of the gay lifestyle, the play also demonstrates the extent to which society dehumanizes men through its overt homophobia. As such, the play largely demonstrates that a homosocially-oriented social structure is responsible for problematizing homosexuality.

To be fair to Williams, a more subtle and complex way of viewing subjectivity would seem to be needed when the critic interprets his plays. I realize traditional theories of representation consider the physical embodiment of the subject on stage as representation, but I believe the opposite can also be the truth, as Foucaultian logic would suggest. The gay subject represented without question in *Cat* is Skipper, Brick's dead friend with whom he shared an "uncommon" relationship. Although some readers have suggested that Skipper may not even be homosexual, the play indicates the opposite. There is nothing to suggest that Skipper's self-perception is to be questioned. He has, after all, drunk himself to death after confessing his love for Brick and failed when trying to "prove" otherwise. Alcohol becomes the means by which both the gay or quasi-gay male characters, Skipper and Brick, run from their inner selves. Skipper is portrayed as a disturbed but clearly homosexual man whose love and admiration for Brick are such that he cannot face the truth Maggie helps reveal to him. Nevertheless, that Skipper has gay (that is, erotic) feelings toward Brick voices the taboo subject of genuine homosexual attraction and love—making the play subversive for its time. Savran acknowledges that with Skipper Williams "begins cautiously to redefine the male homosexual subject" (109) but considers the lack of embodiment of Skipper on stage problematic like Clum and de Jongh.

Even though not embodied on stage, Skipper is clearly a central figure in the drama; therefore, Williams's attempt at gay male subjectivity is implied through his character. Something concerning Skipper's suicide should also be addressed. Admittedly, gay subjects in American drama often commit suicide because of conventions about punishing the nonconformist in American culture and the playwright's fear of repercussions from a rejecting public, as Kaier Curtin's book "*We Can Always Call Them Bulgarians*" shows. With Skipper, however, the issue is far more complex. Brick's rejection plays a large role in Skipper's death, and even though Skipper may find the truth of his own homosexuality difficult to face, the play suggests that social rejection is the root of his downfall—not homosexuality. If Brick had not hung up on Skipper, perhaps he would still be alive, and if Brick had not rejected his friend, he would not be drinking himself to death. In Williams's world the individual is at the mercy of social codes (and Brick is a prisoner of society's norms) which restrict his freedom and happiness, an issue to which I will return later in this essay.

With Brick, Big Daddy, and Maggie, Williams's negotiation of his own gay subjectivity without "coming out" as a gay playwright becomes even more evident. Everything which occurs centers around Brick, who embodies homosexual desire and, potentially, gay representation. True to the playwright's own homosexual nature, Maggie's attraction to Brick's body—and the central focus on Maggie's desire for sexual fulfillment with Brick—places the male body before the audience's (and the author's) gaze. As Mark Royden Winchell has observed, Brick's implied re-consummation with Maggie at the play's end may be a vicarious means through which he can reunite with his dead friend since he had slept with her to "prove" he was not gay (707)—an act which again centers the play on the male body and reinforces Skipper's role as a gay subject. Maggie's comments on Brick's appearance are often repeated—as are her pleas for sexual fulfillment in and revitalization of their marriage.

Laura Mulvey has argued that audiences identify with the male protagonist and enjoy visual display as they observe characters look at each other. However, the latter is shaped by the dominance of the heterosexual male gaze:

> As the spectator identifies with the main male protagonist, he projects his look onto that of his like, his screen surrogate, so that the power of the male protagonist as he controls events coincides with the active power of the erotic look, both giving a satisfying sense of omnipotence. (426)

As Mulvey suggests, Hollywood cinema generally places male subjectivity at the center and focuses on the male's gaze on the female body. On the other hand, in her essay "Dis-Embodying the Female Voice," Kaja Silverman focuses on the problem of the lack of representation of the female voice: "To allow her to be heard without being seen would ... disrupt the specular regime upon which mainstream cinema relies; it would put her beyond the control of the male gaze, and release her voice from the signifying obligations which that gaze sustains" (135). Similarly, Mulvey skirts the issue of male sexual objectification by stating, "According to the principles of the ruling ideology and the psychical structures that back it up, the male figure cannot bear the burden of sexual objectification" (426) and ignores the possibility of the homosexual male gaze in her theory. Each of these feminist theories is centered on the heterosexual paradigm of active/passive (male/female). This is not to criticize Mulvey and Silverman for their heterosexual-oriented views but to point out the possibility that ignoring gay or lesbian subjectivity within the conventional male/female dichotomy might alter conventional views of the gaze. Although Mulvey's and Silverman's theories apply primarily to filmic representation, they nevertheless inform my reading of theatrical and literary subjectivity in Tennessee Williams.

Only recently has the male body as spectacle become acceptable for theory and critical analysis, as Peter Lehman's 1993 book *Running Scared* and Laurence Goldstein's 1994 book *The Male Body* would suggest. To my knowledge, however, little work has been done with addressing the theoretical possibilities of the gay male gaze,[2] which I will turn to only briefly in this analysis and treat more extensively elsewhere. If the heterosexual-oriented cinema places the male subject at its center, would it not be possible that the work of a gay playwright places himself and his own gaze at the center? I think so. The gay male gaze thus redirects the traditional heterosexual man/woman dichotomy to center on the male body, blur the distinction between heterosexual/homosexual, man/woman, active/passive, and subvert traditional American representations of the male (and gay male) subject.

An appreciation of masculine beauty is often associated with gay subjectivity (gay subjects gaze upon male objects) while at the same time it is admired in American society. In his introduction to Williams's *Collected Stories*, Gore Vidal reports that Williams believed he could not write a story without at least one character to whom he was sexually attracted (xxiii). As this comment might suggest, his plays insist on male physicality and beauty, and through this means, further center his plays on gay male subjectivity (his own as well as the gay and quasi-gay characters on stage).

With Brick, Williams subverts traditional representations of the male and places homosexual desire, and the possibility of Brick's being an unresolved gay man, before the audience as central concerns. In *Cat* Brick is clearly eroticized. His masculine appearance appeals to the gay playwright; to the audience, which becomes involved in the subversive (for 1955) eroticization of the male body; to Skipper, who is homoerotically attracted to Brick; and to Maggie, who constantly begs him to sleep with her. In some productions, Brick wears silk pajamas—a clear indication of Brick's erotic appeal—after emerging from a hot shower. In one instance Maggie says, "I can't see a man but you! Even with my eyes closed, I just see you! Why don't you get ugly, Brick, why don't you please get fat or ugly or something so that I could stand it?" (40). While Maggie gazes on her beloved Brick's body, the audience itself is so directed. Through her character Williams eroticizes Brick and thus centers the play on gay male subjectivity.

As a result, though the play may at first appear to be focused on the presumed heterosexual Brick's perceptions of himself in relation to society, the sympathy and audience's identification are focused primarily on Maggie's and the gay playwright's gaze. Without getting too far into the arguments for transvestism in Williams's works, let it be said that the playwright projects his own homosexual desire for Brick's character onto Maggie (blurring male/female, heterosexual/homosexual, and masculine/feminine) and thus converts the male gaze to the female gaze and, ultimately, the gay male gaze. As Robert Gross argues in his recent essay on Brick and the gay spectator: "Maggie's obsession for Brick, articulated in her lengthy speeches throughout the play's first act, encourages us to identify with her and assume her desire" (13). While heterosexual males in the audience may, like Brick, become uncomfortable with Maggie's desire for his body, at the same time, Williams forces them to identify with Brick, the quasi-heterosexual, and thus problematizes their positions as male spectators. They can either identity with Brick, whose heterosexuality is called into question, or with Maggie, whose desires for Brick they most certainly must be forced to assume or acknowledge in a way that might be uncomfortable for them.

Though the object of homoerotic (through Skipper and the playwright's gaze) as well as heterosexual appeal (through Maggie), Brick's potential for embodying the homosexual subject, while strongly implied, is never fully realized. During the McCarthy era Williams could not risk being this subversive, and his fear of being "outed" in an intolerant age was much too great. Nevertheless, the mere possibility that Brick is an unresolved, repressed homosexual who is fighting hard to maintain his idealized view of male friendship and his sexual orientation counters the arguments of Clum criticizing Williams for not allowing the homosexual subject to appear on stage. For if Brick is indeed a homosexual (and, despite Mark Royden Winchell's arguments otherwise, there are strong possibilities within the text for this reading of his character), he would be the most radical statement Williams could have made during the 1950s.

For what reason would Brick's possibly being a gay man be considered radical? Simply because Brick also is the quintessential male ideal in American culture. To suggest that someone exhibiting the qualities of the masculine and homosocially acceptable man in the macho culture of the American 1950s is indeed subversive. Just considering the possibility that Brick is a gay man is a subversive notion in the 1950s, and in some circles it would even be considered so today. This should be evident in the reaction of Robert J. Higgs, the author of a book on the athlete in American literature, who definitively denies any possibility that Brick could be gay because of his masculine virtues (143)—a clear indication of the problematizing of homosexuality but also the reaffirmation of compulsory heterosexuality for a critic whose own idealization of the American athlete would be called into question if American notions of masculinity have little to do with sexual orientation, as is commonly believed. Furthermore, Higgs' reaction reinforces the problem of the homophobic heterosexual male spectator of Williams's plays mentioned earlier. Not only does Williams call into question American views of masculinity and homosexuality, he hints strongly that heterosexual men may be attractive to gay men, that gay men may be both erotically appealing and masculine, and that masculinity/femininity, heterosexuality/homosexuality may merely be constructed norms—not realities.

Like the masculine ideal in America, Brick appears, for much of the play, stoic and controlled. To begin with, Brick's name suggests callousness, repressed emotion, and stubbornness. He is, after all, like a brick wall whom no one, except perhaps Skipper, his true love, and Big Daddy, the man most like him, could penetrate (pun intended). Male homosociality typically defines masculinity in a number of ways, including camaraderie with other masculine men, the frequent use of alcohol, sexual prowess with women, emotional restraint, and athletic success. Brick possesses (or has possessed in the past) all these American male "virtues," with the possible exception of his uncertain experience with women, as Maggie's description of her dates and lovemaking with him might suggest (does Brick date and sleep with a lot of women as the successful male heterosexual is supposed to do?). Nevertheless, the fact that Paul Newman plays the role of Brick in the American film version only reinforces my reading of Brick as the epitome of masculine idealism and the male body at its best.

Ironically, he is drinking himself to death as self-punishment for the loss of Skipper, his one true love—whether Platonic or not. As Eve Sedgwick notes in her study of male homosocial desire, there is a continuum between homosociality and homosexuality many men sometimes fail to comprehend (1–2). Williams recognizes this continuum, and Brick, despite his homophobic protestations to the contrary, may be becoming aware, for the first time, that there is indeed a fine line between male–male intimacy, which he admits he shares with Skipper, and self-acknowledged homosexual feelings.

In fact, Brick is beginning to sense that his old homosocial world has crumbled. As the film version reveals and others, including Dukore, have argued, one of Brick's major weaknesses is his inability to grow up and face the world of adulthood. Part of acceptance of one's self as an adult is the understanding that sexuality helps define identity. In Brick's naive world view, which parallels the view of the 1950s heterosexual male, there are no masculine homosexuals—only those "two sisters" who used to share the bedroom in which he and Maggie have been placed and whose secret from the outside world was "closeted" in the privacy of a huge plantation. By suggesting they shared a form of marriage, however, Williams illustrates the potential for relationships between two men outside conventional definitions of masculinity and compulsory heterosexuality. Brick cannot accept either Skipper, his ideal, as a fellow gay man, nor can he admit the possibility that he possesses tender and homoerotic feelings for his idol. As gay and lesbian theorists have noted concerning the construction of homosexuality before Stonewall, Brick's generation believed that gay men were "degenerates" who acted like women and, by their very existence, assaulted the whole notion of American manhood. Denying the masculinity of Jack Straw and Peter Ochello enables Brick to reassert his own masculinity—but, at the same time and without his awareness, he risks protesting too much that he and Skipper were not gay men in love with each other. As Winchell has suggested, " . . . the thought that he is the object of male lust raises questions of gender identity that may help to account for the vehemence of his objections" (706).

Despite Brick's nervous and vehement denial of the homosexual elements within his relationship with Skipper, the possibility that Brick, the ideal American male, might be gay seems clearly evident. Not only is Brick himself aware that intimate friendship between men is so rare as to be construed as homosexual, but Maggie herself also seems to understand that there is the potential for tender (but Platonic) feelings toward Skipper in her husband, as her reference to legendary Greek friendship indicates. Yet Maggie's confession to Brick that she knows that his feelings for Skipper were "pure" (58) may be interpreted as her own need to deny the possibility that her masculine, ideal husband might be gay. Maggie even admits to Brick that the double dates on which she and other girls would go out with him and Skipper were more "like a date between you and Skipper" (57). Furthermore, she describes Brick's lovemaking style as indifferent and distant. His detachment, as she refers to it, indicates that Brick may perhaps be playing his masculine role all too well at the risk of not understanding his inner self. A frequent visitor to Freudian analysts, Williams clearly portrays Brick as exhibiting all the traits normally associated with latent homosexuality: indifference to women, excessive attention to masculinity, and internalized homophobia. All signs indicate Brick's dispassionate and repressed nature. Despite what some critics have said concerning the appearance of gay characters on stage, Brick may very likely be the first homosexual character embodied in a Williams's play.

Brick's homophobia not only represents his fear of what is the potential for homoerotic feelings within himself but also his fear of the gay "other"— best represented in the play through the references to Jack Straw and Peter Ochello, the monogamous gay couple whose presence is always felt in the bedroom which Brick and Maggie occupy. The mystery surrounding his refusal to sleep with Maggie seems clearly tied to the bedroom, where Jack and Peter have expressed an uncommon affection for one another. The setting, which provides space for the gay male, thus functions to reemphasize the possibility that the hidden truth of homosexuality—even from Brick himself—may be the root of his inability to make love to Maggie. As his ambiguous commentary within the text indicates, Williams does not want the reader to dismiss too easily the possible parallels between the Jack–Peter relationship and the Brick–Skipper friendship. He is far too aware that human sexuality cannot be placed into neat categories. Despite Mark Lilly's facile claim that reading Brick as a gay subject is simplistic and that gay men want to see Brick as gay because there is "safety in numbers" (72), the complexity of Williams's portrayal of this character and the role of homophobia within the play's structure suggests otherwise.

Clearly, Brick fears being labeled a "sissy" himself, but he does not hesitate to label Straw and Ochello "degenerates," "sissies," and "queens." As a genuine subversive in a repressive age, Williams dares to voice terms commonly used to refer to homosexuals not only within American culture as a whole but also in the gay underground of which he is a part. In an article dealing with homophobic discourse, Clum claims that *Cat* is "the most vivid dramatic embodiment of Williams's mixed signals regarding homosexuality and his obsession with public exposure" (170), suggesting that Brick's homophobic reactions to Big Daddy's innuendoes concerning his possible gay orientation receive the last word. Even Savran, who seems to understand the complexity of Williams's gay subjectivity more clearly than Clum, focuses on homosexuality within the play as "self-destructive and cancerous" (101). Admittedly, the play does not describe being gay as an asset, but it is only portrayed as a liability due to society's enforcement of compulsory heterosexuality. Besides, Williams does all he can to validate the existence of gay men and homosexuality during this dark part of American history.

The question is: How are the signals mixed when Williams offers sympathy for gay men through the ghost-like presence of the Ochello–Straw gay space and if Big Daddy is sympathetic to them? Contrary to Clum's misreading in his article on homophobic discourse that attacks Williams for allowing Brick's anti-gay rhetoric to receive the emphasis, Williams mentions the unspeakable: the existence of a monogamous gay couple and overt language to describe and validate the love of homosexuals for one another. To my knowledge no other American play of the 1950s acknowledges the possibility that two men share a bed and no other American play before this time uses the rhetoric of oppression and the oppressed to describe the social predicament of homosexuals. Social conventions are the problem, not gay men or homosexuality.

Though not directly "outing" Brick as a gay subject, Williams never fully "closets" him either. For this reason, all critics who argue definitively against Brick's homosexuality somehow miss the point. While admittedly

Williams suggests in the narrative descriptions that he does not want readers
to simply identify a particular psychological trait and as a result dismiss the
play's mystery, there is also no indication that Williams himself denies the
possibility for this as one aspect of Brick's character. Besides, a scrutinizing,
skeptical critic might not take Williams at his word if one suspects he fears
the repercussions of representing a gay man on stage as a major character in
the homophobic 1950s. Whether Brick's homosexuality is fully resolved (if
sexual orientation is a social construction, is anyone's?) does not answer the
fundamental question the play raises: What does homosexuality have to do
with the gender and sex role of an individual? Williams puts on a good show
of suggesting the possibility of nothing—a pretty radical statement for this
time, indeed.

If a critic is particularly partial to arguing against Brick's homosexual
orientation and concluding that he is, therefore, not a gay subject, this reading still does not account for the positive attitude (at least for 1955) toward
the gay individual Williams posits. None of Brick's hostile, homophobic
rhetoric comes from Big Daddy, whose attitude toward society is fundamentally critical, for he has learned "tolerance." Williams clearly indicates
that Big Daddy, perhaps the most likable character in the play, is both tolerant (but not of Big Mama or his grandchildren) and pro-gay. After all, Big
Daddy supports Brick's friendship with Skipper and defends two gay men
involved in a long-term relationship. Furthermore, he also admits that he
has had homosexual experience himself ("I knocked around in my time")
and does so as if there is nothing of which to be ashamed (115). Presumably, Big Daddy admits here that he is a bisexual subject. Admittedly, Big
Daddy questions whether the friendship between Skipper and Brick was
"normal," but never does he indicate that he expects Brick to be heterosexual
or threaten to cut Brick off because he might be gay. Such openness in treating the homosexual issue during the 1950s is commendable and does not
in any way support the view that Brick's homophobic language gets the last
word. Surely, Big Daddy is far more admirable than Brick, and he preaches
tolerance—just as Maggie, Brick's devoted wife, who fears that he may be
homosexual any way, does as well.

Big Daddy's views of marriage, the family, and the church further serve
to illustrate his awareness that social definitions of normality may force people to lie to themselves and to others in order to conform and receive social
approval. Facing death's possibility, Big Daddy sees no need to conform any
longer. In describing his loveless marriage to Big Mama, he confesses to Brick
his distaste for her and admits he wants to have an extramarital affair. Though
harsh to Big Mama when she eavesdrops on him and Brick, Big Daddy is a
truth teller: "You don't know a goddam thing, and you never did!" (75). Big

Daddy represents an ideal character in Williams's world, for he declares the "truth" as he sees it no matter how harsh and how painful the world where we live—society—might find it. At the same time, he illustrates the problem with patriarchal authority, as Savran points out (106). Williams clearly humanizes the play's most likable character, but at no point does he challenge Big Daddy's notion of truth that it is something which must be faced and something which is at times harsh for the hearer. Trying to get Brick to profess his own truth, Big Daddy admits his favoritism towards him and his extreme dislike of Gooper, Mae, and the "no-neck monsters."

That Big Daddy believes he has just missed death by a narrow margin enables him to see through the illusions of society and recognize that all the "bull shit" society teaches is meaningless thought and social control. Not only has Big Daddy grown "tolerance" on his land, he has also come to view homosexual love as understandable human behavior. After all, he has happily lived on the plantation of Peter and Jack, the monogamous, "married" gay couple whose haunting presence permeates the bedroom of Maggie and Brick, and he has in effect been their surrogate son. He also supports Peter when Jack dies, sympathizing with his grief, and defends them to Brick (116–117). Couldn't this conceivably be the first representation of a gay "family" in American drama?

Big Daddy is, it might be said, the voice for Williams the playwright, who finds social institutions suspect and deceptive. As Big Daddy says, "I've lived with mendacity!—Why can't you live with it? Hell, you got to live with it, there's nothing else to live with except mendacity, is there?" (109). Furthermore, Big Daddy may be Williams's ideal projection of Cornelius, a father from whom he felt alienated, as Lyle Leverich's recent biography clearly demonstrates. If this is the case, Big Daddy responds in a positive, accepting way to his son's possible homosexuality in a manner which Williams would have liked for Cornelius himself to have done. Without Big Daddy's support for Brick's sexual orientation (no matter what it is) and his condemnation of Brick's intolerant language, perhaps Clum's argument about the anti-gay rhetoric would be valid. Here and elsewhere, the play may be seen as an indictment of society and its homophobia, not of homosexuality.

Although some may think that Big Daddy's implied homosexual past with Straw and Ochello may indicate that the relationship between him and the gay couple was not platonic, I see no clear evidence that he was the subject of homosexual exploitation himself, nor does he ever admit anything less than admiration and sympathy for his surrogate parents. Maybe part of what Big Daddy learns from the men is that human sexuality does not come in neat packages and that one should be open to human experience in all its varieties. Furthermore, the argument of Savran and others (101) that Big Daddy's colon cancer demonstrates a form of punishment and Williams's ambivalence about anal sex (and homosexuality) seems to stretch the point. Homosexual experience does not automatically imply sodomy, nor does the fact that Big Daddy has colon cancer necessarily indicate that he is being punished for his participation in homosexual acts any more than for any of his other flaws, including being human and thus subject to mortality. The similar symptoms between bowel cancer and a spastic colon become an important plot device in the play since Gooper, Mae, and the doctor attempt to hide the truth about his impending death from him. And the social attitudes about cancer, which many in the 1950s perceived as a secret not to be shared, and homosexuality make reading Big Daddy's death as a form of punishment problematic. Cancer, like homosexuality, was a taboo subject in the 1950s. At the worst, Big Daddy is being punished for being himself, a reading which would reinforce Williams's awareness of society's intolerance of the individual, and for flaws which all human beings share.

Finally, the events of *Cat on a Hot Tin Roof* occur during a period of widespread gay oppression in the 1950s. While a tolerant society would have been willing to accept the special bond between Jack Straw and Peter Ochello, as well as Brick and Skipper, the most important difficulty to Williams was the problem of mendacity. Even though he is an anti-hero, Brick's character is sympathetic, for he does not really know who he is or what his sexual orientation is; and he is so afraid of admitting failure at achieving the masculine ideal that he will never reconcile his love for Skipper with his inner nature, which he cannot resolve for himself. Brick becomes a symbol not only for a particular type of American male but also for an American society unwilling to confront the truth of homosexuality and individual difference.

Because of an intolerant society, gay identity and relationships in the 1950s were fundamentally problematic—not for the committed gay couple of Jack Straw and Peter Ochello—but for society. If there is anything negative said in *Cat on a Hot Tin Roof* about homosexuality and the gay subject, it cannot ultimately be separated from the issue of society's participation in compulsory heterosexuality, gay bashing, and homophobia. For a man of Williams's generation, he held amazingly progressive views of the gay subject. In his estimation, America during this time sadly could not accept the potential for two men to love each other nor acknowledge the truth about homosexuality. And this shows just how difficult a space a gay subject was forced into. With the increasing mechanization and urbanization of the Old South and its genteel manners and the intolerant climate of the McCarthy era, individual difference had become more and more dangerous. As Williams himself once said in an interview, "Society rapes the individual" (Devlin 146).

NOTES

1. In his early study of homosexuality in American drama and fiction, Georges-Michel Sarotte gives a Freudian reading of Williams's plays, including *Cat on a Hot Tin Roof*. For alternate readings of the play, see C.W.E. Bigsby's *Modern American Drama, 1945–1990*, and almost any book-length study of Williams. See also Bernard Dukore's "The Cat Has Nine Lives"; Robert Bechtold Heilman's "Tennessee Williams' Approach to Tragedy"; Donald Pease's "Reflections on Moon Lake: The Presences of the Playwright"; and Vernon Young's "Social Drama and Big Daddy."

2. My full-length work in progress, *Subverting the Closet: Tennessee Williams and the Evolution of Gay Theatrical Representation*, and "Is There a Gay Man in This Text?: The 'Closeted' Gay Subject, the Male Body, and Homosexuality in *A Streetcar Named Desire*," a paper delivered at the December 1997 Modern Language Association Convention, attempt to theorize the gay male gaze.

WORKS CITED

Bigsby, C.W.E. *Modern American Drama, 1945–1990*. New York and Cambridge: Cambridge U P, 1992.

Clum, John M. *Acting Gay: Male Homosexuality in Modern Drama*. New York: Columbia U P, 1992.

———. "'Something Cloudy, Something Clear': Homophobic Discourse in Tennessee Williams." *South Atlantic Quarterly* 88 (Winter 1989): 161–179.

Curtin, Kaier. *"We Can Always Call Them Bulgarians"*. Boston: Alyson, 1987.

De Jongh, Nicholas. *Not in Front of the Audience: Homosexuality on Stage*. New York: Routledge, 1992.

Devlin, Albert J., ed. *Conversations with Tennessee Williams*. Jackson: U P of Mississippi, 1986.

Dukore, Bernard. "The Cat Has Nine Lives." *Tulane Drama Review* 8 (1963): 95–100.

Foucault, Michel. *The History of Sexuality: An Introduction*. Vol. I. Trans. Robert Hurley. New York: Vintage, 1990.

Goldstein, Laurence, ed. *The Male Body: Features, Destinies, Exposures*. Ann Arbor: U of Michigan P, 1994.

Gross, Robert F. "The Pleasures of Brick: Eros and the Gay Spectator in *Cat on a Hot Tin Roof*." *Journal of American Drama and Theatre* 9.1 (Winter 1997): 11–25.

Heilman, Robert Bechtold. "Tennessee Williams' Approach to Tragedy." *Tennessee Williams: A Collection of Critical Essays*. Ed. Stephen S. Stanton. Englewood Cliffs, NJ: Prentice-Hall, 1977. 17–35.

Higgs, Robert J. *Laurel and Thorn: The Athlete in American Literature*. Lexington: U of Kentucky P, 1981.

Lehman, Peter. *Running Scared: Masculinity and the Representation of the Male Body*. Philadelphia: Temple U P, 1993.

Leverich, Lyle. *Tom: The Unknown Tennessee Williams*. New York: Crown, 1995.

Lilly, Mark. "Tennessee Williams." *American Drama*. Ed. Clive Bloom. New York: St. Martin's P, 1995. 70–81.

Miller, Neil. *Out of the Past: Gay and Lesbian History from 1869 to the Present*. New York: Vintage, 1995.

Mulvey, Laura. "Visual Pleasure and Narrative Cinema." *Screen* 16.3 (1975): 6–18. Rpt. in *Contemporary Literary Criticism: Literary and Cultural Studies*. Ed. Robert Con Davis and Ronald Schleifer. New York: Longman, 1994. 422–431.

Pease, Donald. "Reflections on Moon Lake: The Presences of the Playwright." *Tennessee Williams: 13 Essays*. Jackson: U P of Mississippi, 1980. 261–279.

Sarotte, Georges-Michel. *Like a Brother, Like a Lover: Male Homosexuality in the American Novel and Theatre from Herman Melville to James Baldwin*. Trans. Richard Miller. Garden City, NY: Anchor P/Doubleday, 1978.

Savran, David. *Communists, Cowboys, and Queers: The Politics of Masculinity in Arthur Miller and Tennessee Williams*. Minneapolis: U of Minnesota P, 1992.

Sedgwick, Eve. *Between Men: English Literature and Male Homosocial Desire*. New York: Columbia UP, 1985.

Silverman, Kaja. "Dis-Embodying the Female Voice." *Re-Vision: Essays in Feminist Film Criticism*. Ed. Mary Ann Doane, Patricia Mellencamp, and Linda Williams. Los Angeles: American Film Institute, 1984. 131–149.

Vidal, Gore. Introduction. Tennessee Williams' *Collected Stories*. New York: New Directions, 1985. xix–xxv.

Williams, Tennessee. *Cat on a Hot Tin Roof: The Theatre of Tennessee Williams*. New York: New Directions, 1971. 1–215.

Winchell, Mark Royden. "Come Back to the Locker Room Ag'n, Brick Honey!" *Mississippi Quarterly* 48 (Fall 1995): 701–712.

Young, Vernon. "Social Drama and Big Daddy." *Southwest Review* 41 (1956): 194–197.

R. BARTON PALMER

Elia Kazan and Richard Brooks Do
Tennessee Williams: Melodramatizing
Cat on a Hot Tin Roof *on Stage and Screen*

For those who would evaluate his influence on American culture, the film versions of the plays of Tennessee Williams hold more interest than is ordinarily supposed. Produced for mass audiences, the films presumably offer Williams's intentions only in a distorted or diluted form. Because the playwright did not oversee the productions, students of Williams consider them inauthentic as well. There is some truth in both these judgments. However, Williams's influence on Hollywood and Hollywood's importance for the playwright's career cannot be so easily dismissed. His dramatic texts played a key role as source material in the profitable development of "adult films" in the crisis-ridden Hollywood of the fifties, beginning a trend that would culminate during the late sixties in the institutionalization of the adult film and the ratings system that now defines it. As I have argued at length elsewhere, it would be difficult to imagine this crucial development without *A Streetcar Named Desire, Cat on a Hot Tin Roof, Baby Doll,* and *Sweet Bird of Youth* (Palmer 1997). No doubt, Williams influenced the history of Hollywood much more than the standard film histories acknowledge. Conversely, it is the popular films made from his plays that made Williams more central within American culture than playwrights of similar Broadway stature who were not so well served by Hollywood—Arthur Miller and William Inge especially. If film scholars have slighted Williams, it is only because they

From *The Tennessee Williams Annual Review* 2 (1999): 1–11. Copyright © 1999 by *The Tennessee Williams Annual Review*.

are predisposed to pay little attention to literary sources, to what is strictly "pre-textual" in terms of film production.

The Williams films, particularly the commercially and critically success-ful versions of *Cat* and *Sweet Bird* directed by Richard Brooks, are important in another way as well, one which I intend to explore in more depth here. These two Hollywood blockbusters help us understand how Williams's mod-ernism was adapted to the more traditional tastes of his audiences; this adap-tation was by turns both theatrical and cinematic. Paradoxically perhaps, such "melodramatization" was alternately furthered and resisted by the playwright; and so it was left to Elia Kazan and Richards Brooks, who mounted the stage and screen productions, to complete. In part because of these accommoda-tions, Williams's place within American culture, both highbrow and middle-brow, became and has continued to be more central than those of similarly celebrated contemporaries: notably, Arthur Miller, William Inge, Lillian Hellman, and Edward Albee. For this reason, the interconnected contribu-tions of Kazan and Brooks to the stage and cinematic versions of *Cat* and *Sweet Bird* merit the close attention of Williams scholars. I intend to explore here how *Cat* was melodramatized, leaving the equally fascinating case of *Sweet Bird* for a later occasion.

To begin, a brief theoretical excursus is necessary. Traditionally, film adaptations have been evaluated in terms of their faithfulness. This approach necessarily marginalizes whatever cultural significance and aesthetic value adaptations might possess. So judged, they always fail to achieve their pre-sumed and impossible goal: identity with the very text they displace. Thus adaptations are for many critics always, already defined by the fall into differ-ence and, hence, into an easily derogated derivativeness. It is more useful, I would argue, to approach adaptations in an aesthetically neutral fashion. We should see them, in other words, as versions whose differences from their texts of origin mark the particular conditions of their production and reception. The cinematic adaptations of plays pose a further complexity. Plays involve no original text that could be, properly speaking, "adapted" for the screen. The playscript (though often designed for silent reading as well) is by definition a pre-text actualized only through its production. And this production is work that the cinema, also a performance art, manages as readily as the theater.

The work of production, theatrical or cinematic, is always a fall from the pretextual order of words determined by the expressive urge of the playwright into a collaborative art form shaped by the economic protocols of exchange. In our culture, these protocols define the performance arts. The Broadway theater, it is useful to recall, is just as commercial as the Hollywood cinema, if, of course, in different ways. Brought to the screen, Williams's plays did not suffer a fall from Art into Commerce, as many who have commented on the film versions, including Williams himself, routinely assume. Instead, the plays were simply produced in a different yet related medium.

Because he wished for success, Williams, moreover, was never during the early stages of his career unaffected by economic bottom lines. He was very conscious that he wrote within an institutional context that made the very "publication" of the artistic text dependent upon its demonstrable commercial appeal. Institutional pressures meant that Williams's startlingly modernist dramatic ideas and themes were often (if not always) accommodated to the established tastes and conventions of both the Broadway theater and the Hollywood cinema. After the success of *Streetcar* in both its forms and the stage failure of less conventional works such as *Battle of Angels*, Williams had the opportunity to solidify his position within the American commercial theater. Yet he could do so only if he continued to offer theatrical audiences a playgoing experience that conformed in large measure to their expectations. Similarly, his texts could enjoy a second and popular life on the silver screen (something Williams ardently desired) only if he continued to write what Hollywood could adapt to its own purposes and requirements.

This is not to say, of course, that Williams was a hack eager to write whatever he thought might gain him acclaim and financial success. As a modernist firmly committed to postromantic notions of artistic autonomy and creative expressiveness, Williams inevitably resisted the accommodations he made, feeling that what he had to say would likely be altered for the worse. But as a professional writer eager for the popularity that would allow him to continue his career, Williams not only listened to what others with more commercial sense advised. After the failure on Broadway of *Camino Real* (undoubtedly his most complexly modernist text), he wrote *Cat* with more regard for mainstream tastes. Unlike *Camino*, *Cat* is Aristotelian (driven by plot), melodramatic (dominated by a rhetoric of affect), realist (dependent on credible illusion), and socially conservative (supportive, though not unambiguously, of traditional sexual politics). Here was a more accessible drama that would prove immensely successful in both its theatrical and cinematic forms.

When *Cat* was initially produced on stage, director Elia Kazan pushed Williams even further in the direction of middlebrow taste, reluctantly aided by the playwright, who skillfully rewrote Act III to his director's specifications. As we will see below, the film version by Richard Brooks takes these modifications several steps further, re-shaping the play in ways that caused Williams substantial distress even as the changes made possible a critical and box office success few playwrights have enjoyed on the silver screen. A similar development may be glimpsed in the case of *Sweet Bird*. Interestingly, it is Brooks who here played Kazan's role. Though at Williams's insistence Kazan oversaw the Broadway version, the director was perhaps more reticent to ask the playwright to rewrite after their collaboration on the third act of *Cat* had earned him a quite public, if respectful rebuke.

Williams was determined to include in the printed text of *Cat* his original alongside the Broadway version he had rewritten in response to Kazan's criticisms. In a brief introductory essay, Williams somewhat hesitatingly rejected the director's influence on his writing. Conceiving himself as an artist in the postromantic sense, Williams, though happy to be successful yet again, resented what he felt was the compromise that had made it possible. He confesses with some reluctance that playwriting involves the transformation of private feelings into public art:

> It is sad and embarrassing and unattractive that those emotions that stir him deeply enough to demand expression ... are nearly all rooted, however changed in their surface, in the particular and sometimes peculiar concerns of the artist himself. (3)

But if Williams, as an artist, feels driven to communicate personally and intimately, to his chagrin he must take into account the needs and desires of his audience:

> Of course, I know that I have sometimes presumed too much upon corresponding sympathies and interest in those to whom I talk boldly, and this has led to rejections that were painful and costly enough to inspire more prudence. But when I weigh one thing against another, an easy liking against a hard respect, the balance always tips the same way, and whatever the risk of being turned a cold shoulder, I still don't want to talk to people only about the surface aspects of their lives. (6)

Albert J. Devlin argues that the fictional cadre of *Cat* is meant to "obscure Williams's skepticism for the theatre of 'demonstration'" (190). To put it somewhat differently, the fiction then is an Aristotelian form that enables yet denies the playwright's controlling idea, which paradoxically is anti-Aristotelian. The drama, ostensibly committed to action and change, features a hero who refuses to engage in the agon that confronts him. Obviously, this is an anti-dramatic notion that, taken to its logical conclusion, would shift the work decisively to lyricism. But Williams was not willing to go this far in search of the audience's "hard respect." He devised instead a fiction that made more for an "easy liking," even though he was unwilling at first to work his characters through to the conclusion their interaction implied. Lyricism and struggle were uneasily balanced in the play's first version. Kazan and then Brooks, however, would help the playwright shift his conception decisively toward the dramatic, though the results were, ironically, not to Williams's satisfaction in either case.

In any event, no similar controversy erupted during the initial production of *Sweet Bird* and the play's subsequent publication. There are indications, however, that Kazan was not entirely satisfied with the final shape of the playtext. For he did not, even after the play proved a critical and popular success, refrain from declaring that, much like the original draft of *Cat*, the produced version of *Sweet Bird* was compromised by a major structural fault. It was more like two one-act plays, Kazan said, held together only by Williams's verbal virtuosity. Perhaps diplomatically, he remained silent about what attempts, if any, he made to correct the problem (the issue is discussed in Phillips, 154–5).

In mounting the screen version of *Sweet Bird*, Brooks perhaps set out to finish the revision Kazan was reluctant to undertake. In any event, the changes Brooks made bear close comparison to those Kazan helped effect in *Cat*. The result is not only that the film versions are more similar than their corresponding plays. Interestingly, they also closely resemble the melodramatic structures Kazan created for his own films, especially *On the Waterfront*. The film versions, then, illustrate the accommodation of Williams's ideas to more traditional dramatic structures and themes, to what might well prove popular and hence profitable. The playwright regretted the alterations in his original dramatic conceptions, even though he once said, perhaps tongue in cheek, that the film version of *Sweet Bird* is superior to the produced play. Neither film is by any measure a faithful adaptation. Yet, as we shall see here, *Cat* offers eloquent testimony about the continuing process of accommodation that brought Williams's ideas and characters (as well as the incomparable poetry that gave them life) to the wider audience he was always eager to reach.

Cat on a Hot Tin Roof: The Plantation Myth Redivivus

For the Broadway career of Tennessee Williams, the initial production of *Cat on a Hot Tin Roof* marked a crucial turning point. With this play, Williams rejected the demonstrated unprofitability of his brilliantly mythic *Camino Real*, a play that is the equal of the best postwar European dramas with which Williams was so taken. Reviews that were lukewarm at best and mediocre box office showed him that *Camino* was too marked by intertextual reference, self-reflexive anti-illusion, and allegorical rhetoric to satisfy the tastes of most theatergoers. And, it is hardly surprising, Williams soon turned back to the poetics of affect, illusion, and suspense that had made *A*

Streetcar Named Desire such a success. As Brenda Murphy has demonstrated in convincing detail (Murphy 1992), director Elia Kazan helped Williams carefully modulate audience involvement with and sympathy for both Stanley and Blanche, characters whose differentiated humiliations at play's end are not only intellectually, but emotionally satisfying as well.

It is significant, I think, that Williams's triumph with *Streetcar* resulted substantially from collaboration with Kazan. At the time, Kazan was not only a Broadway giant. Arguably, he was also Hollywood's most skilled director of screen melodrama. Kazan had recently worked box office magic and received critical acclaim for *Pinky* (1949), *A Tree Grows in Brooklyn* (1945), and *Gentleman's Agreement* (1947), all films dependent upon an affecting staging of family and cultural problems that are neatly resolved by characters who learn and grow from their dramatic interactions. This was not an aesthetic that Kazan in any sense discarded after working so successfully with more "literary" material on Broadway, as his film *On the Waterfront* (1954) clearly demonstrates. Here is yet another critical and popular triumph justly famed for its carefully developed and deeply affecting moments of recognition and reversal. Terry Malloy's anguished confession of failure to his brother prepares the way for his tortured perseverance in the final, penitential struggle with union thugs. Terry first colludes with, but then despises and defeats, the mendacity he's been forced to live with, embracing publicly the conventional virtues urged on him by a crusading priest and the girl he loves, who is the sister of a man he helped murder.

The film resembles closely the Broadway version of *Cat*, and this is perhaps the result of Kazan's involvement with both projects. Like Terry Malloy, *Cat's* Brick Pollitt is persuaded by the woman who loves him to face the guilty secret that prevents him from doing what would restore his integrity and position in society. Brick finds that he too has had enough of those lies (including his own) that isolate and destroy. In the end, he is moved to take action that is less public and heroic than Terry Malloy's, but equally effective. Brick endorses Maggie's deception, which, should he turn it into truth, will save him and his family from a perhaps fatal decline into mediocrity. The play ends ambiguously, but on the verge of a supremely melodramatic resolution. Through Brick's apparent transformation, *Cat* comes close to celebrating the social importance of heterosexual coupling. Williams writes large Brick's role within patriarchy since his fruitful union with Maggie would assure the dynastic succession of the aptly named Big Daddy. With *Cat*, Williams thus moves far from the thematics of his earlier stage triumph, *A Streetcar Named Desire*. For there the playwright thoroughly ironizes the heterosexual imperative through the mock triumph of Stanley's reconciliation with Stella at the end of *Streetcar*. The contrast between the two plays is thus startling, to say the least.

Interestingly, the original version of *Cat*'s Act III proves that Kazan was not the one to introduce melodrama into Williams's conception. As first written, the play, paradoxically, is self-reflexively melodramatic in its ostentatious denial of melodrama. What I mean is that the dramatic action moves toward a conclusion it will not finally represent. Maggie's relentless battering and Big Daddy's empathetic interrogation push Brick toward the change of heart that should restore the family to itself. And this is nothing less than the softening of Brick's obdurate refusal to procreate, to mature in the terms demanded by an institutionalized heterosexuality with no concern for the vagaries of desire (as Big Daddy's proud report of passionless, dutiful lovemaking with Big Mama exemplifies). Brick's refusal is nothing less than the textual reflex of Williams's initial refusal to provide in Act III the dramatic structure that the first two acts build toward. That Big Daddy does not reappear is especially significant, for it robs the play's conclusion of its most powerful advocate of acceptance and resignation, even as it obscures the generational continuity and male common cause implied in the reconciliation of father and son that ends Act II. Devlin perceptively suggests that the double, contradictory turning of *Cat* should be traced to Williams's "practice of a deceptive realism that satisfied both the economic law of Broadway and the artistic prompting of Tennessee Williams's endangered career." He goes on to argue that to preserve the "poem of the play," Williams, perhaps with some cynicism, dusted off and made use of an obvious set of themes and characters, "the realistic conventions of the Southern literary plantation" (95).

The plantation myth, merely an undramatized allusion in *Streetcar* but the cultural cadre that provides the plot and characters of *Cat*, shows the imaginative and literary connection between the two plays. Williams invokes yet another form of it in *Sweet Bird*. His use of the plantation myth in *Cat* underlines the more conventional themes of that play. In *Streetcar*, the myth explains the social failure whose implications the play dramatizes in a working class New Orleans far from the aristocratic refinement of Belle Reeve. To account for her penury and rootlessness, Blanche describes the inability of the plantation, because of the family's weak and dissolute males, to sustain itself as an economic unit. For the estate must be sold to pay creditors, depriving Blanche of her home. What her precipitous arrival in New Orleans also signifies is that the plantation, a clear metonymy for patriarchy, has failed to properly monitor sexual desire. The unattached and unsupervised widow of a homosexual driven to suicide by her rejection, Blanche cannot prevent her own slide into a self-destructive promiscuity. With no small poetic justice, she is ultimately punished by Stanley, a rough trade emissary of the lower social orders who scorns her aristocratic airs even as he is eager to share her "fortune." Blanche's demise repeats that of the feckless males in her family, who also managed to lose everything through a failure of self-control. Thus the desire that the play thematizes cannot be institutionalized; it motivates only predation and exploitation, not the building of society. As Stanley's pathetic bondage to Stella exemplifies, moreover, such a desire imparts a power defined most tellingly by the weakness at its very center.

These terms are reversed in *Cat*. Here it is the damaged and dissolute heir apparent whose rejection of his patrimony is deflected, perhaps forever, by a woman who insists, perhaps triumphantly, on the heterosexual imperative, that is, procreative marriage. During the turbulent course of Brick's regeneration, the justice of that imperative is called into question several times: by Maggie's liaison with Skipper, by Skipper's inability to perform, by the mediocre and obnoxious fertility of Gooper and Mae, by Brick's homosocial leanings, and by the aging young man's attachment to an adolescent world of self-satisfaction and boyish pleasure. However assaulted, a fecund heterosexuality defined by familial ties is re-established by the indomitable integrity of Big Daddy, a strong patriarch of the type whose absence from Blanche's family is not even lamented in *Streetcar*. Big Daddy models for his troubled son acceptance of the necessary lies and discontents of family relations. So thoroughly is his identity invested in the destiny of the family that he even manages to accept with equanimity his own approaching death. His hopes for a proper dynastic succession never dim.

Streetcar's engagement with patriarchy, in contrast, produces only the crass and selfish Stanley, whose bellowing and sexual violence inadequately mask his feminization and self doubts (hence his easily wounded pride, his endless theatrical posturing, his irrational, self-abasing possessiveness of Stella). Arriving in Stanley's home, Blanche leaves the plantation behind forever, but discovers no social order that might permit and encourage her rehabilitation, no space that could outside of death, real or symbolic, accommodate her desire. Cut adrift from the world of marital satisfaction Maggie seems able to reinstate, Blanche cannot become again the "right kind" of woman she must once have in some sense been. Her attempt to negotiate a proposal of marriage from Mitch has no chance of success in any case because he, like Stanley, is another feminized male, a mama's boy not yet married since he is hardly marriageable.

Because it deals with failure rather than refusal, *Streetcar* satisfies the average playgoer's need for engagement with both sympathetic characters and a narrative that takes them from ignorance, confusion, and conflict to a "moving" resolution. In contrast, *Cat*'s initial working version, with its weak third act, did not deliver the tight dramatic structure of *Streetcar*. And so Kazan, who was eagerly sought out by Williams to direct again, offered three suggestions for improvement. Each of these was very much in line with his characteristic concern for affect. Big Daddy, so powerfully developed in Act II, was to reappear in Act III; Maggie was to be made more sympathetic; and Brick's unyielding refusal to deviate from self-destruction and reconcile with her was to show some sign of weakening. With Kazan's ideas firmly in place, *Cat* became the playwright's greatest critical and popular success.

In fact, the money he earned from Richard Brooks's immensely profitable film version made Williams financially independent for the remainder of his life. Never again would he have to worry, as he did after the disastrously short run of *Camino Real*, about supporting himself through playwriting or having the opportunity to see what he wrote produced on stage. But the film version of *Cat* required further changes. Williams did not authorize them. Yet they were in some sense authentic and appropriate since they were very much in line with not only the positive version of the plantation myth he had decided to deploy in this play, but also with the significant changes he had effected himself at Kazan's gentle insistence.

Brooks's *Cat*, we could well say, offers more radical versions of the alterations that Kazan inspired. His Maggie is a much more sympathetic character. She cheerfully and readily accepts not only the authority of Big Daddy but also the leadership of her husband once he's made his peace with mendacity. The film's Brick not only endorses Maggie's lie; he finds in her trust of his renewed masculinity the strength to reassert his sexual control, summoning her to their bed at film's end. Brooks's Big Daddy not only helps Brick fight through to a healing understanding of the disgust that disables him. He comes to grips with rejection by his own father, whose failure bequeathed him an irrepressible desire for success, which Brick's unending quest for athletic success mirrors. As Big Daddy heals Brick's psychic wound, so Brick is able to heal his father's. In the film, a strongly emphasized element of Brick's disgust is his anger at Big Daddy for not having been a properly nurturing parent. But because he now learns *in extremis* of his father's similar dissatisfaction, Brick can accept the dying man's Abrahamian demand to be fruitful and multiply. The most important general point to make about Brooks's version is this. Rewriting preoccupied the film's director.

Brooks's approach to the adaptation, we might then say, was much more dramatic than cinematic. In other words, the director put more emphasis on rewriting and re-staging than on devising images that might substitute for dialogue and performance. His two Williams films offer not only little in the way of "opening out" beyond the stage set limitations, but also few silent sequences (except for the effective flashbacks in *Sweet Bird*). A more thoroughly cinematic approach to filming Williams is to be found, for example, in Joseph L. Mankiewicz's version of *Suddenly Last Summer*. Among other fundamental alterations, we might signal the artful use of the changes Brooks made in *Cat* (abbreviated dialogue, some new lines, excised expressionistic devices, more naturalistic acting, etc.), one is perhaps most significant. Wisely, the director re-stages the play so as to lessen the isolation of the characters from each other. That re-staging allows him to take one step further the changes initiated by Kazan.

In the original, the transition from Act I to Act II separates the dialogue between Maggie and Brick from Brick's talk with his father; those dialogues dominate the first two thirds of the play, but are not connected very effectively, either dramatically or thematically to Act III. The film version offers a more fluid dramatic structure that emphasizes the complex interactions of Brick, Maggie, and Big Daddy with the others in the family. The Pollitt house, inside and out, becomes a more plastic playing space, with the characters' restless movements through it indexing their turmoil and transformation. A brief summary will demonstrate.

Maggie and Brick's bedroom conversation is first interrupted by Maggie's departure to greet Big Daddy at the airport. He returns to the plantation alone in her car and chastises Maggie for not yet having three kids and a fourth "in the oven." Upon her return, the couple's quarrel is again interrupted, this time for a parental visit from Big Mama. She upbraids her daughter-in-law for failing to have children and, perhaps, not giving Brick "what he wants." While Maggie attends Big Daddy's birthday party downstairs, Brick learns the truth about his father's cancer from the family doctor. Brick and Maggie then resume their quarrel, which touches a painful nerve when Maggie mentions Brick's feelings ending with Maggie's resolution to do something about having Brick's baby when he can't stand being with her. The party then moves up to Brick's room, where, among other revelations, Big Daddy tells Big Mama how dissatisfied he has been with their marriage.

The others then leave the bedroom to Brick and Big Daddy, where the father's questions about Brick's coldness toward Maggie soon turn into a discussion of the son's self-destructiveness. The two move downstairs to the study; there Brick's refusal to answer his father's questions about Skipper prompts Big Daddy to summon Maggie. Much of the angry interchange between Brick and Maggie that occurs privately in the play's Act I here occurs in Big Daddy's benevolent presence. The father ascertains that nothing happened between Maggie and Brick's best friend; Brick, it turns out, thinks himself to blame for Skipper's death because he did not reassure him of his support and affection. The homosexual implications of Brick's attachment to Skipper, handled more directly if with delicacy in the original, are here effectively explained away. Brick, Big Daddy thinks, cannot embrace adult responsibility:

"the truth is that you never growed up." Brick runs out into the rain to drive away (in a top down convertible awash with the storm) but gets stuck in the mud, a fitting image not only of his immaturity, but also of his inability to escape from the truth and his responsibilities.

Before his abortive flight, however, Brick, refusing to go along with the lie about his father's health, lets Big Daddy know that his condition is terminal. Concerned for his father's pain, Brick slips by the rest of the family, who are squabbling over who should inherit the family business interests, to join his father in the mansion's basement. In this way, Brooks effectively integrates material from Acts II and III, adding to it by having Brick, whose self-imposed isolation from the family is disintegrating, seek out Big Daddy. In a basement full of unpacked art bought on a European junket and Brick's athletic memorabilia, father and son speak for the first time with no lies between them. Brick vents his self-loathing on his own trophies, accuses his father of having more interest in things than in his sons, but then comes to understand how Big Daddy loves him when the old man speaks frankly of his own experience and discontent. Tiptoeing over to the basement stairs, Maggie listens in approvingly on their dialogue. Undisturbed because Big Mama prevents Gooper from going down to investigate, the pair are able to speak as they wish. Eventually, they ascend to the study, there to allay Big Mama's uncertainties about the family's future. Maggie's lie about being pregnant throws into question Gooper's claim to inherit the plantation. But Big Daddy reassumes control over the family. Endorsing her lie, Brick agrees to assume at his father's death the patriarch's responsibilities. He will be helped by his brother Gooper, with whom Brick reconciles. Brick and Maggie then climb together the stairs back to their bedroom, there to re-establish their sexual bond and produce the promised heir, with the husband indisputably at the head of his family.

The melodramatization begun with Kazan's modifications is thus carried through to its logical conclusion. The troubled family is restored to itself. The conspicuous metonymy of that dramatic process is the re-establishment of patriarchal hierarchies. Just as Brick re-asserts his control over Maggie, who is reduced to approving and obedient silence, so Big Daddy takes leadership of the family back from Big Mama, who has proven unable to decide among or properly discipline the disputing females—Mae and Maggie—who unofficially represent the interests of their respective husbands. Gooper accedes to Brick's "natural" possession of superiority and, as a sign of his re-integration, becomes once again the head of his household as he rudely but effectively silences his carping wife. For the first time, Mae is cowed by Gooper's forcefulness and obeys her husband's command.

In the service of a quite conservative agenda, the ambiguities of Williams's original are in these ways simplified. The accommodation involves no small irony. For the very quality that made this Williams property appealing to a mainstream film audience—the story's notorious engagement with a problematic, perhaps perverse sexuality—is thereby preserved in the only form that audience would unproblematically accept. Brick's puzzling and disturbing rejection of Maggie's obvious sexual charms (a reflex of his rejection of his patrimony) motors the narrative but is successfully explained away. For both Brick's "unnatural" connection to Skipper and Maggie's adultery are shown to be mirages, misunderstandings that can be settled, at the urging of a concerned patriarch, by the Pollitts's loving dialogue with one another. The film thus powerfully installs one of the key elements of 1950s ideology—the recuperative power of family solidarity. In the process, Williams's "provocative" drama becomes instead appealingly "naughty." Brooks's *Cat* mounts a titillating but unconsummated and therefore unthreatening challenge to the regnant power of monogamous heterosexuality. Only in this form, as both Elia Kazan and Richard Brooks correctly surmised, could the powerful characters and themes of Williams's most commercial play win favor with a cinema audience, whose ingrained taste for affecting melodrama would be nicely satisfied by a drama more innovative and radical in appearance than fact. Or, to put it differently, Brooks's version of *Cat* became the ideal adult film, Hollywood style, and the model on which his equally successful version of *Sweet Bird* would eventually be based.

Works Cited

Devlin, Albert J. "Writing in 'A Place of Stone': *Cat on a Hot Tin Roof*," in Matthew C. Roudané, ed., *The Cambridge Companion to Tennessee Williams*. Cambridge: Cambridge University Press, 1997, 95–113.

Murphy, Brenda. *Tennessee Williams and Elia Kazan: A Collaboration in the Theatre*. Cambridge: Cambridge University Press, 1992.

Palmer, R. Barton. "Hollywood in Crisis: Tennessee Williams and the Evolution of the Adult Film" in Matthew C. Roudané, ed., *The Cambridge Companion to Tennessee Williams*. Cambridge: Cambridge University Press, 1997, 204–231.

Phillips, Gene D. *The Films of Tennessee Williams*. East Brunswick, NJ: Associated University Presses, 1980.

Williams, Tennessee. *Cat on a Hot Tin Roof*. Revised Edition. New York: New Directions, 1975.

DAVID A. DAVIS

"Make the Lie True":
The Tragic Family in Cat on a
Hot Tin Roof and King Lear

Time goes by so fast. Nothin' can outrun it. Death commences too
early—almost before you're half-acquainted with life—you meet
the other . . .

> Tennessee Williams, *Cat on a Hot Tin Roof* (117)

Men must endure
Their going hence even as their coming hither,
Ripeness is all.
> *King Lear* (V. ii. 9–11)

Families, perhaps the most complicated of human relationships, seem
naturally to lend themselves toward tragedy. Tennessee Williams's family
tragedy of greed, loyalty, and mendacity, *Cat on a Hot Tin Roof* (1955), has
much in common with another timeless family tragedy, William Shakespeare's *King Lear* (1605). Although different in setting, staging, and style,
Williams's play reflects powerful elements of characterization and dramatic
technique from Shakespeare's pattern, exploring the conflicts between
parents and children, between husbands and wives, and between jealous
siblings. As with *King Lear, Cat on a Hot Tin Roof* concerns the imminent
inheritance of an enormous piece of land and the wealth and power that
accompany it, the personality of the family patriarch who established the

From *The Tennessee Williams Annual Review* 5 (2002): 1–11. Copyright © 2002 by *The
Tennessee Williams Annual Review*.

family fortune, and his irresponsible children who will inevitably destroy it with their greed.

Although usually iconoclastic, Williams had great respect for Shakespeare, and he frequently returned to Shakespeare's plays. In an interview in 1974, Williams said, "I began to read [Shakespeare] when I was a child. My grandfather had all of Shakespeare's works, and I read them all by the time I was ten" (Devlin, *Conversations* 269). Precocious in his youth and fascinated with language, Williams found Shakespeare inspiring, and he reread Shakespeare repeatedly during his adolescence, frequently identifying with Shakespeare's tragic characters. In one of his earliest attempts at writing, Williams tried to improve upon Shakespeare's *Romeo and Juliet*, revising the play into rhyming couplets (Williams and Mead 27). Williams did not complete his project to rewrite Shakespeare, but he certainly learned much about dramatic technique at an early age. Later, in 1935, when Williams was twenty-four, he discovered the plays of Anton Chekhov, who Williams would always claim had the greatest influence on his style, but by that time he had already developed a taste for Shakespeare.

During the spring of 1938, his final year at the University of Iowa, Williams had a different kind of encounter with Shakespeare. All students majoring in drama were required to participate in a play, and that year the head of the department chose Shakespeare's *1 Henry IV*. Williams, who, despite his dramatic genius, had little talent as an actor, found himself in a tediously minor role, a member of Falstaff's "Charge of Foot." The director, realizing Williams's lack of talent, saw to it that he only delivered one line. About the experience, Williams recalls:

> throughout the scene in which I appeared I had to sit on the forestage, polishing a helmet, all the while my throat getting tighter and tighter with apprehension at delivering that one line. I simply had to say that somebody had arrived at the gates. But when my cue came, the sound that issued from my constricted throat was quite unintelligible and would always bring down the house—it was like a mouse's squeak. They said it was effective, however. (*Memoirs* 46)

Probably this production squelched any latent ambition Williams held for acting, but he identified with Prince Hal, the profligate heir to the English throne who would soon inspire the imagination of his people.

Critics have noted Shakespearean overtones to Williams's plays, indicating that Shakespeare influenced his dramatic technique, characterization, and dialogue. David Everett Blythe notes that Williams uses a bit of

Shakespearean dialogue from *Othello* in *Night of the Iguana*. Jacob Adler, in "Williams and the Bard," explores "analogous interests, patterns, and techniques" between the two, and he points out similarities in the ways both playwrights incorporated history, violence, insanity, outsiders, and humor into their drama (38). Ultimately, Adler concludes that Williams found *Hamlet* most affecting because of the parallels between Hamlet's life and Williams's life, such as, "A mentally ill girl. A hated (step)father. A young man of exceptional intellect, totally uncomfortable in the world in which he finds himself. A man who (perhaps) pretends to mental illness. A man who in the end is almost attracted to violence" (48). Perhaps Williams's personal identification with Shakespeare's most intriguing character explains his tendency to incorporate Shakespearean allusions into his drama.

Much of the critical dialogue concerning Williams and Shakespeare has focused specifically on one of Williams's most intriguing characters, Blanche DuBois in *A Streetcar Named Desire*. Esther Merle Jackson says that "like Hamlet, Blanche DuBois reveals her inner nature by playing out her conflicted roles: school-teacher, Southern belle, poet, sister, savior, and prostitute," and she suggests that the unbearable tension between these polarities leads both Hamlet and Blanche to their imminent destruction (84). Jacob Adler also finds that Hamlet and Blanche have much in common. He says:

> Neither Blanche nor Hamlet can bear the world as it is. Both have ideals that make meaningful action in an imperfect world almost impossible. Blanche loses her mind, and Hamlet at least pretends to. Blanche dreams of an ideal world of Southern aristocratic culture, as Hamlet had assumed and expected an ideal world of nobility. Much in Hamlet's soliloquies would not be inappropriate to Blanche's feelings.... Blanche is that character in Williams who, like Hamlet in Shakespeare, most clearly becomes an archetype. (43)

Philip Kolin, on the other hand, makes a case for Shakespeare's Cleopatra as a source for Blanche DuBois, and he comments on the parallels between their vanity, coquetry, and destructive sexual desires. Likely, Blanche has been the focus of so much critical attention precisely because she has become an archetypal character, and critics conclude that she, like many Shakespearean characters, symbolizes a particular and perennial aspect of the human condition.

Although *Cat on a Hot Tin Roof* has received less critical attention than *A Streetcar Named Desire*, especially from Shakespearean critics, it nonetheless occupies a privileged position in the American imagination, and it has its own archetypal quality. Most of the criticism of *Cat on a Hot Tin Roof* focuses on the relationships between the play's three main characters and the roles they play within the family. As George Crandell asks rhetorically, "Is *Cat* primarily a story about a troubled marriage (Maggie and Brick), a possibly homosexual relationship (Brick and Skipper), a father and son's inability to communicate (Big Daddy and Brick), or a family squabble over an inheritance (Brick and Maggie versus Gooper and Mae)?" (117). Actually, *Cat on a Hot Tin Roof* is a seminal family tragedy about truth, judgment, and greed, and it has much in common with Shakespeare's *King Lear*. Both plays portray a charismatic family patriarch facing his mortality; both plays concern the tension between an unscrupulous set of siblings and a favored sibling; both plays focus on the transmission of an enormous piece of land; and both plays lead to emotionally traumatic conclusions. Of course, the plays have major dramatic differences. *King Lear* sprawls across numerous settings, involves a military invasion, and includes graphic physical violence, but *Cat on a Hot Tin Roof* takes place entirely on a battlefield more suited to the twentieth century, a bedroom, and includes graphic psychological violence. Another significant difference separates these two plays. *King Lear* climaxes with Lear's tragic death over the body of his beloved daughter Cordelia. *Cat on a Hot Tin Roof*, on the other hand, climaxes with the prospect of a new generation, mitigating the play's sense of desolation.

King Lear's central character lends his name to the play, but *Cat on a Hot Tin Roof* has three central characters, Brick, Maggie, and, of course, Big Daddy. Although he appears on stage only briefly, Big Daddy's presence looms large over all of the characters in the play; they constantly talk to him, about him, or behind his back. C. W. E. Bigsby calls Big Daddy "the image of power, of materiality, of authority," and, indeed, he does rule over his plantation and his family like a king (89). Charismatic and ambitious, Big Daddy acquired his plantation through diligent effort and patience, and, as his relationships with Dr. Baugh and the Rev. Tooker suggest, the community respects his authority, in spite of his coarse demeanor. Unfortunately for Lear, on the other hand, he relinquishes his kingdom to his avaricious daughters in the first scene of the play, diminishing his power and authority for the remainder of the play, but, based on the loyalty his faithful servants show him and the length of his rule, he appears to have been a wise and strong king. The decision, then, to divide his kingdom must have been made under special circumstances, likely precipitated by the impending marriage of his youngest daughter and his advancing age. Big Daddy and Lear find themselves facing exactly the same problem in their respective plays, their legacy. As they face their mortality, they see their families in crisis and their lands in jeopardy, which forces both of them into emotional turmoil.

Big Daddy and Lear share another unique quality that few other people could understand—they both possess enormous wealth. When talking with his son Brick, Big Daddy gloats that he is worth "close on ten million in cash an' blue chip stocks, outside, mind you, of twenty-eight thousand acres of the richest land this side of the valley Nile!" (65). Considering that the play would have taken place soon after World War II, Big Daddy's wealth seems almost absurd, and his children, particularly his sons' wives, lust for their share of the family fortune, which Big Daddy realizes. He says to Brick, "You git a piece of land, by hook or crook, an' things start growin' on it, things accumulate on it, and the first thing you know it's completely out of hand!" (61). In the first scene of *King Lear*, Lear, hoping to prevent future squabbles among his children, divides his kingdom among his daughters based on the pledge of love and affection, and he describes the virtues of each of the three parcels. He gives Goneril an area "With shadowy forests and with champains rich'd / With plenteous rivers and wide-skirted meads," he gives Regan land of equal size and quality, and he proposes to bestow an even richer tract upon Cordelia, which indicates that his holdings are exceptionally vast (I.i.64–65). Indeed, as the king of Ancient Britain, Lear would have been one of the wealthiest men in Northern Europe at the time, and the size of his entourage after his abdication speaks to his largesse. Moreover, the loyalty he inspires in his subjects implies that his rule has been just and benevolent. But for Lear, as for Big Daddy, his fortune and power become his greatest liability.

Big Daddy and King Lear represent the old regime in their respective plays, and, by the time of the dramatic action, they both face their imminent mortality. For three years Big Daddy has suspected that the pain in his gut came from a cancerous tumor, and over that time he has relinquished partial control of the plantation to Gooper and Big Mama, allowing them to usurp power where he ordinarily would not. But in the morning preceding the play's action, the day of his sixty-fifth and, inevitably, his last birthday, he has visited the Ochsner Clinic for a biopsy. Mae and Gooper have conspired to withhold the true diagnosis from him until after his birthday party, so for a brief moment Big Daddy believes that he suffers from nothing more than a spastic colon, despite the wolf's teeth in his guts. He tells Brick:

> Ignorance—of mortality—is a comfort. A man don't have that comfort, he's the only living thing that conceives of death, that knows what it is. The others go without knowing which is the way that anything living should go, go without knowing, without any knowledge of it, and yet a pig squeals, but a man sometimes, he can keep a tight mouth about it. Sometimes he—[*there is a deep, smoldering ferocity in the old man.*]—can keep a tight mouth about it. (68)

Although he feels relieved at the positive diagnosis, Big Daddy has obviously begun to consider his mortality and to consider the disposition of his assets. This latter issue, his estate, seems to concern him even more than his death, because his favorite son, Brick, has become an alcoholic and, thus, could not maintain the plantation, which forces Big Daddy into a dilemma. Big Daddy explains to Brick:

> A little while back when I though my number was up—before I found out it was just this—spastic—colon, I thought about you. Should I or should I not, if the jig was up, give you this place when I go—since I hate Gooper an' Mae an' know that they hate me, and since all five same little monkeys are little Maes an' Goopers.—And I thought, No!—Then I thought, Yes!—I couldn't make up my mind. I hate Gooper and his five same little monkeys and that bitch Mae! Why should I turn over twenty-eight thousand acres of the richest land this side of the valley Nile to not my kind?—But why in hell, on the other hand, Brick—should I subsidize a goddamn fool on the bottle?—Liked or not liked, well, maybe even—*loved!*— Why should I do that?—Subsidize worthless behavior? Rot? Corruption? (81–82)

To defeat his dilemma, Big Daddy hopes to use his remaining time to resolve Brick's problem, to find the reason behind his alcoholism, and to secure the plantation's future. But, while he gets to the heart of Brick's problem, he finds that he has more pressing problems of his own. In the course of their heated conversation, Brick accidentally tells Big Daddy that he will die soon and that Mae and Gooper, and Maggie, are conspiring to take over the plantation. Big Daddy replies with genuine shock, "[*slowly and passionately*]: CHRIST—DAMN—ALL—LYING SONS OF—LYING BITCHES . . .—Lying! Dying! Liars!" (95). Big Daddy finds the revelation of the plot he had suspected all along even more disheartening than his own dire prognosis, which indicates that he cares for his family and his legacy more than his health.

King Lear, hoping to preserve peace in his family and perpetuate his own legacy, proposes to divide his kingdom among his daughters before his death, but fate sends his plans awry, leading to war, suffering, and the end of his line. In his first speech onstage, Lear casts the die, explaining that his advancing years hasten his decision: "Know that we have divided / In three our kingdom, and 'tis our fast intent / To shake all cares and business from our age, / Conferring them on younger strengths, while we / Unburthened crawl toward death" (I.i.37–41). Obviously, Lear has considered his plan well, having previously prepared the map of his kingdom and assembled his daughters and their spouses as well as Cordelia's suitors. His scheme favors Cordelia, his youngest and favorite daughter, because, in addition to her third of the kingdom she also stands to marry a landed foreign nobleman, either the Duke of Burgundy or the King of France, thus, joining two kingdoms. Since his other daughters, Regan and Goneril, have already married English nobles (Lear's own subjects), they only gain their portion of the kingdom as belated dowry. However, Lear's plan to dispense his lands on a simple pledge of affection falls apart when Cordelia refuses to indulge Lear with a cloying speech. Humiliated and enraged, he banishes her and divides her portion of the kingdom between Regan and Goneril. Like Big Daddy, he finds his family and his land in disorder as he faces his mortality, and, rather than facing his twilight securely bound to his beloved daughter, he leaves himself with only the begrudging mercies his Regan and Goneril. Unwilling to indulge their father's lavish entourage, Regan and Goneril quickly strip Lear of his knights and servants, leaving the once powerful king helpless and pitiful before casting him out into the raging tempest. Like Big Daddy, he curses his children's mendacity more than his own mortality, and he bellows with impotent rage, "you unnatural hags, / I will have such revenges on you both / That all the world shall—I will do such things—/ What they are yet I know not, but they shall be / The terrors of the earth!" (II.iv.279–282). Angry and forlorn, Lear charges into the storm, punishing only himself.

The storm, nature's disorder, has significant meaning in both plays. In the original version of *Cat on a Hot Tin Roof*, Williams omitted the storm, but, on the advice of director Elia Kazan, he added a major storm in the Delta for the Broadway production. Just after Mae and Gooper inform Big Mama of Big Daddy's actual condition, ominous storm sounds commence offstage, and servants can be heard frantically preparing for the weather; as Williams's stage directions describe:

> [*Thunder clap. Glass crash, off L.*
> [*Off UR, children commence crying. Many storm sounds, L and R: barnyard animals in terror, papers crackling, shutters rattling. Sookey and Daisy hurry L to R in lawn area. Inexplicably, Daisy hits together two leather pillows. They cry, "Storm! Storm!" Sookey waves a piece of wrapping paper to cover lawn furniture. Mae exits to hall and upper gallery. Strange man runs across lawn, R to L.*
> [*Thunder rolls repeatedly.*] (147)

The storm in the Delta has much in common with the famous storm on the heath in *King Lear*, but Big Daddy, unlike Lear, watches the storm from his veranda. Lear charges into the storm, raging to match the heavens. When asked the King's whereabouts, an observer says:

> [He's] Contending with the fretful elements;
> Bids the wind blow the earth into the sea,
> Or swell the curled waters 'bove the main,
> That things might change or cease, tears his white hair,
> Which the impetuous blasts with eyeless rage
> Catch in their fury, and make nothing of . . . (III.i.4–9)

In addition to focusing the audience's attention on the emotional trauma taking place on stage, the storms underscore the magnitude of the changes taking place within the families and foreshadow the violence, both physical and psychological to come.

The storms also provide the audience with an objective correlative for the internal upheaval taking place within the respective minds of King Lear and Big Daddy. Lear emerges from the storm wet, rumpled, and quite mad. Faced with the precipitous loss of his title, his kingdom, and his family, coupled with his tremendous guilt for ostracizing his only faithful child, Lear reacts violently, incoherently babbling, cursing his daughters, and blaming his fate on women. He says, "Down from the waist they are centaurs, / Though women all above; / But to the girdle do gods inherit, / Beneath is all the fiends': there's hell, there's darkness, / There is the sulphurous pit, burning, scalding, / Stench, consumption" (IV.vi.124–129). Vilifying his ungrateful daughters, Lear traces their malevolent nature to their gender, using the idiom for female genitalia. In a similarly curious episode from the Broadway version of *Cat on a Hot Tin Roof*, Big Daddy wanders back onstage to tell a highly inappropriate joke about a little boy at the zoo watching an elephant:

> So this ole bull elephant still had a couple of fornications left in him. He reared back his trunk an' got a whiff of that elephant lady next door!—began to paw at the dirt in his cage an' butt his head against the separatin' partition and, first thing y'know, there was a conspicuous change in his *profile*—very *conspicuous*. . . . So the little boy looked at it and said, "What's that?" His Mam said, "Oh, that's—nothin'!"—His Papa said, "She's spoiled!" (151–152)

As Big Daddy tells his joke, Big Mama falls into sobs and the other family members look on in amazement. Obviously, Big Daddy does not seem to be in normal humor, and he certainly does not behave like a man who just minutes before learned of his imminent death. Big Daddy, like Lear, allows his circumstances to overwhelm his reason, which, considering the impotence these usually powerful men feel, would be an appropriate defensive mechanism.

Brick uses alcohol as his favorite defensive mechanism, a circumstance that greatly complicates his relationship with Big Daddy. Brick and Cordelia share their respective fathers' affection and favoritism, and they both manage to alienate their fathers, thus contributing to the respective play's dramatic action. Brick seems to be completely oblivious of anyone other than himself as he crawls deeper into the bottle, and he acts surprised when Big Mama tells him that Big Daddy dotes on him and that only he could continue the family legacy. She says, "Oh, Brick, son of Big Daddy! Big Daddy does so love you! Y'know what would be his fondest dream come true? If before he passed on, if Big Daddy has to pass on, you gave him a child of yours, a grandson as much like his son as his son is like Big Daddy!" (117). Gooper, Brick's older brother, bristles at the comment, but he recognizes that Big Daddy has always favored Brick, and he hopes to take advantage of Brick's alcoholism to stake his own claim on the plantation.

Similarly, in the first scene of *King Lear*, Lear proclaims before everyone assembled, including his daughters and their husbands, that Cordelia his been his joy and that he "lov'd her most, and thought to set [his] rest / On her kind nursery" (I.i.23–24). Cordelia's sisters profit at her loss, and, unsatisfied to share dominion over the kingdom, each immediately begins conspiring to depose the other, which makes one wonder if they would not have colluded to acquire Cordelia's land had she received it. Brick and Cordelia, innocently, inhabit a treacherous family dynamic, and only their father's protection prevents their siblings from destroying them, either physically or financially.

Perhaps because of their fathers' protection, Brick and Cordelia have developed idealistic notions of truth that eventually lead to the climax of their respective plays. In the second act of *Cat on a Hot Tin Roof*, Big Daddy presses Brick to divulge the reason behind his drinking, and Brick, evasively, answers "Have you ever heard the word 'mendacity'?," and he goes on to attribute his condition to the accumulation of lies that his life has become and to the liars who surround him, with the exception of Big Daddy (79). Yet, even in his relationship with Big Daddy, neither party has been entirely forthcoming. While they have never explicitly lied to each other, they, as Brick says, have "never *talked* to each other" (83). Brick's emphasis on "*talked*" suggests that his relationship has never developed the intimacy that Big Daddy wished to have, and their one revelatory conversation leads them both to tremendous emotional trauma: Brick faces his sexual confusion, and Big Daddy faces his mortality.[1] Likewise, when Lear asks Cordelia to express her affection for him, she freezes, unwilling to respond in the lavish terms that her unscrupulous sisters have used, and so she simply says "Nothing, my lord" (I.i.87). Her reply seems puzzling, because her sisters have used fawning language, but they speak metaphorically. Goneril says she loves Lear more "than eyesight, space, and liberty," and Regan says that Goneril's words "come too short" to describe her love (I.i.56, 73). Regan and Goneril's conceits seem quite transparent, but Cordelia takes them far too seriously, because she recognizes the falsity between her sisters' love and their words, so she chooses to speak literally, explaining that she loves her father at his due, but not with the elevated language that her sisters use. Lear, offended, asks her "So young, and so untender?," and she replies, "So young, my lord, and true" (I.i.106–107). In both plays, the favorite child's obsession with honesty contributes to the play's tragedy.

In each play, the unfavored siblings' malevolence also contributes to the dramatic action; in effect, they become the antagonists who perpetrate violence, whether physical or psychological, on the favored child and the father. Mae and Gooper, while not so overtly vicious as their counterparts in *King Lear*, appear quite repugnant. Alice Griffin says, understatedly, that they "have few redeeming traits," and, indeed, they manipulate, spy, lie, and connive to get control of the plantation (157). They have come from Memphis to the plantation with their five "no-neck" children ostensibly for Big Daddy's birthday party, but actually they have come expressly to profit from the news of Big Daddy's cancer. Immediately after giving Big Mama the news about Big Daddy's prognosis, Gooper presents her with a dummy trust and demands that she have Big Daddy to sign it, effectively transferring control of the plantation to Gooper and Mae. Big Mama objects, and Gooper callously says, "You jest won't let me do this in a nice way, will yah? . . . I am asking for a square deal, and I expect to get one. But if I don't get one, if there's any peculiar shenanigans going on around here behind my back, or before me, well, I'm not a corporation lawyer for nothing, I know how to protect my own interests" (113). Naturally, Big Mama feels completely alienated by Gooper's behavior, and, since she has more influence on Big Daddy than anyone save Brick, one could surmise that Gooper would only get any share of the plantation through litigation. Regan and Goneril, in a similar moment, learning that Cordelia and the army of France have invaded England for the purpose of securing Lear, quickly mount military action against their sister to prevent her from rescuing her father. Simultaneously, Regan and Goneril conspire with their courtiers to overthrow each other, leading to general strife and mayhem throughout the kingdom. In each case, the unfavored siblings attempt to use force to exact their nefarious, greedy ends, and the resolution comes when their plans have been thwarted.

During the course of these insidious plots, Big Daddy and Lear each have one loyal friend who valiantly represents their respective interests in spite of their cruel mistreatment, Big Mama and Kent. Big Daddy constantly abuses Big Mama, calling her names in public and telling her directly that he finds her repulsive, yet she always lavishes him with love. He even castigates her in front of the family for helping to run the plantation. He says, "Ain't that so, Ida? Didn't you have an idea I was dying of cancer and now you could take control of this place and everything on it?" (57). When she runs sobbing from the room, he shows no concern for her, but, later, when she learns that he really is dying of cancer, she conclusively reveals her devotion to him. In his stage directions, Williams describes how the moment when Big Mama realizes Big Daddy's condition should be acted:

> [*In these few words, this startled, very soft question, Big Mama reviews the history of her forty-five years with Big Daddy, her great, almost embarrassingly true-hearted and simple-minded devotion to Big Daddy, who must have had something Brick has, who made himself loved so much by the "simple expedient" of not loving enough to disturb his charming detachment, also once coupled, like Brick's, with virile beauty.*
>
> [*Big Mama has a dignity at this moment: she almost stops being fat.*] (103)

When Gooper presents his dummy trust, Big Mama refuses him, saying "*CRAP*," just like Big Daddy would. Instead, she begs Brick to have a child who will perpetuate Big Daddy's legacy, leading Maggie to announce her pregnancy prematurely. In *King Lear*, the embattled Kent steps forward to preserve Cordelia from Lear's unjust banishment, drawing Lear's wrath upon himself. Only Kent dares to speak to Lear with reason. He says, "Reserve thy state, / And in thy best consideration check / This hideous rashness. Answer my life my judgement, / Thy youngest daughter does not love thee least, / Nor are those empty-hearted whose low sounds / Reverb no hollowness" (I.i.149–154). Kent foreshadows the play's tragic trajectory, and Lear threatens Kent's life, then banishes him from the kingdom. Knowing that he will be needed more now than ever, Kent contrives to disguise himself as the beggar Caius and to find his way into the King's service. Kent uncovers the conspiracy between Regan and Goneril to eliminate Lear, and he summons Cordelia with the army of France to save Lear. At the play's end, Lear dies in his arms. In these plays of duplicity and intrigue, the loyalty and love of Big Mama and Kent offers a brief glimmer of redemption.

Redemption aside, *Cat on a Hot Tin Roof* and *King Lear* are tragedies, but they have their moments of comic relief. Lear's irreverent fool mocks his condition openly and with impunity, and his absurd commentary fore-shadows the play's tragic conclusion. Hearing that Regan and Goneril have exchanged letters concerning the King, the Fool says, "Fathers that wear rags / Do make their children blind, / But fathers that bear bags / Shall see their children kind. / Fortune, that arrant whore, / Ne'er turns the key to the poor. / But for all this, thou shalt have as many dolors for thy daughters as thou canst tell in a year" (II.iv.47–55). The Fool rightly prophesies that, since King Lear has forfeited his power, his daughters will inflict terrible sadness on him within the year. Like the Fool, Reverend Tooker offers a bit of uncomfortable humor to *Cat on a Hot Tin Roof*. Ostensibly at the plantation house to offer a bit of comfort to the family, he constantly talks of memorial windows and bequests to the parish, revealing himself to be as greedy and mendacious as Mae and Gooper. In one particularly disturbing moment, Big Daddy over-hears Reverend Tooker say to Doc Baugh, "the Stork and the Reaper are run-ning neck and neck!" (54). Obviously, Reverend Tooker knows of Big Daddy's prognosis, which he probably heard from Doc Baugh, and he seems to be equating Big Daddy's death with Mae's sixth pregnancy. But his statement, by the end of the play, proves to have more prophetic import when Maggie reveals her (tentative) pregnancy with an heir to the plantation.

While almost all of the characters in *Cat on a Hot Tin Roof* have cor-ollaries in *King Lear*, one character stands apart, Maggie the Cat. On one hand, Maggie has little in common with the other Pollitts, but, on the other hand, she seems to be an amalgam of Big Mama's devotion, Big Daddy's cha-risma, Mae and Gooper's underhanded determination, and Brick's coolness. Unlike the Pollitts, however, Maggie's multi-faceted personality makes her both tremendously complex and quickly adaptable. Maggie's goal, as revealed in the first act of the play, seems extremely difficult—to make her distant husband love her, to get pregnant, to deal with Brick's alcoholism, and to preserve Brick's interest in the plantation. Amazingly, at the end of the play, she appears to be on the verge of succeeding in all of her goals, which indi-cates that she, more than anyone else, drives the play. Like many of William's most intriguing characters, as Albert Devlin points out in "Writing in 'A Place of Stone': *Cat on a Hot Tin Roof*," she finds herself on the verge of dis-possession, but unlike T. Lawrence Shannon, Blanche DuBois, and Amanda Wingfield, she faces her circumstance with cunning. In a sense, she exists separately from the *Lear*-esque frame play taking place around her. When the plantation appears to be in utter crisis, she assumes control of the situation, leading to the play's ultimate climax. In a blatant lie, she announces to the family that she carries Brick's child, virtually willing herself to be pregnant.

At that moment, Mae and Gooper's plan to take the plantation crumbles, Big Daddy's last wish is fulfilled, and Brick shows a glimmer of interest in life outside his booze. Alone with her husband, she tells him that they are "going to make the lie true" and conceive a child (158). For the first time in possibly years, Brick agrees, passively, to make love to his wife, and Maggie, with an outsider's perspective, comments on the tragic Pollitts: "Oh, you weak, beautiful people who give up with such grace. What you need is someone to take hold of you—gently, with love, and hand your life back to you, like something gold you let go of—and I can! I'm determined to do it—and nothing's more determined than a cat on a hot tin roof" (158). Ultimately, if anyone triumphs in Williams's play, it is Maggie.

Cat on a Hot Tin Roof and *King Lear* conclude with the prospect of a new generation. At the end of *King Lear*, with Lear and all of his daughters dead and no one remaining with a rightful claim to the throne, the Duke of Albany, Goneril's widower could have asserted his own claim on the kingdom, perhaps to be challenged by the King of France. Instead, Albany transfers authority to Kent and Edgar, the faithful defenders of the old regime. Kent, recognizing his own advanced age, defers, giving Edgar sole rule of Lear's troubled kingdom. Edgar accepts his new position with proper solemnity, saying, "The weight of this sad time we must obey, / Speak what we feel, not what we ought to say: / The oldest hath borne most; we that are young / Shall never see so much, nor live so long" (V.iii.324–327). In the wake of terrible suffering and bloodshed, Edgar's ascendancy to the throne gives the play a note of redemption as a new, just regime resolves the anguish plaguing the nation. Maggie's pregnancy lends a similar tone of redemption to *Cat on a Hot Tin Roof*, especially in the Broadway version of the play. The original version ends with Brick, as jaded as ever, merely acquiescing to make love to Maggie, but in the Broadway version, Brick shows genuine interest in Maggie. He even says, as he approaches the bed, the battleground that dominates the stage, "I admire you, Maggie" (158). The play ends here, with Maggie's speech about these weak, beautiful people, but she obviously has assumed power over the entire family at this point. With Big Daddy's death imminent and Mae and Gooper completely out of the picture, she figures, with or without Brick's active assistance, to take control of the plantation and to raise an heir who will, eventually, receive Big Daddy's legacy.

Ultimately, *King Lear* and *Cat on a Hot Tin Roof* are plays about succession. As the old generation faces death, infighting among the young generation coupled with greed, petty jealousy, and dishonesty, leads to tragic ends. In these plays, family members become adversaries, death becomes an opportunity, and sex becomes a weapon. Although remote in temporal and spatial setting, *King Lear* and *Cat on a Hot Tin Roof* have many themes in common, and it seems that Williams kept Shakespeare in mind while writing his play. Yet the similarities between the two plays hardly need to be considered explicitly intentional. Williams may have exploited the family dynamics of *King Lear* for his own purposes, but the extreme relationships in this family have their own seminal value, and almost every audience member in virtually every time, Elizabethan or contemporary, can relate to or conceive of these archetypal characters because every family has its own sense of tragedy.

Notes

1. For more on the theme of homosexuality, see Dean Shackelford's article "The Truth That Must Be Told: Gay Subjectivity, Homophobia, and Social History in *Cat on a Hot Tin Roof.*" *Tennessee Williams Annual Review* 1 (1998).

Works Cited

Adler, Jacob. "Williams and the Bard." *The Tennessee Williams Literary Journal* 2.1 (Winter 1990–91): 37–50.

Bigsby, C. W. E. *A Critical Introduction to Twentieth Century Drama.* Vol. 2. Cambridge: Cambridge UP, 1984.

Blythe, David. "Othello and Night of the Iguana." Notes on Contemporary Literature 27.1 (Jan. 1997): 1.

Crandell, George. "*Cat on a Hot Tin Roof.*" *Tennessee Williams: A Guide to Research and Performance.* Ed. Philip C. Kolin. Westport: Greenwood, 1998. 109–125.

Devlin, Albert, ed. *Conversations with Tennessee Williams.* Jackson: UP of Mississippi,1986.

———. "Writing in 'A Place of Stone': *Cat on a Hot Tin Roof.*" *The Cambridge Companion to Tennessee Williams.* Ed. Matthew C. Roudané. New York: Cambridge UP, 1997. 95–113.

Griffin, Alice. *Understanding Tennessee Williams.* Columbia: U of South Carolina P, 1995.

Jackson, Esther Merle. *The Broken World of Tennessee Williams.* Madison: U of Wisconsin P, 1965.

Kolin, Philip. "Cleopatra of the Nile and Blanche DuBois of the French Quarter: *Antony and Cleopatra* and *A Streetcar Named Desire.*" *Shakespeare Bulletin* 11.1 (Winter 1993): 25–27.

Shackelford, Dean. "The Truth That Must Be Told: Gay Subjectivity, Homophobia, and Social History in *Cat on a Hot Tin Roof.*" *Tennessee Williams Annual Review* 1 (1998): 103–118.

Shakespeare, William. *King Lear. The Riverside Shakespeare.* Ed. G. Blakemore Evans. Boston: Houghton, 1974. 1255–1305.

Williams, Dakin and Shepherd Mead. *Tennessee Williams: An Intimate Biography.* New York: Arbor, 1983.

Williams, Tennessee. *Cat on a Hot Tin Roof.* New York: Signet, 1955.

———. *Memoirs.* Garden City, NY: Doubleday, 1975.

JEFFREY B. LOOMIS

Four Characters in Search of a Company: Williams, Pirandello, and the Cat on a Hot Tin Roof Manuscripts

W hile discussing Friedrich Nietzsche's *The Birth of Tragedy*, Michael Hinden wrote: "Tragedy incarnates pain, annihilates structure, threatens hope, and yet . . . also has the power to sweep us up in the tow of powerful personalities whose grand passions and embellished language draw us into solidarity with—what?—dream images, really: towering characters who are at bottom insubstantial and subject to dissolution before our eyes, uniting us in collective emotion" (Hinden 113). Hinden's words remind me of how, in *Six Characters in Search of an Author*, Pirandello portrays a grand ensemble of "towering characters"—huge-spirited beings who do, nonetheless, eventually "dissol[ve]" into "collective emotion." Pirandello also reveals to us the author's terror in dealing with some of these characters: those who will not cooperatively *join* the collective ensemble but instead assert their will to dominate over the other characters, and the constellation of themes, and the total scheme of the plot, and the stagecraft devices, and all else.

I was reminded again of this Pirandellian perspective when reading, during recent summers, more than twenty draft versions of Tennessee Williams's *Cat on a Hot Tin Roof*, besides other related Williams documents, at five different U.S. research libraries. There I saw how twenty-four years of work on the *Cat* writing project caused Williams at times to be plagued by would-be dominator characters (who sometimes had living human allies, chiefly Elia

From *Magical Muse: Millennial Essays on Tennessee Williams*, edited by Ralph F. Voss, pp. 91–110. Copyright © 2002 by the University of Alabama Press.

109

Kazan, to abet them in their quest for primacy over other characters within the cast). By contrast, the 1975 final revision of *Cat* has, I think, achieved a wonderfully balanced ensemble of the various characters—one that Kazan sometimes helped to evoke, by urging Williams to develop Maggie and Big Mama as characters more completely, but also a balance that Kazan for a long time apparently contravened, through insisting that the character of Brick needed to make personality-altering, and evidently somewhat noisy, onstage transformations. To a degree, the character of Big Daddy also sometimes threatened to overdominate the *Cat* ensemble in certain versions of the play text—whether this threat also came about solely as a result of Kazan's ardent interest in Big Daddy or whether it perhaps resulted from Williams's taunting of Kazan's zeal to magnify this character.

But in any case, the drafts of *Cat* do reveal several directions in which this script could have gone and sometimes *did* go—all of which might, indeed, prove intriguing to deconstructionist, would-be revisionist readers of the text. Like such a deconstructionist reader, I can find *other* Williams plays—especially *The Rose Tattoo*—inviting me to treat draft variants of the play often as really "playable" alternatives to the published drama. Contrariwise, though, in the case of the *Cat* manuscripts, many drafted alternatives seem only chaotic approximations of the ultimately polished American Shakespeare Festival production version published by New Directions in 1975. Such drafts' qualities of chaos resemble the inanity that the Pirandellian *Six Characters* at times nearly impose upon the Author character in that play. Therefore, I cannot but be *conservatively* minded toward the manuscript history of *Cat on a Hot Tin Roof*. I find the entire manuscript progress toward the 1975 *Cat* altogether necessary—and would never be able to laud most of the earlier assaults that were made on the playwright from, or on behalf of, overly "towering" characters.

Williams first created the Pollitt family of characters in "Three Players of a Summer Game," a short story he began in Venice in 1951 and revised many times before the Pollitts found their way to the stage in *Cat*. The story occurs in the 1920s, so the character known there as Brick (and at first as Brick *Bishop*, not *Pollitt*) would have had a fictively historical birth date less like that of the later-to-be-dramatized Brick than like that of the play's Big Daddy. The short story's characters also have rather different fictive biographies from the playscript cast, and in the story it is a rather masculine, perhaps even lesbian Maggie who refuses to have sex with Brick (Texas 1—Subfolder 7: 3,7).

Such details, however, do not seem most important about the "Three Players" short story in its many drafts. What does stand out in the oft-revised tale is its constant Pirandellian sense of life's inherent theatrics: for example,

"Mr. Brick Bishop had bought the corner lot to use as a stage to put on . . . his brave play [at adulterous courtship of another woman] . . . mainly in defiance of the wife who never came to see it" (Texas 1—Subfolder 8: 3). On at least one occasion, too, Williams (like Pirandello?) enunciates a clear belief that the writing process alone is what makes literary characters thrive: "and of course there has . . . been time enough, now, for Mary Louise's thin pretty mother [Brick's fictional adulterous paramour] to become no more than the shadow that she is here [on the page]" (Subfolder 8: 6).

In a fairly early revision of the dramatized full-length *Cat* (the Texas 11 manuscript, on which green-inked comments by the play's stage director Elia Kazan appear), Williams demonstrates that he shares Pirandello's understanding (as defined by Della Terza 29, 31 and Brustein 107–108) of *umorismo*: that inborn, darkly comic matrix of a life where one must struggle between obvious self-division and the social roles one is forced to play. In the Texas 11 manuscript, Maggie declares, very near the drama's final moments, "If I looked in the mirror right now, I'd say 'Who're you?' and yet, at the same time, know more about myself than I've ever known" (Texas 11; addendum, 4). Perhaps Williams was here sketching a direct or indirect response to Kazan's observation, after reading earlier versions of the script, that Maggie is "heartbreaking," "tender and dear and desperate and funny and so touching!" "a wonderful, loyal, single-loving girl who has no defenses, leaves herself wide open to hurt" (Harvard 4/1: 11). And Williams himself became more and more convinced that Maggie was complicated, not just a brazenly sex-driven wife. To be sure, she did, in the very early Texas 10 manuscript, taunt a standoffish, maddeningly prudish Brick with the hot-blooded words, "I'll be sleepless tonight while you slumber peacefully on the shores of Echo Spring. And just my luck, the moon will fall over the sofa that you sleep on. Oh, I could teach the Chinese a trick or two about torture!" (Texas 10: 33). Granted, even in the Texas 10 manuscript, Williams was giving Maggie words that defined perspectives other than the merely sexual: "You'll discover that I'm not unkind, not really. I'm only a bitch because I long to be loved by someone who doesn't love me" (Texas 10: 41); "The only comfort is love, the only protection is love, the only refuge is love" (40). Yet even in the Texas 11 revision, Williams hasn't seen as much complexity as he gives her in the 1975 final version, where her ultimate statements tell Brick that "what [he] want[s] is someone to—. . . take *hold* of [him]" (*Cat* 1975: 173; emphasis mine); in Texas 11 she remains more clearly manipulative by nature, declaring to Brick, "What you want is someone to . . . take *control* of you" (Texas 11: addendum, 4; emphasis mine).

Williams obviously had doubts in these manuscript treatments about deemphasizing Maggie's sexual self-flaunting—although he eventually did so. Kazan repeatedly told him (Harvard 4/1: 1: 5A, Texas 11/1: 14) to drop an early revision schema in which Maggie and Brick both wear pajamas, hers translucent. At one point, Williams may specifically have used Maggie's revealing costume in order to help signify that Brick retained some heterosexual tendencies; for example, Texas 15's act 1 revision declares that Brick looks at her in the pajamas and "is probably not aware that [he] is licking his lips and twisting them at the same time, into a grimace of—*what*?" An alternate presentation of the same episode, however, collected on the same page of the same manuscript, has Brick react to Maggie's sheer apparel with more "twist" than "lick" of lips (Texas 15/2: 2). Yet Mae, Brick's sister-in-law, who intrudes upon the couple's paired pajamas scene, still finds it "sexy" (Texas 15/2: 5). It was in the script as late as December 9, 1954, the date clearly ascribed to the Columbia 1 manuscript, where the double-pajamaed party is mentioned (Rewrite, beginning of act 2: 2).

Also, Maggie's "kneeling at [Big Daddy's] feet to claim she is pregnant," in the Texas 15 and Texas 21 manuscripts (Parker 485, 487), is fairly torridly enacted and is thus called "a little indecent" by Gooper, Brick's brother (Texas 15—Subfolder 4: 2). Her sensuous histrionics lead to the point where "Big Daddy explicitly feels Margaret's body before affirming that she has 'life' in her" (Parker 487), and Brick declares, when he and Maggie are alone at the end of the play, "You fell on your knees and begged for some of his money, you made a strong bid for it, without pretendin' you didn't know he was goin'" (Texas 15/4: 6). More energetically yet, he says, in a later variant, "—Life is a damn fire in you, you know that, don't you? Big Daddy felt that[;] it must have burned his fingers when he ran his old dyin' hand down over your body" (Texas 26/3: 40). Still, Maggie does change; she does not *talk* nearly as frankly and constantly about sex in any later version as she does in the very earliest.

Transformations that Williams made in Maggie's character probably resulted mostly from his attempts to please Elia Kazan. Williams tells us, in a "Note of Explanation" from the 1955 published edition of *Cat*, that, "while [Kazan] understood that [Williams] sympathized with her and liked her [him]self," Kazan felt that she "should be, if possible, more clearly sympathetic to an audience" (*Cat* 1955: 124–25). Kazan also "felt that the character of Brick should undergo some apparent mutation as a result of the virtual vivisection that he undergoes in his interview with his father in Act Two" (*Cat* 1955: 124). In some of the stabs Williams made at incorporating Brick into the play differently from the way he had appeared in the earliest versions, or from the way he would appear in the very latest, the New Directions publication of 1975, the playwright turned him into a surprisingly articulate near-rationalist or into a sort of gushily sweet, shame-ridden child. These portraits of Brick do not fit him into the character ensemble nearly as well as do the earliest and very latest (both quite similar) delineations of his person-ality—for, as Williams himself declared in the famed 1955 "Note of Expla-nation," "The moral paralysis of Brick was a root thing in his tragedy, and to show a dramatic progression would obscure the meaning of that tragedy ... [as well as the fact that] a conversation, however revelatory, [n]ever effects so immediate a change in the heart or even conduct of a person in Brick's state of spiritual despair" (*Cat* 1955: 125).

In some versions of the antecedent work that gives rise eventually to *Cat*, the 1951–1952 short story "Three Players of a Summer Game," Brick demonstrates a wild sort of compassion fused with anger, much like the oxy-moronic amalgamation of behaviors that we encounter in the Big Daddy of *Cat on a Hot Tin Roof.* When Mary Louise, the daughter of his extramarital girlfriend Isabel, is taunted by neighborhood girls, Brick defends her, yelling for a hose to be turned on these youngsters, whom he meanwhile calls (with no very great show of compassion) "a bunch of little bitches, the same as their mothers, a bunch of mean little bitches" (Texas 4—Subfolder 4: 3). Brick is hardly admirable and allusively Christlike in his response—as is, by contrast, Mary Louise's mother Isabel, when she tells the bratty children (Subfolder 4: 4), "You're just children, you don't know what you're doing, you don't under-stand anything, you don't understand what you're doing!" This early narrative version of Brick, not very different from the dramatis personae version of "A Place of Stone" or of the 1975 final *Cat*, has some tendency to kindhearted-ness but does not demonstrate this kindheartedness without simultaneously revealing some markedly unpleasant wrath.

The "moral[ly] paraly[tic]" Brick, as he is defined by Williams in his 1955 "Note of Explanation," is thus already foreshadowed in the Brick of the ear-lier short story "Three Players of a Summer Game." He is, like plenty of other characters in twentieth-century American literature, a stereotypically drink-obsessed male southerner—and as debilitated as any by his boozing. Accord-ing to the manuscript writer Williams, the "Defiance" that Brick wanted to emphasize as the theme of his life's "play" was "somehow invalidated" by his tippling, which left him in a frequent mental fog (Texas 1—Subfolder 3: 2).

In this narrated musing of 1951, as in the earliest version of the *Cat* playscript (Texas 10—Subfolder 1: 3; Subfolder 4: 10), Williams describes a character, appropriately named Brick, with red hair and alabaster skin, though most actors who have played Brick have not had these physical traits. On the other hand, we find this Brick's somber character traits familiar—even though Williams's short story manuscripts sometimes have him dance on a publicly viewed croquet lawn in giddy near-nakedness, dressed only in necktie and undershorts, spraying himself with a garden hose (Texas 4—Subfolder 3: 9). By contrast with such actions, Brick is in general already a demoralized,

existentially dread-ridden gloomster not very prepared to make quick alterations in his behavior, whatever the quickening motivation might be. Hence
Williams's attempts to please Kazan, by repeatedly refocusing Brick, eventually provide not focus but a blur.

Having myself acted the role of Big Daddy, in two 1982 mountings of
Cat on a Hot Tin Roof at West Virginia's University of Charleston, I can testify that act 2 can become emotionally wrenching in performance. I will never
forget the shock of seeing Terry Wetmore, the actor who played Brick in
both Charleston productions, suddenly break into tears after having grasped
the intense kinship that Brick and Big Daddy might feel after completing a
long sequence of confessions and revelations. Terry broke into tears only once,
though, and I sense that any Brick would only rarely let loose the floodgates
of interpersonal sympathy. Yet at the same time, Terry did, albeit on only one
occasion, reveal a potential for profoundly self-scouring catharsis in Brick.

A Brick stammering toward change would, however, I think, do so mostly
through visceral behaviors, rather than through analytical preachments. Therefore, I believe that Williams's best tentative (albeit eventually unused) alterations in Brick's portrait occur in the Texas 21 and Texas 26 manuscripts.

In the first of these, Brick utters guiltily, after having spitefully revealed
to his father that the old patriarch is dying, "I've done it!" "—done it" (Texas
21/3: 3). Brick soon afterward cries out, according to the Texas 21 manuscript (3: 3), "I see him out in the yard" (3: 3), and he calls out, to "a figure
dimly visible," "Big Daddy" (3: 3C). At about the same place as these Texas
21 stammerings, in the Texas 26 revision of Texas 21, he tells Maggie, who
was shocked to find him standing on his broken ankle without the support of
his crutch, "*Experiencing pain!*—is part of—life" (Texas 26/3: 16). Again, he
seems to be viscerally shrieking out his anguished guilt, in a way that seems
fairly plausible to expect from a son who has just undergone an hour of bitter
intergenerational epiphanies.

Also in the Texas 26 variant, though, Williams has Brick shout at Maggie, "Maggie, don't give me that crutch! I nearly killed you with it for a crime
I committed!" (3: 16). This outburst, like so many of the revisions Williams
tended to give to Brick for Kazan's sake, reflects more apparent rationality
of tone than one would expect from a man who has lived for a long while in
grief for Skipper, a very close friend, and in general besotted misery. Other
such passages manifest themselves in Texas 21: "Gooper, I got violent in this
room a while back and I struck hard at somebody with this crutch and I'm not
responsible if this, this, this!" (3: 33). "[He halts, stammering, with a seman-
tically incomplete utterance.]—I am—false! Broken.—Fell off the goddam
roof [Maggie's] still scrambling up . . . Truth is something desperate, and she's
got it!" (3: 34). Even his remark about possibly being "impotent," at the point

of capitulating to Maggie's scheme for putting the two of them once again into bed together (Texas 21/3: 35), seems to me to rest on the borderline of a pseudorationality inappropriate to his character. To many, Brick will seem falsely rationalistic when he stumbles into bed with Maggie while also loudly pronouncing his fears of "impotence" (Texas 21/3: 35). And besides, in some revised drafts, Brick voices supposed deep repentance but mostly by mere echoing of his father:

> Look, look. I don't want anything that I'm not fit for, and I'm fit for nothing, **nothing but rot and corruption**. A goddam **fool on the bottle** is not worth subsidizing, as Big Daddy put it[;] I'm not worth endowing. False! Broken! **I dug my old friend's grave and kicked him in it!** A while ago I almost killed my wife for a crime that I had committed! **I hung up!** Said nothing, **I just hung up!** Hell, I'd been taught by all of your kind all my life that the thing to do is hang up when somebody makes a desperate call for something that *shocks*, or *disturbs you*, even! I want nothing! All I ask about whatever arrangement you come to is what you'll grow on **twenty-eight thousand acres of the richest land of the valley Nile,** what will grow on it, but a crop of lies? **Twenty-eight thousand acres** of lies and lies and more lies? That's all I—(Texas 26/3: 21; Big Daddy's act 2 words in bold)

When I read this particular manuscript speech at a gathering of scholars, Jon Rossini, of Texas Technological University, wondered whether Brick's sincerity would not actually seem to increase when he repeats as his own so many of Big Daddy's words from their powerful act 2 confrontation. The issue, of course, may be not so much our desire for Brick's sincerity as our wish for an aesthetically attractive array of speeches, not overly repetitive. Perhaps, to be sure, Williams did not intend Brick to be repeating Big Daddy's words. At times, after all, in the massive collection of *Cat on a Hot Tin Roof* drafts, Williams will assign a familiar speech from the play to a character who does not utter it in any version of *Cat* that we commonly know. In the example I have quoted here, though, he appears fairly clearly to announce that Brick is repeating verbal material that we have very recently heard Big Daddy relay to *him* (for Brick directly announces that he speaks "as Big Daddy put it"). And so it seems to me that to have Brick echo Big Daddy so much detracts from the play's aesthetic shimmer, while also making his speech sound potentially "canned" in its emotions.

Another, although somewhat opposite, way in which Williams dealt with Brick, in the course of revising his play's original drafts, was to portray him as a creature whose grace (of physique, and, supposedly, of spirit) caused him to inspire much love in others and simultaneously to inspire envy in some love-*deprived* creatures—like his plain-visaged, and very plain-spirited brother, Gooper, as well as his own wife, Maggie, who cannot ever forget her torment-filled childhood, with its emotional and monetary deprivation. An extensive passage, which I have dubbed Maggie's *envy disquisition*, appears in quite a few extant manuscripts of *Cat* (Texas 15 and 21, NYPL 2, Harvard 2) and includes the following declarations by Maggie:

> (*Taking center stage, panting with vehemence*)—Yes, [Gooper,] I did say envy, I said envy. You admitted!—You admitted as much when you said you'd always resented Big Daddy's partiality to Brick. That was truthful, understandable, excusable. I respected you for it;—you noticed I held my tongue, which is something I don't often hold? It isn't easy, it's far from bein' easy, to live in someone's shadow, a husband's, a brother's shadow, because he's blessed by nature with somethin' you have to *sweat* for, and still can't get. . . .
>
> It's love, it's bein' loved, Gooper! You've never been loved, Little Daddy. Don't you know that you have never been loved, in spite of all your—your lively behavior, your sociable, affable nature, you've just—never been loved, Little Daddy. But Brick had something about him, he had a light about him, a, a, a—natural grace!—about him that made him . . . loved, much loved, by many! many! I know. I lived in his shadow. (I was eclipsed by his beauty!) And I envied him, too. But now he's sick, he's wounded,—(winged by the huntress Diana!). So now, I beg you, don't vent your envy on Brick, try to contain your envy or—vent it on me, yes, vent your envy on me, I'm tough, *real* tough, I— (Texas 15—Subfolder 3: 2; second paragraph actually rewritten, somewhat less compactly, in Subfolder 3: 3)

Williams probably wrote this text not so much in order to prove Brick noble as to show Maggie expressing more emotional commitment to her husband than we might always have felt from her. Intriguingly, Williams thus makes Maggie seem *less* "tough" even as she claims for herself a particularly hidebound toughness. But the passage makes Brick sound more wimpish than ever would appear appropriate—more like Blanche's victimized homosexual poet-husband Allan, in *A Streetcar Named Desire*, than like the sexually ambiguous but still often boisterously rebellious Brick. Granted, even the final 1975 version of *Cat* retains some echo of this *envy disquisition*, for Maggie declares, in that inscribed text, that Gooper and his wife Mae are "venting

... malice and envy on [Brick,] a sick boy" (*Cat* 1975: 157). She seems to be using medical terminology there, however, mostly as a rhetorical flourish.

One more means by which Williams made Brick seem to respond to Big Daddy was to have Brick, during Big Daddy's act 3 reappearance, speak to, and physically touch, his father with affection. Some of the mildly affectionate speeches are still in the 1975 ultimate script, where the two men interchange some comments about Big Daddy's ribald elephant joke and then (with even more unity of spirit) castigate the "obnoxious odor" of "mendacity" that permeates the room (*Cat* 1975: 164–66). The physical touches, however, manifest themselves only in earlier texts—such as Harvard 1 (2: 44), where Brick's head, for example, "drops" to Big Daddy's shoulder in act 2, just after he has blurted out the truth about Big Daddy's cancer; or in Harvard 2 (3: 30), where the stage directions record, first, that "Brick moves across room on crutch, sits beside Big Daddy on table and rests one hand lightly on his father's shoulder. The OLD MAN does not glance at him: blinks just once: his wry smile increases." Similarly, on the same page, we read, "He chuckles. BRICK chuckles with him, staring steadily at his father's profile with a soft, vague smile of affection." Besides, in the New York Public Library's manuscript called NYPL 2, Brick expresses affection with his hand on his father's shoulder and then "laughs hugely" at the elephant story (3: 29–30). The manuscript called NYPL 4, which became the basis for the 1975 published version of *Cat*, by contrast has Big Daddy remark, "You didn't laugh at that story, Brick" (3: 25). Brian Parker, the scholar who has done the most extensive work of cataloging the various *Cat on a Hot Tin Roof* drafts, proclaims as uncharacteristically "sycophantic" Brick's occasionally recorded jovialities and shoulder slappings with Big Daddy during the elephant joke episode (Parker 487–88). I do not believe that Brick's motivation needs to be read as sycophantic. But I do think that Williams probably eventually realized that the physical touching was something that Big Daddy and Brick would never have practiced very regularly, so that it would be an unlikely sudden addition to their interpersonal repertoire of behavior, even at this crucial juncture in their lives. Williams must also have eventually judged that Brick would not laugh at the elephant joke, even if he believed it perfectly legitimate for Big Daddy to tell it, since its subject is an elephant with a noticeable erection, and Brick fears, or already frequently experiences, impotence.

It is obvious that Kazan's agenda for revising *Cat* in a certain way did affect Williams greatly as he treated Brick's character in successive drafts. Few of the revisions that Williams tried out, concerning Brick, look like much more than means for making Brick's personality even more dominant than it already was in the play (and in fashions that were more than somewhat confusing to the stage action, since the would-be revisions were guided by the goal of appeasing Kazan's somewhat overly schematic attitude toward character development).

On the other hand, Big Mama is the character who may have been most valuably aided by Kazan's suggestions to Williams. Kazan inked the following notations onto a historically early manuscript now at Harvard: "[Big Mama is] terribly touching here. She's still completely and helplessly adoring of BIG DADDY and still wants him badly" (1: 17); "Couldn't we *see* a bit of Big Mama's 'TAKING OVER'[?]" (2: 9; emphasis mine).

It thus seems fitting that the one episode that proves both the ardor of Big Mama's love for her mate and her personal acumen for tough-minded businesswomanlike dealings is the scene where Big Mama refuses to let Gooper talk any further about the "Basis! Plan! Preliminary! Design!" that he has created for dividing the Pollitt estate (*Cat* 1955: 147; *Cat* 1975: 159–60). By shouting a Big Daddy-like "CRAP!" to such sneaky business shenanigans (1955: 147; 1975 160), Big Mama appears to prove her likely ability to run all the business affairs of the plantation. She may also thus prove that, if she did seem to take over that activity, during the years when Big Daddy first became dreadfully sick with cancer, she most likely did so rather fully out of love and not out of any strong desire for power. But her scene of blunt retort to Gooper is not in the Harvard 4 manuscript, the textualization of her story that Kazan probably first read, nor does it appear in the equally early Texas 10. It has, however, found its way into the script by the time of Texas 15 (Subfolder 3: 5). This is surely one of the most beneficial additions ever made to the play.

Kazan also had commented, on the Harvard 4 manuscript leaves (1: 19), that Big Mama "always laughs like hell at herself." It seems no wonder that she does so, in terms of one of the play's most idealistic constellations of themes—for she provides a "funny" (both quirky and smile-producing) answer to Big Daddy's question (already in the early text of Texas 10: 61 and still in *Cat* 1975: 80) "Wouldn't it be funny if [love] was true[?]." He asks this as Big Mama protests that she really did love him during all their years together, especially perhaps during the period when his disease—as he naturally, even according to himself, "let things go" (Texas 10: 74)—led him to deep insecurities, and indeed to a near-paranoia, about her supposed seizing of total control.

Cat does not finally assert that love is always enduring, or beneficent, or perfectly sound. Brick's and Maggie's marital troubles will not very likely end in a "happily ever after" following the play's final curtain. And even Big Mama's love has some dangerous tendencies to codependent support of a very difficult man, one who is at least verbally abusive to those who care for him. Still, Big Mama's love at least looks to be rather firmly "true" and to deserve the beautiful culminating expression it receives in a speech that Williams vividly revised from an earlier and more prosaic specimen of the statements:

> Oh, time goes by so fast, it goes so fast you don't know where it's gone to. . . . We all got to love each other, we all got to love and stay close as we can to each other. . . . Specially now that death has moved[—]into this place! (Texas 10: 131; Harvard 2/3: 22 [with bracketed dash]; Delaware 1)
>
> Time goes by so fast. Nothin' can outrun it. Death commences too early—almost before you're half-acquainted with life—you meet the other. . . . Oh, you know we just got to love each other, an' stay together[,] all of us, just as close as we can, [e]specially now that such a *black* thing has come and moved into this place without invitation. (1955: 148–49; 1975 161–62 [with bracketing])

I have admired both this speech's expression and its sentiments for many years. Nonetheless, the speech, and the entire role of Big Mama, may carry (as a binary opposition?) incipient hints of a characterization focused more upon cloying sentimentalism than upon stalwart love. And it is noticeable that Amanda Wingfield, in Williams's *The Glass Menagerie*, whose stalwart love can easily become obfuscated by her cloying sentiments, does sigh, and berate her son Tom, with the words "We have to do all that we can to build ourselves up. In these trying times we live in, all that we have to cling to is—each other" (Williams, *The Glass Menagerie* 171). On the other hand (perhaps because of actresses who have so convincingly enacted the vigor of Big Mama's personality), I share what was evidently long ago Elia Kazan's primal instinct: enthusiasm for her character.

She is not, however, the only character who makes the Texas 15 manuscript intriguing. Williams, in this folder, appears to have been testing methods by which to satisfy Kazan's demands that Big Daddy reappear onstage in act 3, rather than vanishing completely after his act 2 dominance. I am not certain that some of these draftings are not intentionally excessive so as to mock Kazan's entire push for textual changes. The revisionary sketches involved are, all the same, highly striking to encounter.

In Texas 15, first of all, Williams does try out Big Daddy's return to recount the risqué elephant tale. He tests that option here much as, in Texas 29 (3: 24), he will later examine the viability of having the old man come back on in order to harrumph, along with Brick, about the "obnoxious odor" produced by "mendacity" in Gooper's would-be manipulation of the family's future fortunes. Both the elephant joke and the condemnation of an "obnoxious odor" are finally combined in the 1975 edition of the ultimately revised play (163–66).

But the Texas 15 materials also include a fascinating, albeit also grotesquely overwrought, scene in which Big Daddy, actually starting at the very end of act 2 but continuing into act 3,

> removes a hunting rifle or shot-gun from a glass case or cabinet in the room, loads it, and instead of going out the hall door, goes out upon the gallery. At this point the curtain rises for the first time to the full height of the proscenium, exposing the roof of the house and the belvedere, a white-fenced square at the center of the roof, open to the night sky, dappled by leaf-shadows from trees as tall as the house. Big Daddy mounts a flight of stairs from the gallery to the roof, the back wall of the set becoming transparent at this point to show his ascension. He speaks the last line of the act on the belvedere, the moon on his face. . . .
>
> ACT THREE
>
> Curtain remains all the way up. In his seat on the belvedere Big Daddy remains dimly visible throughout Act Three, but light and shadow, alternating with clouds' passage under the moon, sweep his lonely figure up there like spasmodic waves of pain in his body. When the spasm grips his bowels, he rises from the wood bench and his hands clench fiercely on the white balustrade of the belvedere and through his clenched teeth, each time, he says to himself and the sky: "A pig squeals: a man keeps a tight mouth about it."—This seems to be the last thing left in his heart, the ultimate dictum by which he has chosen to die, and it serves him well, for even though he bites his lips till they bleed, he never cries out in his anguish. He is not yet dying up there, but "the pain has struck" and he suffers "without the needle." He's probably suffered before, but never before with the certain knowledge of doom, which is going to be unmercifully slow, in the belvedere or below. Did he take the gun up to kill himself or to defend his position away from, above, all liars? He probably doesn't know which: it doesn't matter. There's nothing in him but rage and hate and pride to the end of the play. (Subfolder 5: 3)

Williams, evidently immediately upon writing some of this material, balks at it enough to call it "a bit corny" (Subfolder 5: 3). He, indeed, also crosses out a huge portion of drafted paragraphing, in which, among other draft ideas, he had included Big Daddy's addressing of the moon, first, with the "mocking" comment of "Hello, moon!" but "then, the grin turning fiercer, add[ing] . . . 'You filthy bitch!'—distorting his face up at it like a grey stone gargoyle" (Subfolder 5: 3). Here he also plucks a magnolia blossom—playing the guessing game, with a gradual depletion of plucked blossoms, "God loves me!—he loves me not." Finally, and surprisingly or even shockingly, he asks, "Who loved me? Big Mama and Peter Ochello!—Ha ha ha ha ha ha!—Big Mama and—Peter—Ochello, that ole-bitch . . . dead now! Hunh!—Sup with him in Hell or—Heaven. . . . (Wherever good old aunties go!) Brick? No. Brick loves his liquor!—Oh, well. Big Daddy has 28,000 acres of the richest land this side of the Valley Nile! What's anyone's love?" (Subfolder 5: 3).

These virulently cynical lines Williams did, I repeat, excise from even the draft copy. He did not, by contrast, censor the following passage, quite opposite in content and tone to any obsessive concern with 28,000 acres of real estate reminiscent of the Nile Valley: "[He behaves n]ot always mockingly, sometimes with a lingering pride of possession, but sometimes as if he would like to seize it between his two clenched hands and crush it like a rotten pulp between them, as if he identified this prodigious growth of property with the malignancy in his flesh" (Subfolder 5: 4).

I find it keenly relevant that Williams would seem to be validating this passage, in which Big Daddy appears to equate materialism with disease, but that he would simultaneously use his editing pencil to repudiate a segment of words wherein Big Daddy deemed materialism to be the sum total of life. For as much as Williams finds the materialistic, and particularly the sexual, part of life to be undeniable, I think he may still find spirit more ultimately intriguing.

To be sure, this assertion does not deny that, for example, more places exist in the *Cat* script where Williams subtly tantalizes us with hints about Big Daddy's ambiguous materialism of the body. More than once, certainly, he implies that Big Daddy had been loved—somehow, ambiguously—by Peter Ochello (the homosexual former landowner of what is now Big Daddy Pollitt's plantation). In the Texas 10 version of the early *Cat* manuscript "A Place of Stone," Maggie (30) speculates that Big Daddy "must have had [Brick's] looks" in order ever to gain a job with Ochello and his lover and plantation partner Jack Straw. Recent examiners of *Cat*, like John Clum (170–71), have been willing to read some possible actual confession of homosexual activity into Big Daddy's admission that he had "knocked around," "bummed this country," "slept in hobo jungles and railroad Y's and flophouses in all cities" (*Cat* 1955: 85–86; *Cat* 1975: 117). There is also Williams's cannily ambiguous use of the word "coupled," in the following familiar stage directions from both published editions of *Cat*: "[Big Mama reviews the history of her forty-five years with Big Daddy, her great, almost embarrassingly true-hearted and simple-minded devotion to Big Daddy, who must have had something Brick has, who made himself loved so much by the 'simple expedient' of not loving enough to disturb his charming detachment, also once *coupled*, like Brick, with virile beauty.]" (*Cat* 1955: 103; *Cat* 1975: 144; emphasis mine).

All this textual data, implying sexual ambiguity on Big Daddy's part, was most likely material about which Williams deliberated in multivalent ways. I suspect that he probably did wish to encode a subtext, for Big Daddy as much as for Brick, that would make his two main male characters' sexual preferences somewhat uncertain. But he also encoded, in the portraits of both men (and of their female mates, too—even the money-desperate Maggie) subtexts that repulse the notion that any kind of materialism, including sex, is ultimately the most important human value.

According to a passage that has remained constant in Brick's act 2 discussion with Big Daddy, Brick paradoxically seems to find every college football player filled with "disgust and confusion"; he makes this judgment even though he proclaims himself "[un]fit for" such "contests" any longer (Texas 10: 102). In the very early Texas 10 manuscript (10: 102—as also in Delaware 1/2: 44), Brick goes on to discuss how he had taken private showers, in a separate cubicle away from his university football team, in order to wash off [his] naked body all the sweat and disgust and confusion,'" "all contact and all disgust that comes from contact." These latter references would suggest his potential questioning of his sexual preferences, and yet he surely is not meanwhile judging every football player in the world to be a bisexual. Instead, he seems to imply principally that American competitive life causes people to lose their spiritual bearings among daily competitive "mendacity," which he elsewhere, probably in every textual variant of *Cat*, condemns as a source of "disgust" (*Cat* 1955: 79; *Cat* 1975: 108).

Big Daddy, like Brick, is disgusted, definitely, with a lie-crowded world. Numerous worldlings, like Gooper and Mae, seem to dedicate themselves to trafficking in lies, and they thus produce a Dionysian tragic "stawm," one that particularly weathers the Pollitt plantation during act 3 (1955: 149–50; 1975: 163). Yet a hyperventilating Dionysian colossus of a Big Daddy, bulked against the panorama of his plantation while threatening all around with a rifle, was not, I think, what this play most needed. It needed, instead, the antithesis to such bluster that was already also present in the play: the Big Daddy who had tenuously learned, in act 2 with Brick, that "being friends is telling each other the truth" (1955: 94; 1975: 130). Two often-alienated kinfolk there realized that it would be best, if not necessarily funny, for love to *tell* true.

Therefore, Williams may principally have created Big Daddy's rage on the belvedere scene so as to *defy* Kazan—very cagily defying him, by creating a too much "towering" Dionysian character, one who would not fit any more comfortably into a full plot and ensemble cast than does The Father in Pirandello's *Six Characters*. Such a character, at least (in the alternate Big Daddy reappearance scene that Williams was preparing at the same time), might tell an off-color elephant joke and thus, by displeasing the censors, perhaps destroy Kazan's plans for featuring Big Daddy in act 3 at all.

But Williams, it appears, kept musing (over a long, long period) on this drama. Hence he eventually revised *Cat* as much as Pirandello revised *Six Characters*—with a keen "artistic instinct," one that protected the play against the "molestation" of inappropriate transformations (Moestrup 185). The elephant joke (along with audience attitudes toward ribaldry) evolved, so that the joke became more workable in the script. Eventually, Big Daddy's dramatized character no longer exposed what Pirandello labeled as his inner, tormented, chaotic psychological "face"; instead, his act 3 reappearances represented him behind the guise of what Pirandello deemed a sly social "mask," one that could successfully dupe even the daily-dominoed Gooper and Mae (Oliver 12). The old Mississippi patriarch, indeed, came skillfully to copractice metatheatrical role-playing along with Maggie, supporting her beneficent lie about being pregnant and thus perhaps vanquishing the ugly nonbeneficent lies of Mae's and Gooper's greed (1955: 153; 1975 167–68).

Meanwhile Brick, especially by the time of *Cat*'s 1975 final revision, has returned to being a figure who dwells primarily in the Pirandellian realm of inner psychological "face" rather than negotiating busy social interactions as a rationalistically masked man. Oddly enough, Brick's characterizations did not work any better in the play ensemble when he wore gregarious but false social masks, for Kazan's sake, than Big Daddy's characterization worked, with full effectiveness, as he fulminated with fustian from his rooftop belvedere. Hence (even though he was not writing about *Cat on a Hot Tin Roof*) the critic Jorn Moestrup may well be correct in surmising that there exists some wondrous (albeit highly arcane) "artistic instinct" that can, luckily, free an oppressed art work from assaultingly wrong-headed strategies of modification.

Perhaps it is aesthetically appropriate, then, that in the belvedere scene draft filed with the manuscript called Texas 15, Williams combined Big Daddy's tortuous spasms of pain with Brick's and Maggie's bedroom fadeout by "the rose-silk lamp" (Texas 15—Subfolder 5: 4). He declared, in addition, that "the play says only one [fully] affirmative thing about 'man's fate': that he has it, still in his power, not to squeal like a pig but to keep a tight mouth about it" (Texas 15—Subfolder 5: 4). On the same page, nonetheless, Williams judged love . . . *possible*; not proven or disproven, but *possible*."

Works Cited

Brustein, Robert. "Pirandello's Drama of Revolt." In *Pirandello: A Collection of Critical Essays*, edited by Glauco Cambon. Englewood Cliffs, N.J.: Prentice-Hall, 1967.

Clum, John. "*Something Cloudy, Something Clear*: Homophobic Discourse in Tennessee Williams." *South Atlantic Quarterly* 88.1 (Winter 1989): 161–79.

Della Terza, Dante. "On Pirandello's Humorism." In *Modern Critical Views: Luigi Pirandello*, edited by Harold Bloom. New York: Chelsea House, 1989.

Hinden, Michael. "The Five Voices of *The Birth of Tragedy*." *Comparative Drama* 22.2 (Summer 1988): 97–113.

Moestrup, Jorn. *The Structural Pattern of Pirandello's Work*. Odense: University of Odense Press, 1972.

Murphy, Brenda. *Tennessee Williams and Elia Kazan: A Collaboration in the Theatre*. Cambridge: Cambridge University Press, 1992.

Oliver, Roger W. *Dreams of Passion: The Theatre of Luigi Pirandello*. New York: New York University Press, 1979.

Parker, Brian. "A Preliminary Stemma for Drafts and Revisions of Tennessee Williams's *Cat on a Hot Tin Roof*." *Publications of the Bibliographical Society of America* 90.4 (December 1996): 475–96. (Parker provided the labeling numbers that I am including for all the *Cat* manuscripts; I have added the label Harvard 4 for a manuscript evidently acquired after he visited that Boston site. These Parker/Loomis numbers are not, however, used at any of the research collections; the additional catalog data I here provide will help collection users find specific drafts.)

Pirandello, Luigi. *Six Characters in Search of an Author*. [*Sei personnagi in cerca d'autore*]. 1922. Translated by Edward Storer. Mineola, N.Y.: Dover, 1998.

Williams, Tennessee. *Cat on a Hot Tin Roof*. New York: Signet/New American Library, 1955.

———. *Cat on a Hot Tin Roof*. New York: New Directions, 1975.

———. (Columbia 1) Manuscript Collection Tennessee Williams/23 pp. of rewrites (dated December 9, 1954), probably typed by TW. Tennessee Williams Papers, Rare Book and Manuscript Library, Columbia University, New York City.

———. (Delaware 1) Manuscript 115, Tennessee Williams/Box 1, F9/*Cat on a Hot Tin Roof*; or, *A Place of Stone* (a play) n.d./typescript, 118 pp./bound in blue folder. Special Collections, University Library, University of Delaware, Newark, Delaware.

———. (Harvard 1) Manuscript 91.3/*Cat on a Hot Tin Roof*/manuscript (mimeographed) (New York and Key West 1955). Harvard Theatre Collection, Pusey Library, Harvard University, Cambridge, Massachusetts. (Copy 21 of the playing script revised by the author/lacks act 3.)

———. (Harvard 2) Manuscript 91.1/*Cat on a Hot Tin Roof*/typescript unsigned/(Key West 1955)/additions and revisions by Tennessee Williams. Harvard Theatre Collection, Pusey Library, Harvard University, Cambridge, Massachusetts.

———. (Harvard 4) *Cat on a Hot Tin Roof*. 152 leaves/typescript (carbon) with cuts and annotations throughout, in pencil by T. Williams and in green ink by "EK" (Elia Kazan) and some typescript. Harvard Theatre Collection, Pusey Library, Harvard University, Cambridge, Massachusetts. (I myself have assigned the manuscript number and have declared the green ink markings Kazan's [on the basis that green inkings by Kazan also appear in Texas 10 and because the initials "EK" actually appear in marginal notations within Harvard 4]. There exists another Harvard manuscript of *Cat* that Parker names Harvard 3, so that Harvard 4 seems a natural numbering for the additional manuscript.)

————. (NYPL 2) NCOF+/93–7995/*Cat on a Hot Tin Roof*/121 pp., mimeograph on bond by Hart Stenographic Bureau/gift of Roger Stevens/1955? Billy Rose Theatre Collection, New York Public Library, New York City.

————. (NYPL 4) NCOF/93–7796/119 leaves mimeographed by Studio Duplicating Service, Inc./title page has "property of: American Shakespeare Theatre, Stamford, Connecticut"/ANTA Theatre, New York, 1975? Billy Rose Theatre Collection, New York Public Library, New York City.

————. (Texas 1) Manuscript (Williams, Tennessee) Works/"Three Players of a Summer Game"/Typed ms./drafts/incomplete with autograph revisions and autograph note [78 pp.]/1951 (Venice). Harry Ransom Humanities Research Center, University of Texas, Austin.

————. (Texas 4) Manuscript file (Williams, Tennessee) Works/"Three players of a summer game" (short story)/Typed carbon copy manuscript (33 pp.) with typed insert [9 pp.] and autograph emendations on 10 pp./1952 April/insert dated May 9, 1952, by Audrey Wood. Harry Ransom Humanities Research Center, University of Texas, Austin.

————. (Texas 10) Manuscript file (Williams, Tennessee) Works/*"A Cat on a [Hot] Tin Roof"; or, "A Place of Stone."* Typed ms./early version with heavy revisions, inscribed to Andreas Brown on back of "Characters" page. Harry Ransom Humanities Center, University of Texas, Austin.

————. (Texas 11) Manuscript file (Williams, Tennessee) (A play)/Typed carbon copy ms. [31 pp.]/inc. with autograph emendations on 2 pp. and autograph notes by Elia Kazan on 14 pp./n.d. Harry Ransom Humanities Center, University of Texas, Austin.

————. (Texas 15) Manuscript file (Williams, Tennessee) Works/*Cat on a [hot] tin roof*/ Composite typed ms./incomplete [33 pp.] with typed carbon copy inserts [13 pp.] and autograph emendations on 22 pp./n.d. Harry Ransom Humanities Center, University of Texas, Austin.

————. (Texas 21) Manuscript (Downing, R.)/Misc./Typed and autograph/*Cat on a Hot Tin Roof*/mimeograph/stage manager's script with typed inserts and autograph notes and revisions [169 pp.]/n.d./includes two versions of act 3. Harry Ransom Humanities Center, University of Texas, Austin.

————. (Texas 26) (the second, revised version of act 3 in Texas 21 above). Harry Ransom Humanities Center, University of Texas, Austin.

————. (Texas 29) Manuscript (Downing, R.)/Misc./Typed and autograph/*Cat on a Hot Tin Roof*/Typed ms./Stage manager's copy with T. inserts and A. notes [121 pp.]/ n.d./Bound in hard notebook cover. Harry Ransom Humanities Center, University of Texas, Austin.

————. "The Glass Menagerie." *The Theatre of Tennessee Williams.* Vol. 1. New York: New Directions, 1971.

BRUCE MCCONACHIE

Cat *and the Grotesque in the Cold War*[1]

Tennessee Williams erected an ironic shrine to the comforts of narcis-
sistic consumerism in *Cat on a Hot Tin Roof* (1955). According to his stage
directions, the single setting for the play, a spacious bedroom in a plantation
mansion, features:

> a monumental monstrosity peculiar to our times, a *huge* console
> combination of radio-phonograph (hi-fi with three speakers),
> TV set and liquor cabinet, bearing and containing many glasses
> and bottles, all in one piece [...]. This piece of furniture (?!), this
> monument, is a very complete and compact little shrine to virtually
> all the comforts and illusions behind which we hide from such
> things as the characters in the play are faced with. ... (xiii–xiv)[2]

Cat exposes the "monstrosity" of Williams's characters' "comforts and illusions" but does not rid the stage of them. Like the console itself, the playwright's grotesque characters and situations refuse destruction or resolution;
their monstrosity endures (and even multiplies) to the end.

Williams deploys the rhetoric of the grotesque in *Cat on a Hot Tin Roof*.
As Mark Fearnow points out in his study of the theater of the 1930s, the
genre of the grotesque "fixes experience but does not convert it to meaning. A

From *The Tennessee Williams Literary Journal* 5, no. 1 (Spring 2003): 47–64. Copyright ©
2003 by *The Tennessee Williams Literary Journal*.

grotesque representation provides a degree of distance from a contradictory moment but does not resolve the contradiction" (9).[3] Audiences can enjoy grotesque plays in the theater because they take pleasure in the "naming" of a contradictory person or situation; their fascination with the grotesque object thus carries an electric charge of recognition, horror, and delight. Unlike more normative dramatic genres, grotesque plays provide the audience with no stable subject position from which to enjoy and judge dramatic action. Audiences alternately identify with and reject the major characters that are the carriers of the grotesque. Fearnow traces the whiplash effect of the grotesque in a variety of films and plays from the 1930s, including horror films and the movies of the Marx Brothers, *Tobacco Road*, and the tragi-comedies of Robert E. Sherwood. Tennessee Williams continued this residual dramatic tradition into the 1940s and '50s.

By 1955, Williams had explored a variety of grotesque characters and situations in several of his major plays. *The Glass Menagerie* (1945), for example, named the grotesquerie of Tom's guilt, keeping the memory scenes of the play at an ironic distance from the present through Tom's monologues, "magic-lantern slides," and the ambiguous characterizations of Amanda, Laura, and the Gentleman Caller. Although *Streetcar* (1947) was closer to melodrama, the open-ended quality of the concluding scene suggests that Williams wanted his audience to refrain from moral judgments and focus on the grotesque incoherence of Stanley's triumph, Blanches madness, and Stella's baby. In *The Rose Tattoo* (1951), the obsessions of its protagonist, Serafina, constantly threaten to push the action from sexual comedy into farcical grotesquerie. Critics have generally understood *Camino Real* (1953) as an allegory about the endurance of romantics confronted by the corrosions of time. But time, according to Williams himself, has always been a motive for the grotesque. "The influence of life's destroyer, time, must be somehow worked into the context of [a play]," said Williams in 1978. "Perhaps it is a certain foolery, a certain distortion toward the grotesque which will solve the problem" (*Live* 54). As in *Camino*, the weight of time distorts the actions of all the major characters in *Cat*.

Williams also understood the Broadway potential of the "Southern grotesque" and used it to advantage in *Cat*. By the logic of the Great White Way, Williams had suffered three flops in a row by 1953, with *Camino* damned or dismissed by nearly all of the critics who mattered. As Albert J. Devlin relates, Williams decided to give the Broadway audience what it wanted on the surface of *Cat*, but to plant some explosives under its facade that would destabilize and perhaps (for some spectators) even destroy normative cultural assumptions (97–104). Consequently, *Cat* has many of the trappings of a southern romance: the plantation house, dutiful darkies, minor characters trimmed to fit regional stereotypes, decadent wealth, an aging patriarch, encomiums to "the land," and, of course, frustrated sexuality. On initial inspection, *Cat* probably seemed to the Broadway audience of 1955 a combination of mint julip and "corn likker," brimming with equal portions of a sunny and a benighted South, of *Gone With The Wind* and *Tobacco Road*. Stylistically, too, Williams hewed closer to realism than he had since *Streetcar*. Flannery O'Connor notes that "anything that comes out of the South is going to be called grotesque by the Northern Reader [sic], unless it is grotesque, in which case it is going to be called realistic" (40). Knowing his prospective audience for *Cat*, Williams opted for realist grotesquerie.

Like O'Connor, Williams understood the regional prejudices of his Northern spectators and used them to trap his audience into questioning many of the primary assumptions of containment liberalism. In effect, Williams deploys realist grotesquerie in *Cat* to challenge the cultural imperialism of the North. When Williams introduced himself to his agent Audrey Wood in 1939, he called himself a wily "descendent of Indian-fighting Tennessee pioneers" (Devlin 100). Like Oscar Wilde in the midst of imperial London, Williams cajoles his spectators into embracing their prejudices and then explodes them. His primary weapon is southern orality, spoken by two of his most grotesque characters, Maggie and Big Daddy. As post-colonial scholar Helen Gilbert affirms in her "De-Scribing Orality: Performance and the Recuperation of Voice," "performative orality" has the potential to defamiliarize conventional language and to focus audience attention "on 'voice' itself as a site of contestation" (9). In *Cat*, grotesque personal narratives challenge fact-based language as the only mode of truth telling. The result is polyvocality—what Bakhtin termed *heteroglossia*—that disperses meaning, especially the kinds of univocal meanings prevalent during the 1950s. *Cat*'s emphasis on the grotesque relativity of truth undercuts the Platonic certainties of the Cold War.

The grotesque runs riot through *Cat*. Characters constantly compare each other to animals—Big Mama charges like a "rhino"; Big Daddy eats like a "horse", Mae and Gooper's children are either pigs, monkeys, or "no-neck monsters"; and Magpie, of course, is a cat. Like jackals and vultures watching a dying elephant, these animals feint and threaten each other in an attempt to bite off the biggest piece of Big Daddy's estate following his imminent death. As Big Daddy notes, a powerful odor of "mendacity" pervades the play and none of the major characters escapes its stench. Big Daddy's first-born and his wife, Gooper and Mae, may be the most mendacious, but Brick lies to Big Daddy about his colon cancer, Maggie lies about being pregnant with Brick's child, and Big Daddy lies to his family to support Maggie's lie. Even the final scene in the bedroom, when Maggie declares her love for Brick and determines to make the lie of her pregnancy come true, may also be mendacious. In short, the play adamantly refuses to allow spectators to make dramatic meaning out of its major theme; if all of the characters are mendacious and mendacity encompasses life itself, the term defines everything and nothing. The audience, implicitly mendacious as well, is allowed no stable ethical position from which to judge the mendacity of others.[4]

Williams's embrace of the grotesque is best seen in the pre-production scripts of *Cat* and in his reading version of the play, which contains two third acts, one preferred by Williams and the second, the "Broadway Version," taken directly from the stage manager's prompt book for Act III of the 1955 production. In a "Note of Explanation" added to the published play in 1955, Williams praised the collaborative efforts of director Elia Kazan, whose suggestions for script revisions had helped to shape the final texts of *Streetcar* and *Camino Real* as well as *Cat*. Williams also reported, however, that he and Kazan had differed substantially on revisions of *Cat*. In his "Explanation," he listed three major reservations Kazan had noted in a letter to him commenting on the first draft of *Cat*: 1) Big Daddy's disappearance from the play after Act II; 2) Brick's intransigence, even after his conversation with Big Daddy in Act II; and 3) Maggie's lack of sympathetic appeal to the audience. Williams stated that he had agreed with Kazan about Maggie and revised the script accordingly, but had resisted Kazan's first two suggestions: "I didn't want Big Daddy to reappear in Act Three and I felt that the moral paralysis of Brick was a root thing in his tragedy, and to show a dramatic progression would obscure the meaning of that tragedy in him . . ." (125). In the end, Williams compromised on the first two points as well: Big Daddy makes a brief appearance in Act III and Brick moves toward a reconciliation with his father and his wife in the Broadway version of the play. Apparently Williams felt that he needed Kazan—even though Kazan had presided over *Camino*'s "flop"—and Williams was willing to accede to Kazan's suggestions in order to get him to direct the production.

Whether Williams violated his artistic integrity by compromising with Kazan, whether Kazan was partly to blame for insisting on changes before he would agree to direct the play, or whether, as Brenda Murphy alleges, this mode of collaboration simply continued their past working relationship, it is clear that Williams's preferred version(s) of the script embraced a vision of theatrical grotesquerie that Kazan did not wholly share (97–130).[5] Kazan's suggested changes, if entirely carried out, would have moved the play into a melodramatic father-son conflict based on the revelation of a "guilty secret." As David Savran emphasizes, Williams, like Chekhov, resisted the dramatic conventions of liberal tragedy, in which a secret from the past dooms a bourgeois subject (e.g., Hedda Gabler, Willy Loman) to destruction. In the melodramatic version of this structure, the subject is threatened by the secret's revelation but finally triumphs over its devastating effects. Lillian Hellman, William Inge, Arthur Miller, and many other cold war playwrights relied on the structural devices of liberal tragedy (88–95).[6]

Evidently from Kazan's perspective, *Cat* shared enough affinities with the conventions of liberal tragedy and its melodramatic offspring to lead him to suggest revisions that pushed the play sharply in that direction. In his "Note of Explanation," Williams implied that Kazan urged the three changes to make the play more commercially acceptable, a charge Kazan denied later in his autobiography (543–44). While Kazan may indeed have believed his suggestions would improve the play artistically, they also had the effect of molding the play into the kind of melodrama that had been successful on Broadway. As in a dozen other dramas during the 1950s focused on a troubled boy, the revised *Cat* seen by Broadway audiences suggested that Brick was on his way to resolving his guilty secret about his past problems, settling his relationship with his father, reforming his addictions, and "proving" his heterosexuality with his wife. These changes led to what critic Eric Bentley, in his review of the production, termed the "uncoordinated double vision" of *Cat* (22). Although Williams, under Kazan's prodding, sanded down some of the grotesque edges of his characters and painted over the homosexual hues of Brick's past relationship with Skipper, the Broadway script did not alter the fundamentally grotesque situation of the Pollitts squabbling while Big Daddy dies. Kazan's direction, however, generally sought to impose stable meanings where Williams's script reveled in irony and contradictions. The result, as Bentley suggested, was a production that pulled the audience in two different directions—on the one hand, toward an open fascination with these modern grotesques and their cynical values and, on the other, toward a closed, melodramatic appreciation that patriarchy must survive regardless of the cost.[7]

The "uncoordinated double vision" of the production was apparent in the response of the opening night critics. Several reviewers reacted primarily to Williams's grotesquerie. "The play functions like a snake charmer," said William Hawkins. "It holds one's hypnotized and breathless attention, while it writhes and yowls and bares the souls of its participants with a shameless tongue" (342). "You are torn between fascination and revulsion, but you are held," stated John McClain (344). Richard Watts noted *Cat*'s "sadistic probing into lost souls, its neurotic brooding, its insight into decadence, its torrent of language, both lyric and lewd" (343). Like Hawkins and McClain, Watts was fascinated with the characters and situations but rarely moved to melodramatic pity. Watts confessed, however, that he had "great difficulty" believing in the final reconciliation between Maggie and Brick: "It seems

almost a happy conclusion, yet the final impression is one of doom" (343).
Watts could name the contradiction but did not attempt to resolve its inherent grotesquerie.

Other critics, led by Kazan and probably their own history of playgoing
to expect dramatic closure, were put off or frustrated by the apparent moral
relativity of the play. Robert Coleman complained of the play's "cynical finish"
(343) and John Chapman, who called *Cat* another of Williams's "perceptive
and sympathetic dramas of frustration," wrote: "When it was over I felt frustrated myself—felt that some heart or point or purpose was missing" (343).
Expecting to experience pity and compassion for an empty boy caught up
in a melodramatic situation, Coleman and Chapman did not know what to
do with the grotesque elements of the play that did not point toward clear
dramatic meaning. Brooks Atkinson's review, however, ignored the play's grotesquerie to focus on its revelation of "honesty." Classifying *Cat* as liberal
tragedy in the tradition of Ibsen and O'Neill, Atkinson wrote: "To say that
it is the drama of people who refuse to face the truth of life is to suggest a
whole school of problem dramatists" (344). The Broadway critics, then, were
divided in their understanding of the generic nature of *Cat*. While most gave
the production favorable notices, some experienced the show as theater of the
grotesque while others responded to it as liberal tragedy or melodrama.

Stylistically, Williams had conceived of *Cat* as a realist play, with a setting that looked like a bedroom and stage movement that approximated real
life. Kazan, on the other hand, worked with his designers and actors to give
the production mythic proportions. Kazan convinced Jo Mielziner to design
a bed-sitting room in a plantation mansion that featured a diamond-shaped
raked stage with only a few pieces of furniture on it and Greek columns
painted on a scrim background. The relative openness of the ground plan
allowed Kazan to arrange his performers in a series of formal poses. In his
review, Bentley suggested that Kazan's staging was an attempt to "conquer
that far outpost of the imagination which we call Grandeur":

> Just as there is less furniture and less scenery, so there is a
> less natural handling of actors, a more conscious concern with
> stagecraft, with pattern, with form. Attention is constantly called
> to the tableau, to what, in movies, is called the individual "frame."
> You feel that Burl Ives [cast as Big Daddy] has been *placed* center
> stage, not merely that he *is* there; in the absence of furniture, a
> man's body is furnishing the room. When the man lifts his crippled
> son off the floor, the position is held a long moment, as for a time-
> exposure. My wife nudges me at this point, and whispers, "Why, it's
> a Michelangelo." (emphasis in original) (22).

The grandeur of Kazan's (neo)classicism worked against the play's grotesqueries.

These tableaux vivants also smothered much of Williams's mocking irony. At the turning point of the play, for instance, when Maggie lies about her pregnancy to the assembled Pollitts, Williams crafted dialogue that parodied the biblical Annunciation of Christ: "I have an announcement to make," states Maggie. "A child is coming, sired by Brick and out of Maggie the *Cat*! I have Brick's child in my body, an' that's my birthday present to Big Daddy on his Birthday" (153). Rather than underlining the joke, Kazan had Burl Ives stand behind Maggie and press his hands into her belly as though he were passing the Life Force from his dying body into hers. In Kazan's handling of the scene, this was a mythic moment, with Ives in a flowing white robe, looking god-like in his majesty, and Barbara Bel Geddes as Maggie, the passive recipient of His power. Such "grandeur," however, ignored the absurdity of figuring Big Daddy as the Holy Ghost and Maggie as the Virgin Mary.

The moment, like the other formal tableaux of the production, also betrayed Kazan's itch to involve his spectators in conventional allegorizing. Williams's delight in grotesquerie was an outgrowth of his romantic orientation, hence generally incompatible with *allegoresis*, the attribution of allegorical meaning by readers or spectators. As Brenda Murphy relates, Kazan began to shift the general focus of the production from the Brick–Maggie storyline to the father-son relationship soon after he read Williams's pre-production script in 1954. On his copy, Kazan crossed out a quotation from Yeats that explained the initial title that Williams had given his play, *A Place of Stone*, and penned a note linking the play to the poetry of Dylan Thomas. Williams took up this suggestion and changed the epigraph in the printed play to Thomas's well known passage:

> And, you, my father, there on the sad height,
> Curse, bless, me now with your fierce tears, I pray.
> Do not go gentle into that good night.
> Rage, rage against the dying of the light. (iii)[8]

The raging, cursing, and finally the blessing by Big Daddy of his son would be the focus of Kazan's production. Of course romantic treatments of this theme are possible, but the passing of patriarchal authority from one generation to the next clearly evoked allegorical meanings for Kazan.

Several of the tableaux that Kazan arranged depicted the power of patriarchy. These pictures had wide cultural resonance, appearing in newspaper advertisements for the production and pictorial spreads in *Life* magazine as well as on stage (Clipping File). The picture of Maggie in a slip on her knees clutching at Brick's legs as he balances on a crutch and pats her head was widely reproduced. Visually, it suggests a dutiful, if frustrated, wife and a long-suffering but dominant husband, perhaps irritated by his wife's sexual demands. By emphasizing Maggie's sexual frustration and Brick's physical disability, the picture effectively avoids the problem of Brick's lack of attraction to his wife; their sex life, it appears, will be fine as soon as Brick gets off his crutches. Both the images of Big Daddy knocking the crutch out from under Brick's arm and sending him sprawling and of Big Daddy cradling Brick's head on his chest as he raised him from the floor suggested the power and perversity of the patriarch and the dependency of his son. Here was an Old Testament deity of unknowable wrath and enormous love; sons might curse or embrace such a father, but they must finally obey him. These images of physical strength deter any questions about Big Daddy's homosexual past. Maggie on her knees in front of the standing figure of Big Daddy and the image noted above of Big Daddy infusing Maggie with life clearly subordinate Maggie's interests to Big Daddy's desire to preserve the family name through a male grandson. These are archetypal images of women serving as counters in an economy of exchange controlled by men. Maggie's final purpose in the play is reduced to her biological ability to carry a Pollitt heir.

To turn *Cat* into a play about patriarchal power, Kazan needed actors who could embody the emblematic type as well as enact the psychological complexities of their characters. So eager was Kazan to fill the role of Big Daddy with an actor who looked the part as he had conceived it that the director took a chance with Burl Ives. When Williams objected that a folk singer in his first major acting role on stage might not be able to handle the challenges of the part, Kazan brushed aside the problem and insisted that Ives would be fine. His casting hunch paid off. Ives's power and presence impressed nearly all of the critics, William Hawkins, for example, calling him a "rock mountain" in the role (qtd in Watts 343). In the film version of *Cat*, which closely mirrored Kazan's and Ives's stage interpretation of Big Daddy, Ives sacrifices subtlety for massiveness of emotion and effect. With Ives in the role, Big Daddy became a mythic patriarch who could, without irony, lay just claim to "twenty-eight thousand acres of th' richest land this side of the valley Nile!" (65).

Kazan's decision to cast Barbara Bel Geddes as Maggie was also a gamble, but a strategic one on his part to contain the grotesquerie of the role. In his pre-production script, Williams had made Maggie a more desperate and calculating character, more "poor white trash" than Kazan had wanted. His casting of Bel Geddes, like his suggestion to Williams that Maggie be more sympathetic, was part of Kazan's general strategy to shift Maggie from a greedy and conniving woman to a wholesome mother-wife eager to help her husband regain his heterosexual desire. Before *Cat*, Bel Geddes had played naive ingénues, such as the girl too-sweet-to-be-seduced in *The Moon Is Blue* in 1951. (Soon after *Cat*, she would play motherly helpmates, like Jimmy Stewart's left-behind girl friend in *Vertigo*.) While subsequent Maggies, following Elizabeth Taylor in the film version, have often been known for their steamy sensuality, none of the Broadway reviews used language that came close to that description for Bel Geddes. Instead, she was "appealing and authoritative" (McClain 344); "vital, lovely, and frank" (Atkinson 344); her monologue in Act I of *Cat*, a "scene of devastating honesty" for one reviewer (Kerr 342) and "a luminous and appealing job" for another (Chapman 343). In Bel Geddes and Kazan's hands, Maggie had more purr than scratch.

The model for this Maggie in Kazan's mind was probably Laura Reynolds in *Tea and Sympathy*, which Kazan had recently finished directing before reading and commenting on the pre-production draft of *Cat*. In Robert Anderson's melodrama, a sexually frustrated young wife leaves her husband to seduce and comfort an Empty Boy confused about his sexual identity. Williams's initial ending of *Cat* unambiguously positioned Maggie "on top" in her relationship with Brick, an ironic reversal of her attempt to incite Brick's advances in Act I. Under Kazan's urgings, Williams played with different endings for the drama, finally settling on dialogue for the "Broadway Version" that essentially positioned Maggie as another Laura seeking to help another confused boy toward heterosexual manhood: "You weak, beautiful people who give up with such grace. What you need is someone to take hold of you—gently, with love, and hand your life back to you [...]. I can! I'm determined to do it—and nothing's more determined than a cat on a tin roof—is there? Is there, Baby?" (158). Bentley commented that the ending of the play carried "the outward form of that *Tea and Sympathy* scene without its content" (22).

Tea and Sympathy had raised the accusation of homosexuality but dodged its full cold-war implications. Because the boy in question is not homosexual after all, the play could treat the false accusation as if it were simply another McCarthyite witch hunt motivated by fear. Williams, fully aware of the homophobia of the dominant culture, crafted a play that explicitly endorsed the toleration of sexual deviance and implicitly suggested that sexual orientation cannot be contained by the hetero-homo binary. In his *Homosexuality in Cold War America*, Robert J. Corber effectively argues that Williams, like Gore Vidal and James Baldwin, "stressed the construction of gay male subjectivity across multiple axes of difference, thereby promoting a model of political solidarity that was rooted in a collective experience of oppression rather than membership in a particular community" (4). Instead of promoting a gay male consciousness in isolation from other oppressed groups, says Corber, Williams drew on the experience of radical groups in the 1930s to write plays and short stories that might appeal to others who crossed conventional lines of race, class, and gender. Consequently, Williams was "not interested in establishing that homosexuality constituted a fixed minority identity but looked forward to the end of 'the homosexual' as a category of individual" (4).

In retrospect, Williams's strategy of theatrical grotesquerie might have provided an acceptable rhetoric for some Broadway spectators to question their culture's construction of sexuality. An audience reacting, by turns, in horrified disgust and comic delight to Big Daddy's sexual voraciousness and Maggie's attempts to work off her frustrations might have viewed Brick's innocence about his sexual identity as simply one more problem of animality in the family barnyard. Critics complained that Williams had failed to clarify Brick's past relationship with Skipper, but in truth the Broadway script is just as straightforward about Skipper's attraction to Brick and Brick's horror in discovering it as it is about Maggie's failed attempt to seduce Skipper and Big Daddy's liaison with Jack Straw and Peter Ochello. The pre-production script, however, does provide more details about these matters than the dialogue spectators heard in the theatre in 1955. In it, Big Daddy speaks fondly of the sexual relationship between Jack Straw and Peter Ochello, the two lovers who owned the plantation before him and with whom he shared his own body to become their heir apparent. The early script also clarified the triangular relationship that evolved among Skipper, Brick, and Maggie after their marriage. Cut from the production was Maggie's long speech about how shut out she felt from the affection shared by the two boys, who continued to play football together after college. In the pre-production version, Brick is more withdrawn and volatile, suggesting that his despair over Skipper's suicide had as much to do with his loss of a potential lover as with his guilt over his own refusal to prevent Skipper's death. Significantly, however, the early script is no more forthright about pinning Brick to a single sexual orientation than the later one.

Nonetheless, by pushing the script toward liberal melodrama, Kazan invited the critics to probe the play for the originary moment in the "guilty secret"—possibly Brick and Skipper's lovemaking—from which the plot of the play, in the conventional structure of liberal tragedy, should unfold. Brick does reveal one "guilty secret" in the course of telling his story to Big Daddy: He hung up on Skipper after Skipper confessed his sexual attraction for him and this rejection led soon after to Skipper's death. Several critics, however, believed that Brick's confession hid other secrets yet to be told. Among the first-night reviewers, McClain, Chapman, and Kerr were puzzled—Kerr was even annoyed—that the production had not spelled out the entire truth about

Skipper and Brick. Kerr found in *Cat* a "tantalizing reluctance—beneath all the fire and, all the apparent candor—to let the play blurt out its promised secret" (342). In a follow-up Sunday editorial in the *Herald Tribune* entitled "A Secret is Half-Told in Fountains of Words," Kerr continued to pick at the play: "The boy who has lost a friend and abandoned a wife cannot say what private wounds and secret drives have crippled him." Finally for Kerr, the production evaded its responsibility to the audience: "Listening, we work at the play in an earnest effort to unlock its ultimate dramatic meaning, but the key has been mislaid or deliberately hidden" (n.p.). Building on the psychological truism for his time that essential truth might best be found in "private wounds and secret drives," Kerr simply asked the production to meet the expectations it had aroused. His complaint was the logical response to Kazan's decision to direct the play as though it were a liberal melodrama. Behind the evasions of Kerr's own rhetoric was a simple question: Is Brick now or has he ever been a homosexual? If so, this "hidden key" would unlock the play's apparent mysteries and evasions. Animated to expect an essentialist answer to the question of Brick's sexual orientation, Kerr pursued McCarthyite tactics in his dogged probing of the play for dramatic truth and meaning.

The "is he or isn't he" response to Brick's problems countered Williams's hope that *Cat* might promote a more fluid understanding of human sexuality. It also sunk Kazan's desire to lead the audience to answer the question in the negative when they witnessed Ben Gazzara in the role. During his short career as a Broadway actor, Gazzara had gained the most renown by 1955 as a bully in a play set in a military school. Certainly Kazan had other reasons for casting Gazzara, but the actor's rugged good looks and deep voice must have figured in his choice of the relative newcomer: Gazzara was the complete opposite of effeminate. Further, Kazan knew that "method" actors like Gazzara could project a confused sexual identity as a part of their general narcissism—a confusion Gazzara would deploy later the same year when he starred in *A Hatful of Rain*—without losing, and potentially even enhancing, audience sympathy for the actor-character. While only one of the opening night critics (Chapman 343) decided that Gazzara's Brick was a "queer," several others, like Kerr, questioned his sexual identity in either/or terms.

The chief exemplar in the play of masculine desire undefined by the homo-hetero binary, of course, is Brick's father, Big Daddy. As he tells Brick in the published version of the play, he "knocked around" (85) in his youth and, despite his disgust for Big Mama, dutifully laid her "regular as a piston" (80) during their long marriage. Even on his deathbed, he continues to have a "lech" (19) for Maggie and dreams of a young mistress that he could "hump" from "hell to breakfast" (72). Although Williams softened this language for Broadway, the production still made it clear that Big Daddy's homosexual attachments as a young man did not define or contain him; his lusts were gargantuan enough to override all conventional categories of sexual positionings and couplings. David Savran notes that Williams probably intended Big Daddy's bowel cancer to represent the devastating results of his early sodomy. This may be so, but it is not clear that many in the audience would have made this connection between homosexuality and disease. Further, the play generally presents Big Daddy's death not as the preventable result of some past sin, but as the inevitable fall of a giant; mortality is simply a part of *Cat*'s grotesque world. Big Daddy's bowel cancer adds a note of absurdity to his imminent death, but it does not undercut the play's commitment to tolerance. If Big Daddy cannot be classified as a homosexual, the play suggests, neither can Brick.

Rather than incite the audience to pigeon-hole Brick's sexual orientation, *Cat* wants them to examine the effects of his homophobia. Brick's need to cling to a rigid binary between homo and heterosexuality—his desire to elevate his relationship with Skipper to a "pure an' true thing" (90) above sexual desire— has deformed him. Brick's disgust with Skipper and himself has led him to compulsive alcoholism and self-mutilation; his broken leg and broken soul are the result. The Empty Boy of *Cat*, Brick has all the innocence, grit, vulnerability, and physical strength of his postwar type, but these qualities, rather than evoking the spectator's guarded hope for Brick's eventual enrollment into heterosexual manhood and patriarchal prosperity, arouse the audience's suspicion that Brick may never be fit to assume the place his father and wife initially expect him to fill. If the Empty Boy remains a compulsive, wounded narcissist, the play asks, who will take his place in the patriarchal order? As grotesque realism, *Cat* does not need to answer this question forthrightly; Williams's refusal to resolve the problem, in effect, throws it back into the audience's face.

Sexual innocence in most plays about American boys was typically an endearing quality. For the comedy in *The Seven Year Itch* to work, for example, the American Adam must be less experienced and less eager than the Girl. Williams, on the other hand, shows the corrosive results of perpetuating an innocence that verged on willful ignorance about male sexual orientation. The culture of liberal containment turned its back on the 1949 Kinsey Report to demonize homosexuality as a threat to cold war national unity. *Cat* demonstrates that Brick's ignorance and rigidity not only affect him, they also paralyze major institutions of American society—marriage, the family, and the mechanisms of patrilineal inheritance. As occurs in many of Williams's dramas, the characters are stuck in stasis while time, the destroyer, marches on, forcing the characters into ever more absurd contortions. Arthur Miller famously critiqued *Cat* for Brick's indecisiveness on social issues (189–93). Like all grotesque plays, *Cat* is finally, formally indecisive, but along the way it also demonstrates the perverse results of "ignorance effects" about sexual orientation (Sedgwick 8).[9]

Despite Kazan's desire to kneed the play into liberal melodrama, the yeast of Williams's grotesquerie caused it to rise into odd shapes in performance. Early in his thinking about *Cat*, Kazan decided to stage the play more presentationally than Williams had written it. In Mielziner's slightly raked setting, a corner of the bedroom floor jutted beyond the proscenium arch and into the auditorium. Kazan wanted Burl Ives as Big Daddy to be able to walk downstage, ignore the other characters, and address the audience directly during several of his long speeches in Act II. Kazan probably expected that this staging would increase spectators' sympathetic response to Big Daddy and to his point of view; he may also have wanted the folk singer to be able to tell stories in a mode that was comfortable for him. Kazan gave Barbara Bel Geddes several opportunities for presentational storytelling during her long speeches in Act I as well. One result of such staging was to pull the audience out of its immediate involvement in the plot and characters of the play and encourage them to enjoy the immediacy of a good story well told. Ironically for Kazan, his presentational staging probably made the "liberal tragedy" of Brick's dilemma less interesting to the audience by decentering and dispersing the energies of the drama even as it heightened their enjoyment of Bel Geddes's and Ives's tales of Southern grotesquerie.

Nearly a third of Williams's dialogue in Acts I and II is taken up with storytelling. Like in Chekhov, Williams's favorite playwright, the major characters in *Cat* need to narrate events about their past to come to terms with a present that is frustratingly, absurdly static; their tales, in other words, are realistically motivated. Maggie's stories include her narration of Mae and Gooper and the no-necks at dinner, the tobacco juice tale about an embarrassing incident for a cotton carnival queen, Sonny Boy Maxwell "burning holes" (38) in Maggie's clothes with his eyes, several stories focused on the poverty of her youth, and Maggie's versions of what happened with Skipper. Big Daddy relates tales about his own past with Straw and Ochello, his trip with Big Mama to Europe and Africa, and his battles with mendacity. Their storytelling, especially Big Daddy's, finally leads Brick to tell his version of what really happened in his final telephone conversation with Skipper.

Preceding Brick's confession that his refusal to help Skipper led to his suicide, then, are many other stories that shape audience expectations about the kinds of truth that storytelling can reveal. In effect, Williams used the oral tradition to undercut the hegemony of literate speaking; he destabilized the kind of enunciation that legitimates the credibility of a revealed secret in the performance of a play. According to the linguistics of Émile Benveniste, there are two possible modes of utterance on stage, as in all social situations: *histoire* and *discours*.[10] The mode of *histoire* implicitly claims transparency and objectivity; this kind of utterance underwrites the reliability of most statements about the past in well-made plays. In contrast, *discours* is subjective and specific to place and time; listeners can never be sure if its truth claims transcend the immediacy of the speaking situation. Although modern plays usually deploy a mix of both modes, playwrights are generally careful to mark some speech as *histoire* during moments of exposition, reversal, and revelation. In *Cat*, however, Williams anticipated Harold Pinter and other late modernists by refusing to provide reliable information about the past of his characters. Consequently, even Brick's tortured revelation about Skipper's sexual orientation and his own refusal to provide help cannot be understood by spectators as stable knowledge, uninflected by the subjectivity of Brick's memory. Most realist plays encourage spectators to believe that they can attain an objective, dispassionate understanding of the action. Williams's reliance on *discours* and his undercutting of *histoire* during *Cat*, however, reposition the audience as subjective interlopers with incomplete information, a positioning that heightens the grotesquerie of the play. The dominance of personal narrative and the impossibility of objective knowledge in *Cat* finally call into question the reliability of hegemonic forms of cold-war information.

Maggie's story about the cotton queen and the tobacco juice typifies Williams's use of *discours* in Act I of *Cat*:

> Why, year before last when Susan McPheeters was singled out to' that honor, y'know what happened to her? Y'know what happened to poor little Susie McPheeters?
>
> BRICK (*Absently*). No. What happened to little Susie McPheeters?
>
> MARGARET. Somebody spit tobacco juice in her face.
>
> BRICK (*Dreamily*). Somebody spit tobacco juice in her face?
>
> MARGARET. That's right, some old drunk leaned out of a window in the Hotel Gayoso and yelled, "Hey, Queen, hey, hey there Queenie!" Poor little Susie looked up and flashed him a radiant smile and he shot out a squirt of tobacco juice right in poor Susie's face.
>
> BRICK. Well, what d'you know about that?
>
> MARGARET (*Gaily*). What do I know about it? I was there, I saw it.
>
> BRICK (*Absently*). Must have been kind of funny.
>
> MARGARET. Susie didn't think so. Had hysterics. Screamed like a banshee. They had to stop th' parade an' remove her from her throne. [. . .] (21–22)

To tell her tale effectively, Williams gives Maggie many of the stylistic devices of "personal narrative"—complex rhythms, tonal patternings, alliteration, and repetition (Bauman; Finnegan; Langellier; Ong). These devices mark her storytelling as *discours* rather than *histoire*. While most spectators will probably believe that something like this event really did happen to Susie McPheeters, they will also understand that Maggie has stretched and altered the story to make it more entertaining. Moreover, they will realize that the point of the tale has to do with the ongoing relationship between Brick and Maggie, not with the weight of a real past incident on present circumstances.

Likewise, Williams gives Big Daddy several stories in the mode of *discours* that also point toward present and future relationships rather than the formative influence of an objective past bearing down on a tenuous present. In the middle of his story about a trip abroad with Big Mama, Big Daddy recalls a specific incident in Morocco:

> But listen to this. She [i.e., an Arab woman] had a naked child with her, a little naked girl with her, barely able to toddle, and after a while she set this child on the ground and give her a push and whispered something to her.
>
> This child come toward me, barely able t' walk, come toddling up to me and—Jesus, it makes you sick t' remember a thing like this! It stuck out *its* hand and tried to unbutton my trousers!
>
> That child was not yet five! Can you believe me? Or do you think that I am making this up? I wint back to the hotel and said to Big Mama, Git packed! We're clearing out of this country. . . .
>
> BRICK. Big Daddy, you're on a talkin' jag tonight.
>
> BIG DADDY (*Ignoring this remark*). Yes, sir, that's how it is, the human animal is a beast that dies but the fact that he's dying don't give him pity for others, no, sir. [. . .] (66).

Given Burl Ives-Big Daddy's massive presence on stage, plus his often orotund and didactic language, his stories probably carried more authority than Maggie's. Audiences confronted with "Do you think I'm makin' this up?" likely credited the general truthfulness of Big Daddy's statements about this past event. Nonetheless, they also realized that the present rhetorical situation—a father trying to rescue his son from paralyzing guilt about an unusual sexual encounter—probably influenced Big Daddy's memory. His utterances, whether in storytelling or earnest conversation, were centered more often in the mode of *discours* than *histoire*.

Further, as with Maggie's tales about her poor childhood, the audience listening to Big Daddy came to understand the transformative potential of personal narrative. By telling tales about his past poverty and relations with Straw and Ochello, Burl Ives-Big Daddy transcended a desperate past that might have continued to haunt him but is now safely storied away. In performance, Bel Geddes and Ives used *discours* to transform the past problems of their characters into present opportunities for instructive stories. Both actor-characters set an implicit example for Ben Gazzara-Brick Pollitt; he must be able to tell the tale of Brick and Skipper's phone call, to transform it into personal narrative, before he can put the event behind him and live in the present. He does this, falteringly and incompletely, at the end of his long conversation with Big Daddy, an act of storytelling that prepares him for further transformations at the end of the play. It is important to underline here that Williams is not advocating the transformation of facts about the past into fictions for the present. All of the storytellers of *Cat* tell a truth about past events, even if it is not the entire truth based on all of the facts. In effect, the play demonstrates the moral triumph of *discours* over *histoire*, the humanistic necessity of transforming objective truths into personal ones through storytelling. Dwelling on objective truths about the past can damn individuals to guilt and recrimination. Personal narratives, however, can liberate.

Indeed, the world of *histoire* in *Cat* is the world of mendacity. When literal, objective statements are made, devoid of personal narrative—when the truth is only a matter of "just the facts, ma'am," as it was in the popular television hit, *Dragnet*—Williams demonstrates that no one can be trusted. Utterances from characters that would usually stand as *histoire* in most Broadway plays are not reliable in *Cat*. The audience soon learns that both the reverend and the doctor, typical *raissoneurs* in a well-made play, do not speak the truth in *Cat*. Nor do lawyers and their wives, also normally credible; Gooper and Mae, the chief advocates of literal truth telling, consistently select objective facts that suit their purposes. Of course, Maggie's lie about her pregnancy and Big Daddy's affirmation of it is the biggest whopper of all! What makes their mendacity acceptable to the audience is its timing and Williams's rhetoric. By affirming the value of *discours* and undercutting the importance of *histoire* throughout the action, plus demonizing Gooper and Mae, Williams prepares the audience to acquiesce to Maggie's lie and even to celebrate her acquisition of Big Daddy's estate. The triumph of Maggie and Brick felt "right" to the audience because of the truth of their *discours*; they may have lied within the world of *histoire*, but so did everybody else.

By winning the ears and hearts of Northern audiences with their grotesque personal narratives, Maggie and Big Daddy challenged the authority of *Dragnet*-voiced *histoire*, the voice of liberal culture in the North. As Helen

Gilbert notes, "the appropriation and abrogation of the colonizers' linguistic codes are essential to post-colonial writing" (2). Gilbert discusses the effectiveness of Aboriginal plays and actor-storytellers, with their distinctive tonalities, rhythms, and accents, in subverting the official English of the dominant culture in Australia. Their alterity, she writes, "prevents the seamless application of writing to the oral [and] enacts an important mode of resistance for oral cultures against the hegemony of literate ones" (4). Hence, "performative orality" becomes "the endless deferral of the authority of writing" (4). As in the current dominant culture of Australia, containment liberalism in the United States in the 1950s depended on the authority of writing and counted on orality to be easily translatable into the black and white objectivity of the written word. *Cat*, however, featured two Southerners with garrulous tongues, Maggie and Big Daddy, whose peculiar accents and rhythms gave voice to stories that were much more alive in the on-stage telling than they could ever be in the silent reading.

As Gilbert affirms, the *discours* of personal narrative disperses the validity of official, fact-based language less by overturning *histoire* than by its mere existence as another mode of truth telling. The polyvocality of *Cat*, central to the play's embrace of the grotesque, undercuts the possibility of an allegorical reading of the play. Kazan may have been reaching for univocal "grandeur," but the reviews suggest that Williams's storytellers frustrated the desire for narrative closure. To be sure, some in the audience tried to force the round peg of the play into the square hole of *Dragnet* positivism and patriarchy. But others seem to have enjoyed its grotesquerie and consequently may have been led to a more mature understanding of the fluidity of cultural and sexual identities. Williams could not directly confront the domination of liberal containment culture, any more than he could openly question the homo-hetero binary, and expect his plays to flourish on Broadway. Through the residual path of the grotesque and its voice of personal narrative, however, he could examine the ignorance effects of the worship of the American boy, the consumerism fuelled by boyish narcissism, the self-disgust and mendacity at the heart of cold-war homophobia, and the positivistic basis of patriarchal power. Plus, Williams could open these wounds without appearing to "take a stand" on any of the issues he had raised. The grotesque has its uses in politically repressive times.

After opening on March 24, 1955, *Cat on a Hot Tin Roof* played for 694 performances. No doubt its reputation for sexual titillation helped to keep it alive. George Jean Nathan advised New Yorkers who craved "a dirty show" in June of 1956 not to go out of town in search of one, but to "stay right here on Broadway in New York and go to *Cat on a Hot Tin Roof*" (n.p.). Nathan was hardly alone in emphasizing *Cat* as a sexual turn-on; advertising for the show featured an attractive man in pajamas and an alluring female in a slip. The critics also anointed *Cat* with several prestigious awards. For the 1955 season, Williams's play won the New York Drama Critics' Circle Award, the Donaldson Award, and the Pulitzer Prize. The promise of high culture and sleazy (hetero)sex in an exotic milieu has often proven a potent combination in luring audiences to Broadway shows. How many of them left *Cat* with their cold-war expectations and assumptions destabilized or even undercut cannot, of course, be known. Williams's southern grotesquerie and, ironically, Kazan's presentational style had provided the ingredients for a different kind of experience than most of the spectators probably anticipated.

Notes

1. I have excerpted this article from my forthcoming book, *Producing and Contesting Containment: American Theater in the Culture of the Early Cold War, 1947–1962* (Iowa City: Iowa U P, 2003), and made very few changes to the text.

2. This edition of the play has two versions of Act III, Williams's preferred version and the Broadway Version, "as played in the New York Production" (126), along with Williams's "Note of Explanation" (124–25) on the inclusion of both versions. Subsequent citations are from this edition of the play.

3. Many critics, of course, have discussed Williams's interest in grotesquerie, but none, to my knowledge, has analyzed his plays as examples of a rhetorical genre of the grotesque. Probably the first to note the generically mixed nature of the play was Mary Hivor who asked, "If the battle for inheritance be the core of the plot, how could we have anything but comedy?" (126). On grotesquerie in the South, see also Inge. Williams's attraction to the grotesque has fundamentally to do with his romanticism, as first explored by Jackson (9–42).

4. Like many other critics, Christopher Bigsby calls "mendacity" the major theme of *Cat* but cannot resolve the major contradiction centered on this theme: "Maggie is as involved in this process [what Bigsby earlier termed ' . . . hypocrisy, cant, greed and self-interest'] as anyone. She genuinely cares for Brick but her urgency and her energy seem to derive precisely from a refusal to let go of the inheritance that she believes to be hers by right. And she, too, is capable of lying. To [critic] Benjamin Nelson, hers is a "'life-lie told in the face of death,' and yet the precise distinction between those lies which generate life and those which do not is never clearly established, the more so since Maggie's lie is a desperate bid to forestall Gooper's bid for the estate" (82–83). Other critics who discuss the play as an examination of "mendacity" include John V. Hagopian, Philip C. Kolin, and Kenneth Tynan.

More generally, critics' attempts to make meaning out of *Cat* have led in several contradictory directions. In his overview of criticism on the play, George W. Crandell states: "Williams's ambiguity regarding both the theme of the play and Brick's sexual identity continues to puzzle critics who debate what the play is really about. Not surprisingly, the focus of critical attention also shifts among various relationships. Is *Cat* primarily a story about a troubled marriage (Maggie and Brick), a possibly homosexual relationship (Brick and Skipper), a father and son's inability to communicate (Big Daddy and Brick), or a family squabble over an inheritance

(Brick and Maggie versus Gooper and Mae)?" (117). Of course, the play is "really about" all of these relationships, but I would suggest that none of them, individually or together, yields a coherent meaning.

5. Although I disagree with some of Murphy's conclusions about the Williams-Kazan collaboration on *Cat*, as I have noted in the text, I am deeply indebted to her original scholarly work on the 1955 production.

6. Savran, of course, relies on Raymond Williams's discussion of liberal tragedy in *Drama from Ibsen to Brecht*, 34–74, 268–76.

7. Maurice Zolotow also noted "the failure of artistic control" in Kazan's conception of the play (93).

8. The published play acknowledged this epigraph as a quotation from "Do Not Go Gentle Into That Good Night," from *The Collected Poems of Dylan Thomas* (New York: New Directions, 1952).

9. As Sedgwick points out, the closeting of homosexuality generates "ignorance effects" that have been "harnessed, licensed, and regulated on a mass scale for striking enforcements" (5).

10. Helen Gilbert notes that Benveniste's *histoire/discours* distinction, though useful, "should not be set up as absolute binaries" (4). Nor does Williams deploy these modes as opposites; some of the information related by a character through *discours* does prove to be reliable within the world of the play.

Works Cited

Atkinson, Brooks. "Theatre: Tennessee Williams' [sic] Cat." Coffin 344.

Bauman, Richard. *Story, Performance, and Event: Contextual Studies of Oral Narrative.* Cambridge: Cambridge UP, 1986.

Benveniste, Émile. *Problems of General Linguistics.* Miami: U of Miami P, 1966.

Bentley, Eric. "Theatre." *New Republic* 132 (4 April 1955): 22.

Bigsby, Christopher. *A Critical Introduction to Twentieth-Century American Drama.* Vol 2. Cambridge: Cambridge UP, 1984.

Chapman, John. "*Cat on a Hot Tin Roof* Beautifully Acted But a Frustrating Drama." Coffin 343.

Clipping File, "*Cat on a Hot Tin Roof.*" New York Library of Performing Arts.

Coffin, Rachel, ed. *New York Theatre Critics' Reviews, 1955.* Vol. 16. New York: Critics' Theatre Reviews, 1956.

Coleman, Robert. "*Cat on a Hot Tin Roof* Is Likely to Be a Hit." Coffin 343.

Crandell, George W. "*Cat on a Hot Tin Roof.*" *Tennessee Williams: A Guide to Research and Performance.* Ed. Philip C. Kolin. Westport, Ct: Greenwood, 1998. 109–125.

Devlin, Albert J. "Writing in 'A Place of Stone': *Cat on a Hot Tin Roof.*" *The Cambridge Companion to Tennessee Williams.* Ed. Matthew C. Roudané. Cambridge: Cambridge UP, 1997. 95–113.

Fearnow, Mark. *The American Stage and The Great Depression: A Cultural History of the Grotesque.* Cambridge: Cambridge UP, 1997.

Finnegan, R. *Oral Poetry: Its Nature, Significance, and Social Context.* 2nd ed. Bloomington: Indiana UP, 1991.

Gilbert, Helen. "De-Scribing Orality: Performance and the Recuperation of Voice." *Post-Colonial Drama: Theory, Practice, Politics.* London: Routledge, 1996.

Hagopian, John V. "*Cat on a Hot Tin Roof.*" *Insight: Analyses of Modern British and American Drama.* Vol. 4. Ed. Herman J. Weiand. Frankfurt: Hirschgraben, 1975. 269–75.

Hawkins, William. "Cat Yowls High On 'Hot Tin Roof.'" Coffin 342.

Hivor, Mary. "Theatre Letter," *Kenyon Review* 18 (1956): 125–126.

Inge, Thomas M. "The South, Tragedy, and Comedy in Tennessee Williams's *Cat on a Hot Tin Roof.*" *The United States South: Regionalism and Identity*. Eds. Valeria Lerda and Tjebbe Westendorp. Rome: Bulzoni, 1991. 157–65.

Jackson, Esther Merle. *The Broken World of Tennessee Williams*. Madison: U of Wisconsin P, 1966.

Kazan, Elia. *A Life*. New York: Doubleday, 1988.

Kerr, Walter F. "Theater: *Cat on a Hot Tin Roof.*" Coffin 342.

———. "Theater: A Secret Is Half-Told in Fountains of Words." *New York Herald Tribune* 3 April 1955. Clipping File n.p.

Kolin, Philip C. "Obstacles to Communication in *Cat on a Hot Tin Roof.*" *Western Speech Communication* 39 (1975): 74–80.

Langellier, Kristin M. "Personal Narratives: Perspectives on Theory and Research." *Text and Performance Quarterly* 9 (1989): 243–76.

McClain, John, "Drama Socks and Socks," Coffin 344.

Miller, Arthur. "The Shadows of the Gods." *The Theatre Essays of Arthur Miller*. Ed. Robert A. Martin. New York: Viking, 1978. 189–93.

Murphy, Brenda. *Tennessee Williams and Elia Kazan: A Collaboration in the Theatre*. Cambridge: Cambridge UP, 1992.

Nathan, George Jean. "Theatre Week," *New York Journal American* 9 June 1956. Clipping File n.p.

O'Connor, Flannery. "Some Aspects of the Grotesque in Southern Fiction." *Mystery and Manners: Occasional Prose*. Eds. Sally and Robert Fitzgerald. New York: Farrar, 1961. 36–50.

Ong, Walter J. *Orality and Literacy: The Technologizing of the Word*. New York: Routledge, 1988.

Savran, David. *Communists, Cowboys, and Queers: The Politics of Masculinity in the Work of Arthur Miller and Tennessee Williams*. Minneapolis: U of Minnesota P, 1992.

Sedgwick, Eve Kosofsky. *Epistemology of the Closet*. Berkeley: U of California P, 1990.

Tynan, Kenneth. "*Cat on a Hot Tin Roof.*" *Curtains. Selections from the Drama Criticism and Related Writings*. New York: Atheneum, 1961. 204–05.

Watts, Richard Jr. "The Impact of Tennessee Williams." Coffin 343.

Williams, Raymond. *Drama from Ibsen to Brecht*. New York: Oxford UP, 1969.

Williams, Tennessee. *Cat on a Hot Tin Roof*. 1955. New York: Penguin, 1985.

———. *Where I Live: Selected Essays*. Eds. Christine R. Day and Bob Woods. New York: New Directions, 1978.

Zolotow, Maurice. "The Season On and Off Broadway." *Theatre Arts* 39.6 (1955): 22–23, 93.

WILLIAM MARK POTEET

Cat on a Hot Tin Roof

"When a football player loses his supreme confidence in his super-
masculinity, he is in deep trouble."

—Vince Lombardi

Brick Pollitt, the former college and professional football star in Tennessee Williams' *Cat on a Hot Tin Roof*, is in deep trouble. *Cat on a Hot Tin
Roof*, first performed in 1955 and arguably Williams' most commercially
successful play, represents one day in 1954 in the life of the Pollitts, one
of the Mississippi Delta's wealthiest cotton-growing families. As with *A
Streetcar Named Desire*, Williams' characters here have become so deeply
embedded in American culture (both popular and high) that almost everyone can picture the earthy, swaggering Big Daddy in a crumpled white linen
suit or the voluptuous and striking Maggie, dressed in a slip and stalk-
ing the bedroom in feline fervor. The viriley beautiful and semi-drunken
Brick, his foot in a cast and his morally frozen body sheathed in icy white
silk pajamas, also quickly comes to the collective mind. In *Cat on a Hot
Tin Roof*, Williams' theater of memory has evolved into a brighter, though
still subjectively dense, location. Unlike *Streetcar*, in *Cat on a Hot Tin Roof*
the theater of initiation does not have to borrow its masculinity from any
other homosocial quarter; the play draws its concepts of masculinity and
homosexuality directly from the most homosocial of American institutions,

From *Gay Men in Modern Southern Literature: Ritual, Initiation, and the Construction of
Masculinity*, pp. 35–62, 213–14. Copyright © 2006 by Peter Lang Publishing.

organized sports. As the famous Green Bay Packers' coach Vince Lombardi indicates in the above quotation, from Brian Pronger's *The Arena of Masculinity: Sports, Homosexuality, and the Meaning of Sex*, in the American psyche football isn't just a game, it is the very arena of "supreme confidence" and "super-masculinity."

A critical examination of *Cat on a Hot Tin Roof* presents two crucial problems that must be dealt with at the onset, one textual and the other more subjectively problematic; and both have an important bearing on the theaters of memory and initiation. The play has two very different concluding third acts, and Brick's sexual orientation is purposefully confusing. With his penchant for obfuscation and contradiction, the playwright himself is of little help on either issue. The conventional, standard rationale for the revised third act is found in Williams' "Note of Explanation" inserted between the acts in most published editions of *Cat on a Hot Tin Roof*. Williams maintains that he succumbed to the "creative influence on the play" by its original Broadway director Elia Kazan, who had successfully worked with Williams on both the stage and film productions of *A Streetcar Named Desire*. Apparently, to ensure a more publicly palpable version of *Cat*, Kazan suggested three basic revisions of act three: Big Daddy (who disappears at the end of act two) be reintroduced; Brick should undergo some sort of change, with the emphasis toward positive; and Maggie should become a more sympathetic character.[1] In the revised act three, commonly differentiated as the "Broadway version," Williams makes the suggested changes—and creates a longstanding critical debate that proves more frustrating than enlightening.

In his "Note of Explanation" for the revised third act of *Cat*, Williams writes that Kazan felt the need to change the character of Brick because, "of the virtual vivisection that he undergoes in his interview with his father in act two" (124). Ironically, Kazan appears to have had no compunction to request this same "virtual vivisection" on Williams' original script. However, Marian Price explains that for all the critical consternation caused by Kazan's suggested revisions, Williams himself is more to be held responsible. What began as mere artistic opinion and advice from Kazan prompted Williams to believe that the original version of the play would not become a commercial success, something Williams strongly desired as a public affirmation of his work. Elia Kazan stated several times that when he realized Williams' reluctance to make the changes he simply told the playwright to "leave it as it is." Price argues that her reading of the play "supports the idea that Williams actively embraced the suggested revisions, made them his own, and confidently awaited the play's triumph."[2] She goes on to posit Williams' personal guilt over artistic compromise and homosexuality as the motivating factors of his misplaced blame of Elia Kazan.[3]

To complicate matters further, there are actually four extant published versions of act three of *Cat on a Hot Tin Roof*.[4] For a 1974 Broadway revival of the play, Williams again rewrote the polymorphous third act, keeping the original intact and only allowing Big Daddy to appear and tell an off color joke. By the time the revival had made it to the stage, Williams had produced an "acting-version" that returned to the old Broadway third act, minus Big Daddy's joke.[5] Given that the primary dramatic action of all of the various versions of act three is the comic bickering over an inheritance, Roger Boxill points out rather facilely, but perhaps trenchantly, that "no version of Act III quite works, because the final act is an afterthought."[6] Aside from the post-structuralist concept of meaning never being firmly fixed, the reader/viewer expects the traditional text itself to remain fixed; these types of textual cruxes always present the daunting (and often prosaic) necessity of a compare-and-contrast critical approach. However, while most modern critics tend to get mired down studying the differences in the original and Broadway versions of act three, none have noticed a more informative approach to the problem. Williams' third act revisions for the 1974 Broadway revival of *Cat* hold the answer, particularly in light of the ways that masculinity inform the play. The only fundamental revision Williams makes to the 1974 script is the insertion and excision of Big Daddy's joke.[7] Given the fact that Williams was more than well aware of the critical controversy caused by *Cat*'s unstable third act, it seems incredibly telling that when given the chance to correct the constantly perplexing problem he is more concerned with a dirty joke than Brick's sudden and unexplained change or Maggie's added sympathy. Most critical studies of the play either ignore or dismiss Big Daddy's joke as superfluous to act three. Ruby Cohn, who deems Big Daddy a "colorful character," believes that "his elephantine joke diffuses the dramatic drive."[8] In *A Streetcar Named Desire* the dirty joke actually *infuses* the dramatic drive, bringing into play sexuality, the homosocial, and masculinity—three of the primary dynamics that Williams attempts to bring together in act three of *Cat on a Hot Tin Roof*.

If Blanche DuBois is clearly the protagonist in *A Streetcar Named Desire*, then which character fills that role in *Cat on a Hot Tin Roof*? The play's title obviously indicates Maggie, but the title alone proves deceptive. According to David Savran:

> Among the *dramatis personae*, at least three—Maggie, Brick, and Big Daddy—bear the intense desire and undergo the kind of transformations usually associated with protagonists. To grant a privilege to any one character's point of view is to misread the designs of interdependence and complicity that Williams so painstakingly constructs as a solitary enterprise.[9]

Maggie's tenacity, Brick's ambiguous sexual orientation, and Big Daddy's impending death all represent the complex "interplay of live human beings in the thundercloud of a common crisis," as Williams states in his stage directions for *Cat* (85). There is no question of Maggie's tenacity, a cat just trying to stay on a hot tin roof. Big Daddy is surely dying of bowel cancer. But just how ambiguous is Brick's sexual orientation?

Williams approaches the topic of homosexuality very differently in *Cat* than he does in *Streetcar*. As Mark Royden Winchell points out, "Williams's treatment of homosexuality in *Cat on a Hot Tin Roof* represents an advance over the clichés of *A Streetcar Named Desire*."[10] Gone is the sensitive and nervous young poet Allan and his worldly older friend, replaced by the macho football player buddies Brick and Skipper. These two represent early prototypes of male characters that Williams will continue to incorporate into his dramatic canon. According to Robert Emmet Jones:

> Although many of the playwright's male characters are stereotypes of contemporary ideas of masculinity—athletes, truck drivers, manual workers, studs, sailors, hustlers—they remain passive sexual objects, and other aspects of their personalities are rarely explored.... And they are types fantasized about by homosexuals.... Williams expresses the homoerotic longing that these men might harbor homosexual or bisexual tendencies themselves.[11]

Fortunately, Brick Pollitt, though he does "remain a passive sexual object," is one of the few early Tennessee Williams homoerotic characters whose personality is explored. Unfortunately, for all of the furtiveness and secrecy concerning Brick's true sexual nature, that exploration proves difficult and complicated. However, it is this very concept of secrecy, the choice not to know, that leads to a better understanding of homosexuality in *Cat on a Hot Tin Roof*.

Writing in 2002, and from a distinctly twentieth-century perspective on the subject of homosexuality, Harold Bloom believes that without the energy supplied by Maggie and Big Daddy's characters Brick would, "freeze the audience, particularly now, when homosexuality is no longer an issue for an audience not dominated by Fundamentalists, Reagan Republicans, and assorted other mossbacks."[12] Historically contextualizing popular critical commentary, contemporaneous with *Cat*'s 1955 Broadway debut, sheds a very different light on homosexuality, masculinity, and the homosocial, and how Williams' combined theaters of memory and initiation both followed and helped define the cultural norms of the era.

In his book *Cultural Politics—Queer Reading* (1994), Alan Sinfield demonstrates how the concept of secrecy, so prevalent in all spheres of 1950s

American culture, permeated by fears of post–World War II communism—battered by McCarthyism, influenced the critical reception of *Cat on a Hot Tin Roof*. Sinfield refers to *Cat* as a "scandalous success," but he also points out that popular drama critics of the day had the responsibility of "the nervous restoration of the secrecy that Williams had violated." Sinfield notes that

> This was happening when Brooks Atkinson reviewed the initial (1955) production without mentioning Brick's relationship with Skipper. Walter Kerr, in the *New York Herald Tribune*, acknowledged "the implications" of "an unnatural relationship" but complained that *Cat* exhibits "a tantalizing reluctance" to "blurt out its promised secret." In fact, the play is plain enough; Kerr needs there to be a secret.[13]

For Tennessee Williams, and the viewing public, Brick's homosexuality must remain clouded in secrecy, but it must still be expressed. The theater of memory helps the playwright achieve this goal by constant, yet veiled, allusions to homosexuality by all of the major players in *Cat*. The theater of initiation, powered by its need for continuous reiteration, serves to redouble this concept of talking about homosexuality while *not* talking about homosexuality. Both theaters enable Williams to maintain the open secret.

In twenty-first-century hindsight, it becomes clear to most viewer/readers, especially gay ones, that Brick and Skipper are both, without doubt, homosexuals. In his now famous and often quoted section of stage directions from act two of *Cat on a Hot Tin Roof*, Williams shares the core of his dramatic theory with the reader. In this theory he states that "some mystery should be left in the revelation of character in a play, just as a great deal of mystery is always left in the revelation of character in life, even in one's character to himself" (85). The sole, real mystery in the play is Brick's sexual orientation; this mystery, however, is necessary to maintain the open secret status of homosexuality. Alan Sinfield convincingly argues how and why this concept of the open secret exists:

> It helps to constitute the public/private boundary—the binary that seems to demarcate our subjectivities from a public realm while actually producing those subjectivities—and thus facilitates the policing of the boundary. The secret keeps a topic like homosexuality in the private sphere, but under surveillance, allowing it to hover on the edge of public visibility. If it gets fully into the open, it attains public recognition; yet it must not disappear altogether, for then it would be beyond control and would no longer effect a general surveillance of aberrant desire.[14]

David Savran espouses a similar theory of gay subjectivity and what he refers to as the "guilty secret" of homosexuality, but Savran's theoretical approach to the subject also incorporates the past, represented in Williams' drama by the persistent theater of memory:

> Even more important, this practice acts both to ratify and subvert a psychoanalytical model of personality, for in the same gesture that directs the spectator's hermeneutical gaze toward the withheld secret, it seems to deny the primacy and intelligibility of that traumatic memory, both emphasizing and calling into question the determination of the present by a moment in the past.[15]

As John M. Clum notes about *Cat*, "the tenderness Williams sees as the clear side of his vision here exists only in a stage direction: the cloudiness of homosexuality remains an object of terror, not of the act, but of public exposure."[16] These theories of gay subjectivity represent a direct connection to Tennessee Williams' primary homosexually themed plays, all of which are almost slavishly devoted to memory—the past; and that past is constantly reinforced by the repetition of depictions of masculine, gay initiations.

Even before the dramatic action of *Cat* begins, Williams begins constructing the theater of memory. The only set for *Cat* consists of a large and roomy bedsitting room in the Pollitt plantation house. In the stagecraft "Notes for the Designer" introduction, Williams writes:

> It hasn't changed much since it was occupied by the original owners of the place, Jack Straw and Peter Ochello, a pair of old bachelors who shared the room all their lives together. In other words, the room must evoke some ghosts; it is gently and poetically haunted by a relationship that must have involved a tenderness which was uncommon. (xiii)

We later learn that Straw and Ochello, an apparently unabashedly gay couple, bequeathed the plantation to Big Daddy, whom they took in as a young man and made overseer. As in *Streetcar*, all during the course of the play the reader/viewer will be made aware of a gay past, men in a bedroom. Williams specifically points out that the bedroom must "evoke" the past, and just as the homosexual characters in *Cat* transcend the stereotypical ones of *Streetcar*, the gay "ghosts" have evolved also. Unlike the memories of Allan, which torment Blanche DuBois, Williams goes to great lengths to suggest that the ghosts of Straw and Ochello inhabit a bedroom that is "gently and poetically haunted." Later in the play, during Brick and Big

Daddy's pivotal confrontation, Brick, in a telling assault, will attempt to destroy the memory-theater that "must have involved a tenderness which was uncommon."

These gay "ghosts," these gentle specters of homosexuality, Straw and Ochello, serve multiple purposes in *Cat*. The entire dramatic action of the play is trapped within the matrix of their relationship. Williams constructs a kind of narrowing cultural spiral around Straw and Ochello: from breaking with the societal norms of the mid-twentieth-century South, to owning the plantation, to sharing the bedroom, and finally to the bed itself. In act one, during a discussion about why Maggie and Brick have remained childless, Big Mamma points at the bed and tells Maggie, "—When a marriage goes on the rocks, the rocks are *there*, right *there!*" (37). The bed comes to represent a successful union, the type of union none of the heterosexual (or ostensibly heterosexual) couples in the play can achieve, and it certainly symbolizes Brick's unfulfilled homosexuality. Judith J. Thompson believes that when the original act three of the play is considered, "the fully realized homosexual relationship exemplified by Straw and Ochello represents the only alternative in the play to either loveless heterosexual couplings or tragically suppressed homosexual longings."[17] David Savran reads Big Daddy as a "carrier of homosexuality," and asserts that "not only has Big Daddy inherited the plantation from Straw and Ochello, but he has also inadvertently passed along at least a glimmer of homosexual desire to his younger son, Brick. . . ."[18] For Roger Boxill, Brick's "glimmer of homosexual desire" becomes unequivocal, when he states, about Straw and Ochello, "it is in their very bedroom, moreover, in a setting described as evocative of their benign ghosts, that the present heir, himself a homosexual, is closeted."[19] For a play that the playwright himself and a plethora of critics have adamantly argued is not about homosexuality, there certainly seems to be a lot of "homosexuality" going on—even from page one. For all of the above noted purposes that the Straw and Ochello characters serve in *Cat*, they also function complexly to alter and enhance the way that Williams incorporates the theaters of memory and initiation into the play.

In both *The Glass Menagerie* and *A Streetcar Named Desire*, Williams constructs the theater of memory as a dim stage, not well lighted. He describes the primary set of *The Glass Menagerie* by writing in the stage directions that "the scene is memory and is therefore nonrealistic. . . . The interior is therefore rather dim and poetic."[20] Thus, the bedsitting room set for *Cat* is also described by the playwright as "poetically haunted," and Williams further suggests this hazy quality by noting that the set designer should consider "a reproduction of a faded photograph of the verandah of Robert Louis Stevenson's home on that Samoan Island where he spent his last years" (xiii).

However, Williams also points out that this dimness only represents the background of the play's dramatic action, acts as a sort of atmospheric buffer, when he writes, "for the set is the background for a play that deals with human extremities of emotion, and it needs that softness behind it" (xiii). Indeed, because the foreground of the play is pulled into sharp and bright modernity by "a monumental monstrosity of our times, a *huge* console combination of radio-phonograph (Hi-Fi with three speakers) TV set *and* liquor cabinet, . . . this monument, is a very shrine to virtually all the comforts and illusions behind which we hide from such things as the characters in the play are faced with . . ." (xiii–xiv). Williams does not allow the characters in *Cat* to hide or get lost in the dimness of the background; rather it exists to absorb some of the impact from the well-lighted and modern foreground, where the dramatic action is played out. "That softness behind it," the set, is represented by the ghosts of Straw and Ochello, so that the theater of memory can perhaps take up and contain the stark, vivid, and oftentimes brutal theaters of memory and initiation invoked by Brick, Maggie, and Big Daddy—"*that cloudy, flickering, evanescent—fiercely charged!—interplay of live human brings in the thundercloud of a common crisis*" (85).

Early in act one of *Cat*, Williams introduces the structure of the foregrounded memory and initiation theaters, the trope of boyhood and games which will be extended throughout the play. In the initial stage directions that describe Brick, Williams makes the point that "he is still slim and firm as a boy" (17). Maggie then immediately refers to him as, "boy of mine!" (17). To extend the concept of boyhood and games further and also to suggest a sexual ambiguity (another dynamic embedded into the play), Williams writes of Maggie "her voice has range and music; sometimes it drops low as a boy's and you have the sudden image of her playing boys' games as a child" (18). Williams weaves actual games into the fabric of the play, games such as football, archery, and croquet, to reflect the more psychically sophisticated games the characters play with sexual orientation and power.[21] Alice Griffin, fully accepting Tennessee Williams' necessary prevarication, his collusion in maintaining the "open secret," writes that "in an interview with *Theatre Arts* magazine Williams said that Brick was not a homosexual, that his self-disgust was the result of living so long with lies." After Williams himself, and apparently Griffin also (writing in 1995!), absolve Brick of his imagined sexual transgression, then we are able to see the "true" crux of *Cat*:

> It is now possible to view Brick's character in the context of the play
> as a whole and to see that the question of homosexuality is not the
> issue. The symbolism of games and game playing of winning and
> losing, provides a clue to Brick's disillusionment with the world.[22]

Griffin fails to understand her own clue properly and fully when she argues that Brick's athleticism *only* represents his concept of life, how easily winning can suddenly turn to losing. The game itself then becomes more important than the goal. Brick's goal is twofold and contradictory, to be accepted by his father back into the heteronormative masculine sphere and to reconfigure and reclaim Skipper's memory—how to become/remain a masculine, heterosexual man and still be in love with the memory of his dead friend. No wonder he is so conflicted and emotionally frozen throughout the play; he seems to be playing a losing game.

The study of masculinity has long recognized the influences that organized sports has on the psycho-sexual development of boys. Michael Messner explains:

> For the boy who seeks and fears attachment with others, the rule-bound structure of organized sports can promise to be a safe place in which to seek non-intimate attachment with others within a context that maintains clear boundaries, distance, and separation.[23]

Brick's theaters of memory and initiation have dramatically transformed from that "safe place" into a location where the old rules are tenuous at best, and the structure has collapsed. His attachment to Skipper, despite all of his objections, was intimate. The boundaries were blurred, and the distance was closed. To reachieve proper separation and return to the rules of the game, Brick and Skipper both choose a Draconian route, death: Brick's emotional—Skipper's corporeal.

The memory-theater reconstruction of Skipper begins early in act one. While Maggie is railing at Brick about his drinking, she suddenly asks him, "were you thinking of Skipper?" (25). When he evades the question, Maggie tells him:

> Laws of silence don't work.... When something is festering in your memory or your imagination, laws of silence don't work, it's just like shutting a door and locking it in a house on fire in hope of forgetting that the house is burning. But not facing a fire doesn't put it out. Silence about a thing just magnifies it. It grows and festers in silence, becomes malignant.... (25)

Interestingly, Maggie's analogy perfectly expresses how Alan Sinfield's concept of the "open secret" helps society monitor and control homosexuality. If silence about a "thing" just magnifies it, then it also becomes easier to delineate, identify, and contain. This speech also, of course, draws parallels between Brick's predicament and Big Daddy's terminal cancer, and their mutual failure to communicate. In his book, *The Inward Gaze: Masculinity and Subjectivity in Modern Culture*, Peter Middleton relates an anecdote about watching a group of young boys play a game. He perceives two different themes at work:

> One is the way the fantasy of manhood seems to be created out of a bricolage of fragments from the masculine public world, and the other is the difficulties that males, especially males of different ages, have articulating their relations with one another.[24]

Both of these themes are examined by Williams in *Cat*. The component fragments of bricolage, used in an effort to define masculinity, are identified and assembled (for very varying purposes) by Maggie, Brick, and Big Daddy. Most of act two of *Cat* represents a detailed study of a father and son, two men at odds with one another and desperately trying to communicate. The interplay between the foregrounded theaters of memory and initiation, with the contented gay presence of Straw and Ochello hovering in the background as a buffer, enables the characters to explore the "open secret" of homosexuality in the only location it could be explored at the time—at the edges. However, a playwright of Tennessee Williams' talent has the ability to make those edges crackle.

Maggie is the first character in *Cat* to reconstruct Skipper through the theater of memory. The relationship Maggie remembers between Brick and Skipper is described in classical terms of beauty and nobility, yet at the core of her argument, Maggie proves to be disingenuous at least and purely functional at best. At the end of act one Maggie, in an attempt to help Brick overcome his emotional torpor, recalls to Brick his and Skipper's friendship as:

> one of those beautiful, ideal things they tell about in the Greek legends, it couldn't be anything else, you being you, and that's what made it so sad, that's what made it so awful, because it was love that never could be carried through to anything satisfying or even talked about plainly. Brick, I tell you, you got to believe me, Brick I do understand all about it. I—I think it was—*noble!* (43–44)

Critics tend to make much ado over this speech, especially considering Williams' penchant for rather frank and obvious symbolism and classical allusions. Earlier in act one, when one of Brick's brother Gooper's many children, one of the "no-neck monsters," enters the bedroom wielding a bow and arrow, Maggie explains that it is her Diana Trophy, a reminder of her archery prowess while a student at Ole Miss (28).[25] Thus, the most obvious critical conclusion to draw (and the one that most critics maintain) is demonstrated by Winchell when he states that "one of the ironies of Williams's play is that its two most overtly heterosexual characters—Maggie and Big Daddy—are also the most tolerant of the latent erotic ties between Brick and Skipper." Winchell goes on to argue that Maggie's language in describing Brick and Skipper's friendship "elevates it to a platonic status."[26] However, a more important irony can be discerned from Maggie's hetero-sexual tolerance of latent homoeroticism in her husband, one that passes the platonic for the practical.

The densely complicated structure of the end of act one of *Cat* bears a close reading, because it is within this structure that Williams illustrates how deftly he can shift between and combine the theaters of memory and initiation. And it is in this important scene that the playwright also *frees* Maggie from her often conjectured role of classical goddess-cum-suffering saint. By the end of act one, Maggie is no longer some symbolic representation, some avatar of female acceptance and understanding—she is simply (and complexly) a human woman.

Immediately after Maggie tells Brick that she considers his and Skipper's attachment "noble," she quickly adds, "my only point, the only point that I'm making, is life has got to be allowed to continue, even after the *dream* of life is—all—over . . ." (44). She stresses that this is her only point, and she also repeats an important line from *A Streetcar Named Desire*. When Eunice tells Stella that she must forget Blanche's "story" of Stanley's rape, Eunice says, "don't ever believe it. Life has got to go on. No matter what happens, you've got to keep on going" (133). In the context of *Streetcar*, Alvin B. Kernan calls this "the only truth that Williams will maintain, 'you've got to keep on going.'"[27] It may well also represent the only "truth" that Maggie will maintain. "What is the victory of a cat on a hot tin roof?" she asks herself more than Brick, "I wish I knew. . . . Just staying on it, I guess, as long as she can . . ." (25). In *Cat*, Maggie has a plan, one that represents her neither as a mercenary nor a gold-digging bitch—she wants to survive. This notion of survival informs both Maggie's memory-theater construction of Skipper and her perceived understanding and acceptance of Brick's latent homosexuality.

Shortly before her speech about Brick and Skipper and their "noble" relationship, Maggie tells Brick something about his brother Gooper and Gooper's wife Mae, information Maggie thinks that Brick does not realize:

> Mae an' Gooper are plannin' to freeze us out of Big Daddy's estate
> because you drink and I'm childless. But we can defeat that plan.

> We're *going* to defeat that plan! *Brick, y'know, I've been so Goddamn*
> *disgustingly poor all my life!*—That's the *truth*, Brick! (41)

She then continues to describe her early life as a traditional Southern "poor
relation," replete with family alcoholism, poverty, and lost social position.
To save her marriage to Brick, and their inheritance from Big Daddy, Maggie must take the initiative, which includes helping Brick overcome his
drinking and her having a baby. For Maggie, the most obvious source of
Brick's drinking problem and loss of libido is his guilty memory of Skipper.
Defeating Gooper and Mae's disinheritance plan would hardly profit from
exacerbating Brick's guilt over Skipper's death. Realizing that she cannot
make Skipper's memory vanish, Maggie chooses to valorize it in the only
way possible at the time, by linking it to the classical Greek model of male
friendship.

In *Cat*, Williams employs the only two models of homosexuality available for public consumption in the 1950s, the classical, ephebophilic, and
platonic ideal of Greek friendship and the homophobic, post-psychoanalytic
effeminate identity. When Maggie realizes that it is necessary to confront
Brick's homoerotic feeling toward Skipper, she must choose between the two,
her only options. Later, in his confrontation with Big Daddy, Brick must
also choose between the representations, and he opts for the homophobic.
Maggie's selection of the classical Greek model, however, allows her to both
ameliorate the situation and reiterate a salient point: Skipper is dead. After
Maggie tells of Skipper's downward spiral into depression, alcoholism, and
drug dependency, it seems as if his laurels had already begun to wither quite
dramatically. And Maggie, with her Diana-like archer's prowess, aims right
for the heart of the matter.

Williams intersperses Maggie's act one memory-theater reconstruction of Skipper with images of the theater of initiation, and those images are
repeated and reinforced throughout the dramatic action of the play. Immediately after the speech about the nobility of their friendship, she tells Brick:

> Why I remember when we double-dated at college, Gladys
> Fitzgerald and I and you and Skipper, it was more like a date
> between you and Skipper. Gladys and I were just sort of tagging
> along as if we were necessary to chaperone you!—to make a good
> public impression—. (44)

This scene calls to mind the traditional concept of the gay "beard," when gay
men bring a woman along on a social occasion to give the public impression
of heterosexuality. However, this double date also fits into the parameters

of Luce Irigaray's argument of women being relegated to a commodity by the homosocial interaction of men. Maggie realizes her position in this initiatory dynamic, but she also continues to exploit the homoerotic underpinnings to Brick and Skipper's friendship. When Brick accuses Maggie of naming his feelings toward Skipper "dirty," she says, "I'm not naming it dirty! I'm naming it clean!" (44). Once again, she emphasizes the point that Brick and Skipper's relationship can be safely addressed from the retrospective position of Skipper's death:

> Then you haven't been listenin', not understood what I'm sayin'! I'm naming it so damn clean that it killed poor Skipper!—You two had something that had to be kept on ice, yes, incorruptible, yes!—and death was the only icebox where you could keep it. . . . (44)

For all of the understanding that this speech demonstrates to most critics of the play, it also illustrates the practicality of Maggie's plan. Brick and Skipper's relationship remains "noble" because it is "incorruptible," and it is no longer a threat to Maggie because Skipper is dead.

Maggie next describes in detail the circumstances that lead to Skipper's death. After a football game, one that Brick missed because of an injury, Maggie suddenly told Skipper, "SKIPPER STOP LOVIN' MY HUSBAND OR TELL HIM HE'S GOT TO LET YOU ADMIT IT TO HIM!" (45). This prompted Skipper to make a failed attempt at seducing Maggie, one in which she describes his impotence as, "that pitiful, ineffectual little attempt to prove what I had said wasn't true . . ." (45). It is this encounter that started Skipper's downward drug and alcohol spiral toward death. David Savran points out Maggie's role by stating:

> When she attempts to force her way into the relationship (that decisively unsettles the distinction between homosocial and homosexual desire), making love to Skipper, it is because "it made both of us feel a little bit closer to [Brick]," the common object of desire . . . Since her liaison with Skipper, Brick's repudiation of him, and Skipper's quasi-suicide, Maggie has become the inheritor, the mediator in a now-immobilized erotic triangle between the living and the dead, the woman who desires to be a partner in an impossible and belated erotic fascination, the woman who, in coveting Brick's aloofness, desires his very refusal to desire her.[28]

Savran's remarks, rather unwittingly, constantly return to how death has rendered the entire situation moot—"now-immobilized erotic triangle," and "an impossible and belated erotic fascination." Maggie, while not the simplistic cause of Skipper's death, realizes that it is both the motivating factor for Brick's emotional nihilism, and also represents a way to possibly rectify the damage, by acknowledging the erotic attachment, naming it "clean," and reclaiming Brick's love. She desires much more than his refusal to desire her.

Most critics argue for the fundamental sincerity of Maggie's understanding toward Brick's homoerotic attraction to Skipper, while ignoring some of the direct clues that her understanding is made possible by Skipper's absence. Mark Royden Winchell maintains:

> Had Williams not found Maggie steadily more charming, he could easily have made her into a female Stanley Kowalski. Brick's assumption that she has driven Skipper to his death (much as Stanley helped drive Blanche insane) seems implausible only because Williams convinces us of Maggie's basic sincerity and decency.[29]

And while Maggie is basically sincere and decent, she is not above bending the truth to suit her own needs. This is evidenced by an important incongruity in her memory-theater reconstruction of Skipper. Maggie tells Brick that she and Skipper attempted to make love, "because it made both of us feel a little bit closer to you . . . And so we made love to each other to dream it was you, both of us!" (43). But the play makes it clear that Brick's alienation of affection in his marriage does not begin until after Skipper's death. In act two, Big Daddy bluntly tells Brick, "you started drinkin' when your friend Skipper died" (84). In her concluding act-one speech, Maggie clearly reminds Brick how happy their marriage was before Skipper's death when she says to him, "and we were happy, weren't we, we were blissful, yes, hit heaven together ev'ry time that we loved!" (45). Maggie's sexual encounter with Skipper may have been altruistic on her part, a way to help him feel closer to Brick, but apparently she needed no such liaison to make her feel closer to her own husband.

At the end of her act-one speech, Maggie reiterates both her motives and her position to Brick:

> I'm honest! Give me credit for just that, will you please?—Born poor, raised poor, expect to die poor unless I manage to get us something out of what Big Daddy leaves when he dies of cancer! But Brick?!—*Skipper is dead! I'm alive!* Maggie the cat is . . . *alive! I am alive, alive! I am . . .—alive!* (45–46)

Maggie leaves no doubt about her desires, the love of her husband and the money she believes is rightfully theirs. Her "noble" and classically qualified acceptance of Brick and Skipper's homoerotic friendship seems more expedient than open-minded. She harbors no animosity toward Skipper, especially since he is dead. And her memory-theater reconstruction of Skipper represents a way to reconcile with Brick, to acknowledge and accept. However, Maggie's theater-of-initiation images of Brick and Skipper clearly illustrate the homosocial ramifications of their relationship, the dense and complex blend of latent homosexuality and masculinity. Interestingly, at the very end of act one of *Cat*, Williams prepares the reader/viewer for the next bombardment of highly charged exchanges, the fierce interplay of the theaters of memory and initiation, when Brick and Big Daddy confront one another over mendacity, drinking, women, sports, and homosexuality. The final image of act one, after the verbal fireworks between Maggie and Brick have concluded, is noted by Williams in the stage directions: *"Brick has replaced his spilt drink and sits, faraway, on the great four poster bed"* (47). Faraway indeed, he is absorbed back into the gentle buffer of memory, the symbolic bed, created by the ever present ghosts of Jack Straw and Peter Ochello.

In act two of *Cat on a Hot Tin Roof* Tennessee Williams continues the psychic theater constriction, but here the theater of initiation into masculinity supersedes the theater of memory. The scene is still Maggie and Brick's bed-sitting room, dominated by the large bed, but the room also becomes the site of Big Daddy's sixty-fifth birthday celebration. Brick's physical immobility, a broken leg caused by the previous night's drunken, failed attempt at jumping hurdles at his old high school track, necessitates that the party be brought to him. And just as he does at the start of act one, Williams has one of the characters quickly describe Brick as a boy. Brick's mother, Big Mama, says to him, "oh you bad boy, you, you're my bad little boy. Give Big Mama a kiss, you bad boy you!" (50). With Brick's "boyishness" firmly established, the party soon turns into a fiasco of bickering over Big Daddy's affections (and money) by most of the characters except Brick. These same characters—Gooper, Mae, Maggie, Reverend Tooker, Dr. Baugh—are all complicit in hiding Big Daddy's terminal cancer diagnosis from him. After Big Daddy clears the room, the stage is soon set for his and Brick's act-long confrontation over the exact nature of Brick's problem—what is gnawing at Brick's emotional core. But Brick has the advantage, and the answers, because he possesses more information, and he knows exactly what is gnawing at Big Daddy's core.

The act two scenes which lead to Brick's memory-theater reconstruction of Skipper and his vivid, telling theater-of-initiation images are constantly interrupted and intruded upon to demonstrate how difficult it is for the two

men, father and son, to communicate, difficult but not impossible. Some of
the impediments to communication are represented by the meddling of other
characters. When Big Daddy catches Mae eavesdropping on his and Brick's
conversation, he tells her, 'you was just nothing but *spyin'* an' you *know* it!' (62).
At the beginning of the confrontation, in a spoken aside, Big Daddy bluntly
asks: "*Why is it so damn hard for people to talk?*" (64). It is so damn hard for
these people to talk for myriad complex reasons. It is in the stage directions of
act two when Williams tells us that "*some mystery should be left in the revelation
of character in a play, just as a great deal of mystery is always left in the revelation of characters in life, even in one's own character to himself*" (85). Brick must
also maintain the "open secret" of his and Skipper's homoerotic/homosexual
relationship. To complicate act two further and problematize communication,
we have Brick's famous contention that "mendacity is a system that we live
in" (94). When Big Daddy points out that he and Brick have never lied to
one another, Brick quickly adds, "but we've never *talked* to each other" (83).
However, between the lying and the secrets, the evasions and the furtive suggestions, Brick and Big Daddy do *talk*, and they both manage to shed light on
homosexuality, the homosocial, and masculinity—what it means to be gay, be
closeted, be straight, be young, be old, be dying, all in the Delta heat of that
bedsitting room.

To introduce and diffuse the subject of homosexuality in act two, Williams uses the broadly drawn and comically greedy characters of Gooper and
Mae as a catalyst. When Big Daddy brings up Skipper's death, he tells Brick
"I'm suggesting nothing—. . . But Gooper and Mae suggested that there was
something not right exactly in your—. . . Not, well, exactly *normal* in your
friendship with—" (84). According to Mark Royden Winchell:

> It would be inexact, however, to characterize Mae and Gooper as
> homophobic. They undoubtedly support the official taboos against
> homosexuality, but there is no evidence that they are viscerally
> offended by the thought that Brick is a "pervert." The only emotions
> that seem to move them are avarice and envy.[30]

When Maggie broaches the subject of Brick and Skipper's homoerotic
relationship, it is in an attempt to ameliorate the past and heal the future;
when Mae and Gooper do it, they are exploiting and exacerbating the past
for petty greed. They all have personal ulterior motives for recalling and
reconstructing Brick's sexual history. Big Daddy then becomes the only
character in *Cat* who addresses Brick's homoerotic feelings as a way of
helping, a way of understanding Brick's blank emotional state. The irony
in this situation, of course, exists in the fact that Big Daddy is portrayed

as the ultimate symbol of patriarchal heterosexuality and masculinity. As playwright Arthur Miller believes, Big Daddy represents "the every image of power, of materiality, of authority."[31] A man who has a "lech" for Maggie (19), asks Brick how she is in bed (91). A man who desires a young mistress so he can, "strip her naked and choke her with diamonds and smother her with minks and hump her from hell to breakfast" (72). A man who says about his wife, "but that old woman she never got enough of it—and I was good in bed . . ." (72). However, it is the "secret" in Big Daddy's hypermasculine heterosexual past that enables him to relate to Brick, and that secret abides in the buffering background memory-theater created by the ghosts of Straw and Ochello.

When Brick is aghast at the very idea that people might have thought that he and Skipper were homosexuals, Big Daddy tries to explain and reason with him:

> BIG DADDY [*gently*]: Now, hold on, a minute, son.—I knocked around in my time.
> BRICK: What's that got to do with—
> BIG DADDY: I said "Hold on!"—I bummed, I bummed this country till I was—
> BRICK: Whose suggestion, who else's suggestion is it?
> BIG DADDY: Slept in hobo jungles and railroad Y's and flophouses in all cities before—. (85–86)

More sophisticated members of a 1955 audience probably understood the implications and import of Big Daddy's "bumming" and "knocking" around; most gay men undoubtedly did.[32] With Big Daddy's first remark to Brick, Williams indicates in the stage directions that he speaks *gently*, a word and mood much more befitting the background memory-theater of Straw and Ochello than Brick's turbulent foreground memory-theater construction. And as opposed to hearing understanding in his father's implied homosexual past history, Brick simply hears "queer" and begins his long homophobic tirade:

> Oh, you think so, too, you call me your son and a queer. Oh! Maybe that's why you put Maggie and me in this room that was Jack Straw's and Peter Ochello's, in which that pair of old sisters slept in a double bed where both of 'em died. (86)

Williams then assigns Big Daddy the difficult task of becoming the mediator between the gentle background memory-theater and the homophobic foreground memory-theater. Straw and Ochello's happy, indulged gay past grates against Brick and Skipper's sad, denied gay past. At Brick's denunciation of Straw and Ochello, Big Daddy emphatically says to him: *"Now just don't go throwing rocks at—"* (86). Further to illustrate just how difficult it is for Big Daddy to defend and support an accepted and happy gay history, Williams has him instantly interrupted by the intrusion of Reverend Tooker, looking for the bathroom. As John M. Clum points out:

> Big Daddy will not allow attacks on Straw and Ochello, but his defense is interrupted by Reverend Tooker, *"the living embodiment of the pious, conventional lie,"* an interruption that suggests that it is the pious conventional lie that forbids defense of Straw and Ochello. The interruption is Williams's choice: it allows Brick's homophobic discourse to dominate the scene.[33]

Throughout the remainder of act two, Big Daddy futilely attempts to calm Brick's violent outburst. In the stage directions, Williams tells us that *"Brick is transformed, as if a quiet mountain blew suddenly up in volcanic fame"* (87). Big Daddy tries to allay Brick's homophobic rant numerous times, with lines such as, "I'm just saying I understand such—" (87). However, Brick's sublimated homophobia over his homosexual attraction to Skipper has, like the quiet mountain, reached a critical mass, and no understanding or empathy can stop its eruption. When Big Daddy evokes the gentle, understanding memory-theater represented by the ghosts of Straw and Ochello, the background buffer, Brick quite literally shouts him down, "YOU THINK SO, TOO?" (87). Until the end of the act, Williams shows the power of the wildly homophobic driven by the unfettered masculine dynamics of the homosocial. Brick's dark, introspective theater of memory (where, just perhaps, he loved Skipper) is eclipsed by his bright and vivid theater of initiation, homosocial and brutal (where, just perhaps, he loved Skipper).

The beginning of Brick's homophobic outburst in act two is fueled by such words as *"queer"* (86) and *"sodomy!"* (87), but it is his description of Straw and Ochello's relationship that shatters the buffering background: "Straw? Ochello? A couple of . . . ducking sissies? Queers? Is that what you—" (88). Williams represents the elderly and ill Big Daddy as too exhausted, physically and emotionally, to defend the positive gay history of the bedroom further, when he says to Brick, "Jesus! Whew. . . . Grab my hand!" (88). And Brick's refusal, "naw, I don't want your hand . . ." (88), implies his victory over any memory construction of homosexuality not poisoned by homophobia and the homosocial.

If Maggie's combined theaters of memory and initiation are meant to heal, then Brick's are meant to damage his frozen subjective state further and extend his emotional stasis. To reiterate images of homosexual initiation, Brick, like Maggie, reconstructs his and Skipper's college experiences. However, Maggie's story of the double date, when it seemed more as if Brick and Skipper were a couple, is almost innocent when compared to Brick's college memory and his story of initiation—a vicious fraternity fag bashing. Brick tells Big Daddy:

> Why, at Ole Miss, when it was discovered a pledge to our fraternity, Skipper's and mine, did a, *attempted* to do a, unnatural thing with— We not only dropped him like a hot rock!—We told him to git off campus, and he did, he got!—All the way to . . . North Africa, last I heard! (88–89)[34]

Acts such as this, in part created by the severe homophobic climate of the 1950s, were not only forgiven in young men, they were usually actively encouraged by the prevailing societal norms. After he relates this story, Brick asks Big Daddy, and also those same prevailing societal norms, "why can't exceptional friendship, *real, real, deep, deep friendship!* between two men be respected as something clean and decent without being thought of as—. . . Fairies . . ." (89). It is no wonder that Brick's memory-theater reconstruction of Skipper is so toxic and that his initiation-theater reconstructions are so cruel. In Williams' stage directions, immediately following Brick's pained and dramatic declaration of the word Fairies, he states that "[*In his utterance of this word, we gauge the wide and profound reach of the conventional mores he got from the world that crowned him with early laurel*]" (89). Those "conventional mores," particularly during the period when Williams was writing *Cat on a Hot Tin Roof* and it was a hit on the Broadway stage, help explain not simply 1950s homophobia but also its lasting negative impact on constructions of American masculinity. According to Michelangelo Signorile:

> The fear that swept gay men at the height of the McCarthy Era cannot be underestimated. It exploited a prevailing fear in American culture at large of effeminate men and instilled it further, even among gay men. Not only would men, gay and straight, not want to appear effeminate lest someone think they were homosexual, but the profusely masculine pose that straight men adopted in the 1950s had a profound effect on gay men that lasted for generations.[35]

Brick's homophobic discourse finally reaches a tenuous dénouement when he tries to explain to Big Daddy his and Skipper's relationship in terms of boyhood and sports, as if homoerotic attraction was simply an adolescent indiscretion expressed and sublimated on the football field—the very arena of the homosocial.

Brick's memory-theater construction of Skipper begins with an implied caveat to excuse their behavior and relationship, and in an attempt to make his explanation more feasible, he ascribes it to Maggie: "Maggie declares that Skipper and I went into pro-football after we left Ole Miss' because we were scared to grow up . . ." (90). In his detailed study of masculinity, homosexuality, and American organized sports, Brian Pronger illustrates the roots of Brick's homophobia in the context of professional football:

> By making it known that one is gay, one is making it clear that one thinks there is a different legitimate interpretation of the fundamental myths of our culture. This constitutes a basic rejection of conservatism, of the status quo. Hiding homosexuality, on the other hand, *even if it is known that one is hiding*, indicates that one either agrees with the status quo or at least defers to it.[36]

Brick not only seems to agree with the status quo but has deferred to it to such an extent that he has become blank, unable to feel anything except the brief extremes of rage and hate. To defer to the status quo further, Brick's memory-theater reconstruction of his and Skipper's relationship represents a highly edited and watered-down version of events. Brick's story of Skipper's downfall and death is so sanitized that Big Daddy correctly refers to it as "that half-ass story!" (91). And Brick must confess that the story is truly "half-ass" when he admits to leaving out a drunken telephone call from Skipper in which he told Brick that he loved him. Brick's theater of memory is polluted by this initiatory homosexual declaration of love.

Brick and Big Daddy's confrontation ends act two of *Cat*, and Williams has probed homosexuality as best a 1950s American playwright could at the time. Brick's vehement homophobia represents a way for the play to examine a taboo topic and not obviously approve of it. Most gay men viewing a production of *Cat* in 1955, whether they agreed or not, probably well understood Brick's position, his argument. Big Daddy must force Brick to face the truth about him and Skipper, when he says to Brick, "*You!*—dug the grave of your friend and kicked him in it!—before you'd face the truth with him!" (92). And at the end of act two, when in retaliation Brick tells Big Daddy the secret everyone has hidden from him, his imminent death from cancer, the irony of Brick's comment to him is not wasted on a gay audience: "—And being friends is telling each other the truth . . ." (94).

The multiform concluding third act of *Cat* presents a reader or critic with several problems. In the original version, before Williams made Kazan's suggested changes, one extra memory-theater reconstruction of Skipper exists. This one belongs to Big Mama when she describes the details of Skipper's drug and alcohol induced death (101). This short passage, in which Skipper is represented as basically pathetic, seems primarily expository (and unnecessarily redundant) at best, simply gratuitous at worst; it also appears unchanged in the Broadway version. Big Mama's story is the final mention of Skipper. In both third acts, Straw and Ochello are conspicuously missing by name, and only symbolically appear at the very end, when Maggie attempts to lure Brick into their bed. Even in that manifestation, the Straw and Ochello ghosts have lost their role and power as generators of the buffering background theater of memory. Maggie usurps the homosexual power of their bed, claims it for heterosexuality and her desired impregnation. At the very end of the Broadway version of act three, Williams ironically represents the bed as a sexual shrine of reproduction, an altar, by having Maggie supplicate herself at it: "*then she kneels quickly beside Brick at foot of bed*" (158). Effectively, both theaters of memory and initiation, the homosocial dynamic, and questions of masculinity, all motivating factors for the dramatic action of the first two acts of the play, vanish in the original and Broadway third acts. And they vanish to the detriment of the play, prompting many critics, such as the above mentioned Roger Boxill, to argue that "no version of Act III quite works, because the final act is an afterthought."[37] Williams, who in all probability realized that the problems with act three stemmed from the absence of the dramatic force of the examination of homosexuality and masculinity, attempts to reinsert that dramatic force by reintroducing Big Daddy—creating even more problems and critical conjecture.

Big Daddy's sudden and unexplained reappearance in the Broadway version of act three does appear to be "tacked" on. Thomas F. Van Lann points out, "Kazan wanted Big Daddy brought back in act three because he is such a vibrant and impressive character. But Big Daddy does not belong in act three, for he has nothing more to contribute."[38] But in all of his third-act incarnations, Big Daddy does have something to contribute, the only thing he contributes, a dirty joke. This bawdy story holds some major importance for Williams, as evidenced by the fact that when given the opportunity to rewrite the vexing act three for a 1974 Broadway revival of *Cat* completely, he does nothing more than insert the joke into the original act three, and then remove it again. The subject of Big Daddy's dirty joke demonstrates Williams' attempt to reinfuse act three with the complex mélange of homosexuality, homoeroticism, homosociality, and masculinity which drives the dramatic action of the earlier two acts of the play.

Just as he does in *A Streetcar Named Desire*, Williams has a male character relate a traditional dirty joke to sexualize the situation. And the theme, the hypersexuality of a male animal (a rooster in *Streetcar*), is repeated in *Cat*. On the surface, Big Daddy's joke is rather sophomoric and trite; it involves a father, mother, and young son visiting a zoo. When the son sees that a bull elephant is sexually aroused by a nearby female elephant in heat, he asks his mother about the conspicuous change in the elephant's profile. His mother replies, "oh, that's nothing!" to which his father adds, "she's spoiled!" (152). Throughout his telling of the joke, Big Daddy continuously asks Brick if his language is too vulgar.

> BIG DADDY: . . . Ain't that a nice way to put it, Brick?
> BRICK: Yes sir, nothin' wrong with it.
> > *And*
> BIG DADDY: . . . Ain't I telling this story in decent language, Brick?
> BRICK: Yes, sir, too ruttin' decent! (151–152)

It is evident that the story is meant for Brick's elucidation alone. And while the dirty joke's topic is nominally reproduction, Williams has already displayed his, and Big Daddy's, disgust with heterosexual over-fecundity in all of the references to Gooper and Mae's animal-like brood of children. In act two, Big Daddy tells Brick:

> But Gooper's wife's a good breeder, you got to admit she's fertile. Hell, at supper tonight she had them all at the table and they had to put a couple of extra leafs in the table to make room for them, she's got five head of them, now, and another one's comin'. . . . (61)

Big Daddy's joke cannot relate to Maggie's sham pregnancy; he tells it before her announcement. So why, exactly, does he tell a story whose punch line is exaggeratedly phallic and for Brick's sole benefit?

If one returns to Peter Lyman's previously noted Freudian support of dirty jokes as an intricate factor of male group bonding, then Big Daddy's story becomes a homoerotically charged cautionary tale for his son:

> As Freud observed, the jokes that individual men direct toward women are generally erotic, tend to clever forms (like the double entendre), and have a seductive purpose. The jokes that men tell about women in the presence of other men are sexual and aggressive rather than erotic and use hostile rather than clever

verbal forms; and . . . have the creation of male group bonding as their purpose.[39]

Though all of the major characters are present when Big Daddy tells the joke, it seems clear that he is telling it to Brick alone. And Big Daddy is so careful to make his language appropriate, "clever forms (like the double entendre)," that he even seeks Brick's approval. Brick implores him to make the story more explicit, and thus make it a heterosexual male bonding device, when he says of the usage, "yes, sir, too ruttin' decent!" (152). The joke, as basic as it is, is more clever and playful than aggressive and hostile, so its purpose, according to Freud, is seductive and erotic. However, Big Daddy's purpose is a seduction of Brick's subjective sexuality. The punch line of the joke can only be read in one way, that women do not fully understand or appreciate male sexuality, represented by the elephantine phallus. The dirty story serves an identical purpose if the symbolic phallus is replaced with a biological penis. Evolutionary biologist Jared Diamond, in a very nonsymbolic or representational study of gender responses to penis size, indicates that many women find that "the sight of a penis is, if anything, unattractive. The ones really fascinated by the penis and its dimensions are men. In the showers in men's locker rooms, men routinely size up each other's endowment."[40] Interestingly, Brick's homoerotic friendship with Skipper is based in the sphere of sports, where the locker room represents a homosocial location for men to display their bodies—in the absence of women. So Big Daddy's joke, while on the surface patently heterosexual, in the highly structured telling becomes both homosocial and homoerotic.

The bawdy story allows Williams to subvert traditional male bonding in an attempt to return act three of *Cat* to the subject of homosexuality and masculinity, but the playwright fails. Act three, all of the various act threes, fall rather flat, burdened by superfluous comic repartee and a dearth of substance. Big Daddy's inserted appearance and joke, though a highly complicated construction, is just that, inserted to the point of being clumsily intrusive. The primary reason that act three of *Cat on a Hot Tin Roof* is never "fixed" is because it can't be.

As a study of masculinity and homosexuality, *Cat on a Hot Tin Roof* represents a flawed but, nevertheless, compelling work of drama. Tennessee Williams skillfully probes several gay issues in the play, issues that necessitate his somewhat oblique approach. The play's major importance in Williams' canon is how well it illustrates the playwright's ability to create, construct, and reconstruct characters through the complex theater of memory, and then sexualize those characters by recalled and repeated initiatory scenes. The textual problems with the play are a symptom more than a cause in and of themselves.

The true difficulty with *Cat on a Hot Tin Roof* stems from Williams' inability to balance the various memory-theaters. When female characters alone are given the duty to recreate missing gay characters in Williams' plays, there exists a kind of dramatic equilibrium, as in *A Streetcar Named Desire*. However, in *Cat* the male characters, Brick and Big Daddy, their masculine subjectivities clashing at every word, throw the dramatic balance off to the point of distraction. Interestingly, in all of Williams' major plays written prior to his publicly coming out in 1970, *Cat on a Hot Tin Roof* is the only one in which two male characters discuss the issue of homosexuality. As if to magnify this point, *Cat* is also the only play of Williams that critics, both popular and academic, insist is *not* about homosexuality. When female characters recreate the missing gay men, they seem to be mitigated of their sexual transgressions. It is only when Brick and Big Daddy, the football player and the man's man, masculine avatars, recreate homosexuality that critics get concerned and worried. As if to acknowledge and indicate this perceived problem, in his next play with a missing gay character, Tennessee Williams returns to reconstruction by women alone—and the theaters of memory and initiation reach an art form.

Notes

1. Tennessee Williams, *Cat on a Hot Tin Roof* (New York: Signet, 1955), 124–125. Hereafter cited parenthetically in the text.

2. *Cat on a Hot Tin Roof* won Williams his second Pulitzer Prize far Best Play of the Year in 1955. His first was for *A Streetcar Named Desire* in 1948.

3. Marian Price, "*Cat on a Hot Tin Roof*: The Uneasy Marriage of Success and Idealism," 94.

4. There are actually *five* well-known versions of act three if one takes into consideration director Richard Brooks' 1958 screenplay for the film. Not allowed to make any references to homosexuality, Brooks' version is the most antiseptic. In it, Brick must simply grow up and accept his father's love to become heterosexually happy again—a tidy, predictable, and classic 1950s ending. How wasteful considering the cinematic perfection of casting Paul Newman as Brick and Elizabeth Taylor as Maggie the Cat.

5. Roger Boxill, "*Cat on a Hot Tin Roof*," 20–22.

6. Boxill, 21; Judith J. Thompson, apparently ignoring the fact that all of the versions of act three include the comic battle for Big Daddy's fortune, argues that "the mood of the Broadway conclusion is, rather, essentially comic: an ambience in which sudden conversions and 'miraculous' transformations of character need no justification other than the fact of their happening, with little regard to *how* they come about" (*Tennessee Williams' Plays: Memory, Myth, and Symbol*, 69). What Thompson fails to note is the fact that all of the various act threes are "essentially comic," opening the opportunity for miraculous changes that never happen.

7. Produced by The American Shakespeare Theatre, the 1974 revival of *Cat* was directed by Michael Kahn and featured Keir Dullea as Brick, Elizabeth Ashley as Maggie, and Fred Gwynne as Big Daddy. Another Broadway revival of *Cat* in 1990, directed by Howard Davies, starred Kathleen Turner as Maggie, Daniel

Hugh Kelly as Brick, and Charles Durning as Big Daddy. To illustrate its continuing popularity with Broadway audiences, 2004 saw another revival of *Cat on a Hot Tin Roof* with Ashley Judd as Maggie, Jason Patric as Brick, and Ned Beatty as Big Daddy, and directed by Anthony Page.

8. Ruby Cohn, "The Garrulous Grotesques of Tennessee Williams," 55.

9. David Savran, *Communists, Cowboys, and Queers: The Politics of Masculinity in the Work of Arthur Miller and Tennessee Williams*, 99–100.

10. Mark Royden Winchell, "Come Back to the Locker Room Ag'in, Brick Honey!" 83.

11. Robert Emmet Jones, "Sexual Roles in the Works of Tennessee Williams," 549–550.

12. Harold Bloom, "Introduction." *Modern Critical Interpretations: Tennessee Williams's Cat on a Hot Tin Roof*, 3; Though Bloom greatly admires Tennessee Williams as one of the twentieth century's preeminent dramatists, he does not include *Cat on a Hot Tin Roof* among the playwright's best works. Bloom relegates it to the status of, "more a film script than an achieved drama" (3).

13. Alan Sinfield, *Cultural Politics—Queer Reading*, 53.

14. Sinfield, 47.

15. Savran, 91–92.

16. John M. Clum, "Something Cloudy, Something Clear": Homophobic Discourse in Tennessee Williams," 40.

17. Judith J. Thompson, *Tennessee Williams' Plays: Memory, Myth, and Symbol*, 76.

18. Savran, 53.

19. Boxill, 24.

20. Tennessee Williams, *The Glass Menagerie*, in George McMichael, ed., *Concise Anthology of American Literature*, 2nd ed., 1845.

21. *Cat on a Hot Tin Roof* is loosely based on a short story by Williams entitled "Three Players of a Summer Game" published in *The New Yorker* two years before he wrote the play.

22. Alice Griffin, "*Cat on a Hot Tin Roof*," 112.

23. See Michael S. Kimmel and Michael A. Messner, eds., *Men's Lives*. 2nd ed., 168.

24. Peter Middleton, *The Inward Gaze: Masculinity and Subjectivity in Modern Culture*, 20.

25. In her 2002 book, *Tennessee Williams' Plays: Memory, Myth, and Symbol*, Judith J. Thompson does a yeoman's job of connecting references in *Cat* to: Apollo, Hyacinthus, Hippolytus, Aphrodite, Artemis, Narcissus, the Phrygian Cebele, Osiris, Set, Bast, Castor and Pollux, and Saint Margaret.

26. Winchell, 88, 89.

27. Alvin B. Kernan, "Truth and Dramatic Mode in *A Streetcar Named Desire*," 18.

28. Savran, 107.

29. Winchell, 89–90.

30. Winchell, 84.

31. See Savran, 53.

32. Williams uses a more subtle indication of gay male sexual cruising in his very first play, *The Glass Menagerie* (1945), when the narrator, Tom Wingfield, relates his long hours spent in a dark movie theater. Williams' 1954 short story,

"Hard Candy," describes in detail the homosexual sexual activity in an old movie theater, the Joy Rio. Also, Tom has become a merchant sailor who finds himself, "walking along a street at night, in some strange city, before I have found companions" (1886). To the experienced homosexual man, of any recent era, all of these activities, including Big Daddy's "bumming" around, clearly represent the underworld of secretive gay male sexual expression.

33. Clum, 38.

34. From André Gide to Paul Bowles, Williams also recognizes that modern North Africa has always represented a haven for ostracized Western gay men, though a complex and troubling colonial location/haven.

35. Michelangelo Signorile, *Life Outside: The Signorile Report on Gay Men: Sex, Drugs, Muscles, and the Passages of Life*, 46.

36. Pronger, 117.

37. Boxill, 21.

38. Thomas F. Van Laan, "'Shut Up!' 'Be Quiet' 'Hush!': Talk and Its Suppression in Three Plays by Tennessee Williams," 254.

39. Peter Lyman, "The Fraternal Bond as a Joking Relationship: A Case Study of the Role of Sexist Jokes in Male Group Bonding," 145

40. See Susan Bordo, *The Male Body: A New Look at Men in Public and in Private*, 81.

Chronology

1911	Thomas Lanier ("Tennessee") Williams born March 26 in Columbus, Mississippi, to Cornelius Coffin and Edwina Dakin Williams, one-and-a-half years after his sister Rose Isabel was born.
1911–1919	Family moves often, then settles in St. Louis, Missouri. In 1919, brother, Walter Dakin, is born.
1929	Graduates from University City High School and enters the University of Missouri.
1935	Suffers nervous breakdown. Play he collaborated on, *Cairo! Shanghai! Bombay!* is produced.
1936–1937	Enters and is later dropped from Washington University, St. Louis. Enters University of Iowa. First full-length plays, *The Fugitive Kind* and *Candles to the Sun* are produced. Sister Rose undergoes lobotomy.
1938	Graduates from University of Iowa with a degree in English.
1941–1943	Takes various jobs in different cities.
1944	*The Glass Menagerie* opens in Chicago.
1945	*The Glass Menagerie* opens in New York and wins New York Drama Critics Circle Award.
1947	*Summer and Smoke* opens in Dallas. *A Streetcar Named Desire* opens in New York and wins the New York Drama Critics

173

Circle Award and the Pulitzer Prize. Meets Frank Merlo, who becomes his long-time companion.

1948   *Summer and Smoke* opens in New York. *One Arm and Other Stories* published.

1950   *The Roman Spring of Mrs. Stone*, a novel, published. *The Rose Tattoo* opens in Chicago.

1951   *The Rose Tattoo* opens in New York, wins the Antoinette Perry (Tony) Award for best play.

1953   *Camino Real* opens in New York.

1954   *Hard Candy: A Book of Stories* is published.

1955   *Cat on a Hot Tin Roof* opens in New York; wins New York Drama Critics Circle award and Pulitzer Prize.

1956   First collection of poems, *In the Winter of Cities*, is published. *Baby Doll*, a film, is released and nominated for Academy Award.

1957   *Orpheus Descending* opens in New York.

1958   *Garden District* (*Suddenly Last Summer* and *Something Unspoken*) is produced Off-Broadway.

1959   *Sweet Bird of Youth* opens in New York.

1960   *Period of Adjustment* opens in New York.

1961   *The Night of the Iguana* opens in New York.

1962   Awarded a lifetime fellowship by the American Academy of Arts and Letters.

1963   *The Milk Train Doesn't Stop Here Anymore* opens in New York. Frank Merlo dies. Williams falls into depression.

1966   *Slapstick Tragedy* opens in New York.

1967   *The Two-Character Play* opens in London.

1968   *The Seven Descents of Myrtle* opens in New York.

1969   *In the Bar of a Tokyo Hotel* opens Off-Broadway. Converts to Catholicism. Nervous collapse causes him to stay hospitalized for three months in a hospital in St. Louis.

1970   *Dragon Country: A Book of Plays* is published.

1971   Revised version of *Two-Character Play*, called *Out Cry*, opens in
            Chicago.

1972   *Small Craft Warnings* opens Off-Broadway.

1974   *Eight Mortal Ladies Possessed*, a collection of short stories, is
            published.

1975   *Memoirs* and a second novel, *Moise and the World of Reason*, are
            published. *The Red Devil Battery Sign* opens in Boston.

1977   *Vieux Carré* opens in New York.

1978   *Where I Live*, a book of essays, is published.

1980   *Clothes for a Summer Hotel* opens in Washington, D.C. Mother
            dies.

1981   *A House Not Meant to Stand* opens in Chicago. *Something Cloudy,
            Something Clear* opens in New York.

1983   Williams dies in February at the Hotel Elysée in New York
            City.

Contributors

HAROLD BLOOM is Sterling Professor of the Humanities at Yale University. Educated at Cornell and Yale universities, he is the author of more than 30 books, including *Shelley's Mythmaking* (1959), *The Visionary Company* (1961), *Blake's Apocalypse* (1963), *Yeats* (1970), *The Anxiety of Influence* (1973), *A Map of Misreading* (1975), *Kabbalah and Criticism* (1975), *Agon: Toward a Theory of Revisionism* (1982), *The American Religion* (1992), *The Western Canon* (1994), *Omens of Millennium: The Gnosis of Angels, Dreams, and Resurrection* (1996), *Shakespeare: The Invention of the Human* (1998), *How to Read and Why* (2000), *Genius: A Mosaic of One Hundred Exemplary Creative Minds* (2002), *Hamlet: Poem Unlimited* (2003), *Where Shall Wisdom Be Found?* (2004), and *Jesus and Yahweh: The Names Divine* (2005). In addition, he is the author of hundreds of articles, reviews, and editorial introductions. In 1999, Professor Bloom received the American Academy of Arts and Letters' Gold Medal for Criticism. He has also received the International Prize of Catalonia, the Alfonso Reyes Prize of Mexico, and the Hans Christian Andersen Bicentennial Prize of Denmark.

M. THOMAS INGE is a professor of humanities at Randolph-Macon College. He has written on Faulkner, the Southern Agrarians, American popular culture, and Southern humor. His books include the *Handbook of American Popular Culture* and *The New Encyclopedia of Southern Culture: Volume 9: Literature*, the latter of which he coauthored.

GULSHAN RAI KATARIA is a professor in the English department at Punjabi University, Patiala, India. He specializes in American drama, Elizabethan drama, and twentieth-century literature.

177

ROBERT J. CORBER is a professor at Trinity College, Hartford. He co-edited *Queer Studies: An Interdisciplinary Reader*. He is author of *In the Name of National Security: Hitchcock, Homophobia, and the Political Construction of Gender in Postwar America*.

DEAN SHACKELFORD has taught English at Southeast Missouri State University, where he also has been a director of undergraduate studies. He has published articles on Tennessee Williams, Flannery O'Connor, Harper Lee, Countee Cullen, and others.

R. BARTON PALMER is a professor in the English department at Clemson University. His work includes *Hollywood's Tennessee: The Williams Films and Postwar America*, which he coauthored, and *Twentieth-Century American Fiction on Screen*, which he edited.

DAVID A. DAVIS is an assistant professor at Mercer University. His work has appeared in various journals and covered Southern literature and other topics.

JEFFREY B. LOOMIS is a professor at Northwest Missouri State University. He is the author of *Dayspring in Darkness: Sacrament in Hopkins*. He is researching a book on Tennessee Williams's manuscripts. In addition, his articles have appeared in a variety of books and journals, and he has published book reviews and poems.

BRUCE MCCONACHIE is chairman of the department of theatre arts at the University of Pittsburgh, where he is also a professor. He is a specialist in American-theater history and theater historiography. His books include *American Theatre in the Culture of the Cold War: Producing and Contesting Containment, 1947–1962*, and *Performance and Cognition*, which he co-edited.

WILLIAM MARK POTEET is an independent scholar and writer. He is the author of numerous scholarly essays and also a fiction writer.

Bibliography

Bak, John S. "'Sneakin' and Spyin' from Broadway to the Beltway: Cold War Masculinity, Brick and Homosexual Existentialism." *Theatre Journal* 56, no. 2 (May 2004): 225–49.

Barna, Zsanett. "'How to Let the Cat out of the Bag?': Non-Diegetic Music in *Cat on a Hot Tin Roof.*" *Americana: E-Journal of American Studies in Hungary* 1, no. 1 (Fall 2005): [no pagination].

Bigsby, C. W. E. *A Critical Introduction to Twentieth-Century American Drama.* Volume 2. Cambridge [Cambridgeshire]; New York: Cambridge University Press, 1982–1985.

Bloom, Harold. *Tennessee Williams.* New York: Infobase Publishing, 2007.

Boxill, Roger. *Tennessee Williams.* New York: St. Martin's Press, 1987.

Bray, Robert, ed. *Tennessee Williams and His Contemporaries.* Newcastle upon Tyne, England: Cambridge Scholars, 2007.

Cafagna, Dianne. "Blanche DuBois and Maggie the Cat: Illusion and Reality in Tennessee Williams." In *Critical Essays on Tennessee Williams*, edited by Robert A. Martin, pp. 119–31. New York: G. K. Hall, 1997.

Cañadas, Ivan. "The Naming of Jack Straw and Peter Ochello in Tennessee Williams's *Cat on a Hot Tin Roof.*" *English Language Notes* 42, no. 4 (June 2005): 57–62.

Clum, John M. "'Something Cloudy, Something Clear': Homophobic Discourse in Tennessee Williams." *South Atlantic Quarterly* 88, no. 1 (Winter 1989): 161–79.

Crandell, George W. "*Cat on a Hot Tin Roof.*" In *Tennessee Williams: A Guide to Research and Performance*, edited by Philip C. Kolin, pp. 109–25. Westport, Conn.: Greenwood, 1998.

179

————. "'Echo Spring': Reflecting the Gaze of Narcissus in Tennessee Williams's *Cat on a Hot Tin Roof*." *Modern Drama* 42, no. 3 (Fall 1999): 427–41.

Crandell, George, ed. *The Critical Response to Tennessee Williams*. Westport, Conn.: Greenwood Press, 1996.

Crespy, David A. "Swimming to Chekhovia: Edward Albee on Tennessee Williams—An Interview." In *The Influence of Tennessee Williams: Essays on Fifteen American Playwrights*, edited by Philip C. Kolin, pp. 216–20. Jefferson, N.C.: McFarland, 2008.

Devlin, Albert J. "Writing in 'A Place of Stone': *Cat on a Hot Tin Roof*." In *The Cambridge Companion to Tennessee Williams*, edited by Matthew C. Roudané, pp. 95–113. Cambridge, England: Cambridge University Press, 1997.

————, ed. *Conversations with Tennessee Williams*. Jackson: University Press of Mississippi, 1986.

Fleche, Anne. *Mimetic Disillusion: Eugene O'Neill, Tennessee Williams, and U.S. Dramatic Realism*. Tuscaloosa: University of Alabama Press, 1997.

Gates, Jonathan. "T. William's Language of the Soul in *Glass Menagerie, Streetcar Named Desire*, and *Cat on a Hot Tin Roof*." In *Proceedings: Northeast Regional Meeting of the Conference on Christianity and Literature*, edited by Joan F. Hallisey and Mary-Anne Vetterling, pp. 38–43. Weston, Mass.: Regis College, 1996.

Griffin, Alice. *Understanding Tennessee Williams*. Columbia: University of South Carolina Press, 1995.

Gross, Robert F. "The Pleasures of Brick: Eros and Gay Spectator in *Cat on a Hot Tin Roof*." *Journal of American Drama and Theatre* 9, no. 1 (Winter 1997): 11–25.

————, ed. *Tennessee Williams: A Casebook*. New York: Routledge, 2002.

Holditch, Kenneth, ed. *Tennesssee Williams Literary Journal* 4, no. 2 (Fall 1999).

Holditch, Kenneth, and Richard Freeman Leavitt. *Tennessee Williams and the South*. Jackson: University Press of Mississippi, 2002.

Holditch, W. Kenneth. "Southern Comfort: Food and Drink in the Plays of Tennessee Williams." *Southern Quarterly: A Journal of the Arts in the South* 44, no. 2 (Winter 2007): 53–73.

Hurd, Myles Raymond. "Cats and Catamites: Achilles, Patroclus, and Williams' *Cat on a Hot Tin Roof*." *Notes on Mississippi Writers* 23, no. 2 (June 1991): 63–66.

Isaac, Dan. "Big Daddy's Dramatic Word Strings." *American Speech: A Quarterly of Linguistic Usage* 40, no. 4 (December 1965): 272–78.

Kundert-Gibbs, John. "Barren Ground: Female Strength and Male Impotence in *Who's Afraid of Virginia Woolf* and *Cat on a Hot Tin Roof*." In *Staging the Rage: The Web of Misogyny in Modern Drama*, edited by Katherine H. Burkman and Judith Roof, pp. 230–47. Madison, N.J.: Fairleigh Dickinson University Press, 1998.

Martin, Robert A., ed. *Critical Essays on Tennessee Williams*. New York: G.K. Hall; London: Prentice Hall International, 1997.

May, Charles E. "Brick Pollitt as Homo Ludens: 'Three Players of a Summer Game' and *Cat on a Hot Tin Roof.*" In *Tennessee Williams: 13 Essays*, edited by Jac Tharpe, pp. 39–63. Jackson: University Press of Mississippi, 1980.

Mayberry, Susan Neal. "A Study of Illusion and the Grotesque in Tennessee Williams' *Cat on a Hot Tin Roof.*" *Southern Studies: An Interdisciplinary Journal of the South* 22, no. 4 (Winter 1983): 359–65.

McCann, John S. *The Critical Reputation of Tennessee Williams: A Reference Guide.* Boston, Mass.: G.K. Hall, 1983.

Murphy, Brenda. "Brick Pollitt Agonistes: The Game in 'Three Players of a Summer Game' and *Cat on a Hot Tin Roof.*" *Southern Quarterly* 38, no. 1 (1999): 36–44.

O'Connor, Jacqueline. *Dramatizing Dementia: Madness in the Plays of Tennessee Williams.* Bowling Green, Ohio: Bowling Green State University Popular Press, 1997.

Paller, Michael. *Gentlemen Callers: Tennessee Williams, Homosexuality, and Mid-Twentieth-Century Broadway Drama.* New York: Palgrave Macmillan, 2005.

Price, Marian. "*Cat on a Hot Tin Roof*: The Uneasy Marriage of Success and Idealism." *Modern Drama* 38, no. 3 (Fall 1995): 324–35.

Reck, Tom Stokes. "The First *Cat on a Hot Tin Roof*: Williams' 'Three Players.'" *University Review* 34 (1968): 187–92.

Sarotte, Georges-Michel. "Fluidity and Differentiation in Three Plays by Tennessee Williams: *The Glass Menagerie, A Streetcar Named Desire*, and *Cat on a Hot Tin Roof.*" In *Staging Difference: Cultural Pluralism in American Theatre and Drama*, edited by Marc Maufort, pp. 141–56. New York: Peter Lang, 1995.

Savran, David. "'By Coming Suddenly into a Room That I Thought Was Empty': Mapping the Closet with Tennessee Williams." *Studies in the Literary Imagination* 24, no. 2 (Fall 1991): 57–74.

———. *Communists, Cowboys, and Queers: The Politics of Masculinity in the Work of Arthur Miller and Tennessee Williams.* Minneapolis: University of Minnesota Press, 1992.

Siegel, Robert. "The Metaphysics of Tennessee Williams." *American Drama* 10, no. 1 (Winter 2001): 11–37.

Thompson, Judith J. *Tennessee Williams's Plays: Memory, Myth, and Symbol.* New York: Peter Lang, 2002.

Tischler, Nancy M. "The Distorted Mirror: Tennessee Williams' Self-Portraits." *Mississippi Quarterly* 25 (1972): 389–403.

———. *Student Companion to Tennessee Williams.* Westport, Conn.: Greenwood Press, 2000.

Van Laan, Thomas F. "'Shut Up!' 'Be Quiet' 'Hush!': Talk and Its Suppression in Three Plays by Tennessee Williams." *Comparative Drama* 22, no. 3 (Fall 1988): 244–65.

Wilhelmi, Nancy O. "The Language of Power and Powerlessness: Verbal Combat in the Plays of Tennessee Williams." In *The Text & Beyond: Essays in Literary Linguistics*, edited by Cynthia Bernstein, pp. 217–26. Tuscaloosa: University of Alabama Press, 1994.

Winchell, Mark Royden. "Come Back to the Locker Room Ag'in, Brick Honey!" *Mississippi Quarterly* 48, no. 4 (Fall 1995): 701–12.

Zeineddine, Nada. *Because It Is My Name: Problems of Identity Experienced by Women, Artists, and Breadwinners in the Plays of Henrik Ibsen, Tennessee Williams, and Arthur Miller.* Braunton, [England]: Merlin, 1991.

Acknowledgments

M. Thomas Inge, "The South, Tragedy, and Comedy in Tennessee Williams's *Cat on a Hot Tin Roof.*" From *The United States South: Regionalism and Identity*, edited by Valeria Gennaro Lerda and Tjebbe Westendorp. Copyright © 1991 by Bulzoni Editore.

Gulshan Rai Kataria, "The Hetairas (Maggie, Myrtle, Blanche)." From *The Faces of Eve: A Study of Tennessee Williams's Heroines*. Copyright © 1992 by Gulshan Rai Kataria.

Robert J. Corber, "Tennessee Williams and the Politics of the Closet." From *Homosexuality on Cold War America: Resistance and the Crisis of Masculinity.* Copyright © 1997 by Duke University Press. All rights reserved. Used by permission of the publisher.

Dean Shackelford, "The Truth That Must Be Told: Gay Subjectivity, Homophobia, and Social History in *Cat on a Hot Tin Roof.*" From *The Tennessee Williams Annual Review* 1 (1998): 103–118. Copyright © 1998 by *The Tennessee Williams Annual Review.*

R. Barton Palmer, "Elia Kazan and Richard Brooks Do Tennessee Williams: Melodramatizing *Cat on a Hot Tin Roof* on Stage and Screen." From *The Tennessee Williams Annual Review* 2 (1999): 1–11. Copyright © 1999 by *The Tennessee Williams Annual Review.*

David A. Davis, "'Make the Lie True': The Tragic Family in *Cat on a Hot Tin Roof* and *King Lear*." From *The Tennessee Williams Annual Review* 5 (2002): 1–11. Copyright © 2009 by *The Tennessee Williams Annual Review*.

Jeffrey B. Loomis, "Four Characters in Search of a Company: Williams, Pirandello, and the *Cat on a Hot Tin Roof* Manuscripts." From *Magical Muse: Millennial Essays on Tennessee Williams*, edited by Ralph F. Voss. Copyright © 2002 by the University of Alabama Press.

Bruce McConachie, "*Cat* and the Grotesque in the Cold War." From *The Tennessee Williams Literary Journal* 5, no. 1 (Spring 2003): 47–64. Copyright © 2003 by *The Tennessee Williams Literary Journal*.

William Mark Poteet, "*Cat on a Hot Tin Roof*." From *Gay Men in Modern Southern Literature: Ritual, Initiation, and the Construction of Masculinity*. Copyright © 2006 by Peter Lang Publishing.

Every effort has been made to contact the owners of copyrighted material and secure copyright permission. Articles appearing in this volume generally appear much as they did in their original publication with few or no editorial changes. In some cases, foreign language text has been removed from the original essay. Those interested in locating the original source will find the information cited above.

Index

Characters in literary works are indexed by first name (if any), followed by the name of the work in parentheses.

185